Nikky-Guninder Kaur Singh is [illegible] of Religious Studies and Chair of the department at Colby College in Waterville, Maine. She is Co-Chair of the Sikh Studies Section of the American Academy of Religion. Her books include: *The Guru Granth Sahib: its Physics and Metaphysics* (1981), *The Feminine Principle in the Sikh Vision of the Transcendent* (1993), *The Name of My Beloved: Verses of the Sikh Gurus* (2001) and *The Birth of the Khalsa: A Feminist Re-memory of Sikh Identity* (2005).

'Nikky Singh's latest publication provides an eloquent introduction to Sikhism, grounded in reference to the scriptures and articulate with a sharp awareness of contemporary issues. Students will find Singh's *Sikhism: An Introduction* a clearly organised text, written in an engaging style, and usefully augmented by a substantial bibliography. *Sikhism: An Introduction* is the fruit of many years of immersion in Sikh Studies and of sharing it through the author's university teaching. This excellent illustrated guide to the Sikh tradition offers readers not only key factual material but also Singh's own insights into gender and her substantial attention to the arts, to colonial encounters and diasporic life stories.' – ***Eleanor Nesbitt, Professor of Religions and Education, University of Warwick and author of* Sikhism: A Very Short Introduction**

'A solid and lively introduction to key events in Sikh history, *Sikhism: An Introduction* paints a vivid portrait of Sikh spirituality, arts, politics, gender and family life. This engaging text takes readers from the origins of Sikhism in Guru Nanak's life and teachings to contemporary Sikh life in India and the Sikh diaspora. Nikky-Guninder Kaur Singh's call to Sikhs to reflect on the founding principles of their tradition gives Sikh and non-Sikh readers alike insight into the challenges all religions face as they evolve over time.' – ***Robin Rinehart, Professor of Religious Studies and Asian Studies Program Chair, Lafayette College, Easton, Pennsylvania***

'In this delightful study Nikky-Guninder Kaur Singh introduces the reader to the history, religion, and culture of the Sikhs, highlighting the various issues related to doctrine, worship, ethics, art, architecture, and diaspora. Her bold critique of patriarchal structures of Sikh society is refreshing. Written in accessible style this exciting book will appeal not only to undergraduate students of Sikh studies, religion, medieval Indian history, and literature, but also to lay readers who will gain firsthand information about the youngest world religion.' – ***Pashaura Singh, Professor and Dr. Jasbir Singh Saini Endowed Chair in Sikh and Punjabi Studies, University of California, Riverside***

I.B.TAURIS INTRODUCTIONS TO RELIGION

In recent years there has been a surge of interest in religion and in the motivations behind religious belief and commitment. Avoiding over-simplification, jargon or unhelpful stereotypes, I.B.Tauris Introductions to Religion embraces the opportunity to explore religious tradition in a sensitive, objective and nuanced manner. A specially commissioned series for undergraduate students, it offers concise, clearly written overviews, by leading experts in the field, of the world's major religious faiths, and of the challenges posed to all the religions by progress, globalization and diaspora. Covering the fundamentals of history, theology, ritual and worship, these books place an emphasis above all on the modern world, and on the lived faiths of contemporary believers. They explore, in a way that will engage followers and non-believers alike, the fascinating and sometimes difficult contradictions or reconciling ancient tradition with headlong cultural and technological change.

'I.B.Tauris Introductions to Religion offers students of religion something fresh, intelligent and accessible. Without dumbing down the issues, or making complex matters seem more simple than they need to be, the series manages to be both conceptually challenging while also providing beginning undergraduates with the complete portfolio of books that they need to grasp the fundamentals of each tradition. To be religious is in the end to be human. The I.B.Tauris series looks to be an ideal starting point for anyone interested in this vital and often elusive component of all our societies and cultures.' – ***John M. Hull, Emeritus Professor of Religious Education, University of Birmingham***

'The I.B.Tauris Introductions to Religion series promises to be just what busy teachers and students need: a batch of high-quality, highly accessible books by leading scholars that are thoroughly geared towards pedagogical needs and student course use. Achieving a proper understanding of the role of religion in the world is, more than ever, an urgent necessity. This attractive-looking series will contribute towards that vital task.' – ***Christopher Partridge, Professor of Religious Studies, Lancaster University***

'The I.B.Tauris series promises to offer more than the usual kind of humdrum introduction. The volumes will seek to explain and not merely to describe religions, will consider religions as ways of life and not merely as sets of beliefs and practices, and will explore differences as well as similarities among specific communities of adherents worldwide. Strongly recommended.' – ***Robert A. Segal, Professor of Religious Studies, University of Aberdeen***

Please see the back of the book for the full series list

I.B.TAURIS INTRODUCTIONS TO RELIGION

Sikhism

An Introduction

by

Nikky-Guninder Kaur Singh

I.B.TAURIS
LONDON · NEW YORK

Published in 2011 by I. B. Tauris & Co Ltd
6, Salem Road, London W2 4BU
175 Fifth Avenue, New York NY 10010
www.ibtauris.com

Distributed in the United States and Canada Exclusively by
Palgrave Macmillan, 175 Fifth Avenue, New York NY 10010

First South Asian Edition 2011

ISBN 978-1-84885-321-8

This edition is for sale in the Indian subcontinent only. Not for export elsewhere.

A full CIP record for this book is available from the British Library
A full CIP record for this book is available from the Library of Congress

Library of Congress catalog card: available

Printed and bound in India by Brijbasi Art Press Ltd., New Delhi.

In memory of Ajeet Singh Matharu, a promising young Sikh scholar
(1983–2010)

Contents

Preface

This project is based on the 'polarity of familiarity and strangeness,' which for Hans Gadamer is fundamental to hermeneutics (*Truth and Method*: 295). My bond with Sikhism goes way back to childhood visits to the Gurdwara in Bathinda with my grandmother. In fact I can still feel the specialness of that space with its air of formality, colorful brocades, joyous music, and the hum of the electric fan over a star-filled canopy. In order to understand the Sikh tradition I belong to, I have been studying, writing, and teaching its sacred literature for many years now. But along with familiarity, Gadamer stipulates the condition of 'strangeness' in the hermeneutic activity, which creates a tension that is quite exciting. Having come to a girls' prep school in the USA, I have been dislocated from my home and the familiar world of Sikhism since I was a teenager. The unique nature of this introductory text, however, elicited a more conscious rupture with the literature, ceremonies, art, and historical events that I was familiar with. So I tried to return to them as a 'distanciated other'. And paradoxically, as the intimate became foreign, new insights and new possibilities opened up. The flow of recent publications, conference papers, websites, and media coverage on matters Sikh added to my adventure.

Since understanding is a perpetual activity, we must approach texts and events from our own horizon. 'To acquire a horizon means that one learns to look beyond what is close at hand — not in order to look away from it but to see it better, within a larger whole and in truer proportion' (*T&M*: 305). This introduction is an invitation for more meaningful communications in our global society. It is not intended to be a closure of any sort; I only hope it will generate more familiarity, reflection, and publications on Sikhism.

I want to thank my editor Mr. Alex Wright at I.B.Tauris for giving me this opportunity. I have met him once briefly, 20 some years ago at an AAR Exhibit Hall. I was going around with my manuscript,

Feminine Principle in the Sikh Vision. The word 'Sikh' in the title instantly brought a sparkle in the eyes of Mr. Wright, working for Cambridge University Press at that time. His breadth of vision and sustained interest in Sikh scholarship has been inspirational. I am also very grateful to Harpreet Singh at Harvard for his nuanced reading of the proofs at such short notice, and making valuable suggestions. My thanks to students, friends, colleagues and critics directly and indirectly involved in this project. For the images I thank Bhai Satpal Singh Khalsa, Eliza Browning, Gurumustuk Singh Khalsa, Binky Manpreet Singh, Dr Narinder Kapany, and from Ireland, Harpreet Singh. My thanks to the ever helpful Suzanne Jones and to Mel Regnell for her technical expertise.

The combination of familiarity and strangeness made me discover many fascinating topics and personalities that I so wished to include, but unfortunately I could only cover so much in a single volume. Most of all, I regret my inability to include the young generation of Sikh men and women promoting Sikhism in diverse fields across the continents. Their boundless energy and creativity are truly admirable. I salute each one of them, and especially the young Ajeet Singh Matharu. His tragic death on July 25, 2010 is an enormous loss to the Sikh world. Born in California, educated at Phillips Academy and the University of Southern California, Ajeet was pursing his PhD in history at Columbia University. This summer he was in Chandigarh to study Punjabi. It is hard to come to terms with such scholarly promise crashed in a minute in a car accident. This book is dedicated to the memory of Ajeet.

Nikky-Guninder Kaur Singh

Introduction

In the twenty-first century, religion is so alive. Gone are the notions of religion as something otherworldly and spiritual; its powerful impulse is witnessed in contemporary culture, politics and business. Understanding the modern world requires an understanding of the traditional world religions. Clearly, the domain of a few academic specialists is becoming an existential reality. This volume is an introduction to the north Indian tradition of Sikhism – currently the 'fifth-largest world religion'. It has three aims: to promote a multifaceted study of Sikhism in mainstream academic curriculum; to inform the general public about it; and to remind the Sikh community of its egalitarian foundations.

My first aim is to show that the academic study of Sikhism should move beyond religious studies and engage with the broader humanities and social sciences disciplines. Indeed, Sikhism has made great strides from the time that it was outwardly neglected in textbooks and classrooms. If it was mentioned, it would have been categorized incorrectly as a 'sect of Hinduism' or a 'sect of Islam', or a 'hybridization between Hinduism and Islam'.[1] During my high school, college and even graduate school days in the USA, there were no courses offered on Sikhism. The situation is remarkably different today. Chairs are being endowed in Sikh studies at major American universities. Internationally, there is a steady flow of academic books and journals. Book anthologies and encyclopedias give solid textual space to Sikhism. Conferences on Sikh topics are being organized across the continents, stimulating further research. The energetic and innovative young generation of diasporic Sikhs is exploring new avenues for the understanding and transmission of their heritage.

Yet, for the most part, the study of Sikhism remains confined to classes in religious studies, with the result that its vastly complex and fascinating subject matter remains untapped. The tradition originated (and evolved) historically and geographically between South Asia and West Asia. Therefore, linguistically, culturally, philosophically and artistically, Sikhism should offer a vast store of material for scholars specializing in both Western and Eastern religions. Rich with philosophical doctrines and myths, art and architecture, historical moments, political movements, and unique rituals and symbols, Sikhism offers a variety of source materials to be engaged with across different methodologies and disciplines.

I hope this textbook will facilitate conversations and connections with art history, anthropology, literature, philosophy, gender studies, cultural studies and ethnic studies. I have been teaching at Colby College for over two decades, and find its liberal arts atmosphere most fulfilling. In a recent semester, for example, an Ecology major in my seminar on Sikhism studied the representation of flora in Janamsakhi paintings; a student of literature did an analysis of Guru Nanak's *Jap* and T. S. Eliot's *Four Quartets*. Education, after all, is about making connections, and this textbook aspires to create interwoven patterns of understanding. It is exciting to see Sikh topics reach students in diverse academic disciplines.

I have opted for a thematic approach, which I think will be conducive to familiarizing students with Sikh materials in a way they can relate to, while introducing the study of other religions and cultures. The nine chapters in the book focus on different topics. They are 'microscopic', to give the reader an in-depth understanding of an aspect of Sikhism, and 'telescopic' at the same time, to raise questions and concerns central to contemporary humanities and social sciences. Overall, I have tried to offer a broad, yet intimate, picture of the tradition so that faculty and students can use them in academic departments beyond Asian religions. For example, the chapter on Sikh art could be used in a survey on Asian art in general; the chapter on Sikh rituals, in a course in anthropology; the chapter on gender and Sikhism, in a course on women, gender and sexuality.

My second aim is to familiarize the general public with this vibrant faith and its contemporary relevance. The religion is grounded in Guru Nanak's revelation of the infinite singular Divine (literally the number 'one'), to be savored by everyone through their individual sensibilities. Such an ideal imbues every bit of our secular world with spiritual enchantment. Its ethical structure breaks the oppressive practices and hegemonies of caste, class, ethnicity and gender; *everybody* is autonomous and equal, with the same responsibilities toward the Divine and toward one another. The literary beauty and pluralism of Sikh scripture are remarkable. The entire text expresses the love for the infinite One in the voice of the Sikh Gurus, Hindu saints and Muslim mystics. Its wide range of poetic images and universal musical melodies has the potential to illuminate the minds of readers and listeners in a variety of ways, helping each to become what they want to be. The five symbols worn by Sikh men and women as markers of their Sikh identity draw on this inclusive text and link with their common humanity. As a young world religion, Sikhism can offer a modern approach to perennial problems and contemporary challenges.

Even though so many people work, travel and live in the global village, very little is known about men and women of *other* faiths. The modern geographic or electronic proximity has failed to generate essential human communications. Demographically, large numbers of Sikhs live in Southall (UK), Bobigny (France) and Yuba City (USA), yet these men and women and their children remain perpetual strangers to the local populations. Few outsiders have any knowledge about their world view or customs. After 9/11, at least 200 Sikhs were victims of hate crimes in America, just because they had beards and wore turbans. The fear felt by the uninformed English villagers who fabricated the dark-bearded Sikhs as the *The Devil's Children*, in Peter Dickinson's science fiction, has an eerie resonance today. In spite of a Sikh presence, outsiders are suspicious of their religious symbols – the ceremonial swords, steel bracelets, turbans, uncut hair and beards.

As a cure for our modern malady, scholars in the field of religious studies advise that we move beyond diversity to pluralism – '*we all* talking with each other about *us*' (in the words of Wilfred Cantwell Smith).[2] Three centuries ago, the Tenth Sikh prophet, Guru Gobind Singh (1666–1708), made just such an exhortation. Seventeenth-century India was quite a global hub. Trade and commerce had connected the South Asian subcontinent with both West Asia and East Asia. The Mughal Empire was at its zenith, attracting Muslim poets and artists from places such as Persia, Arabia and Anatolia. Indian silk was in demand among the elite in Malaya, Indonesia and the Philippines. The Mughal period was also tightly linked with the

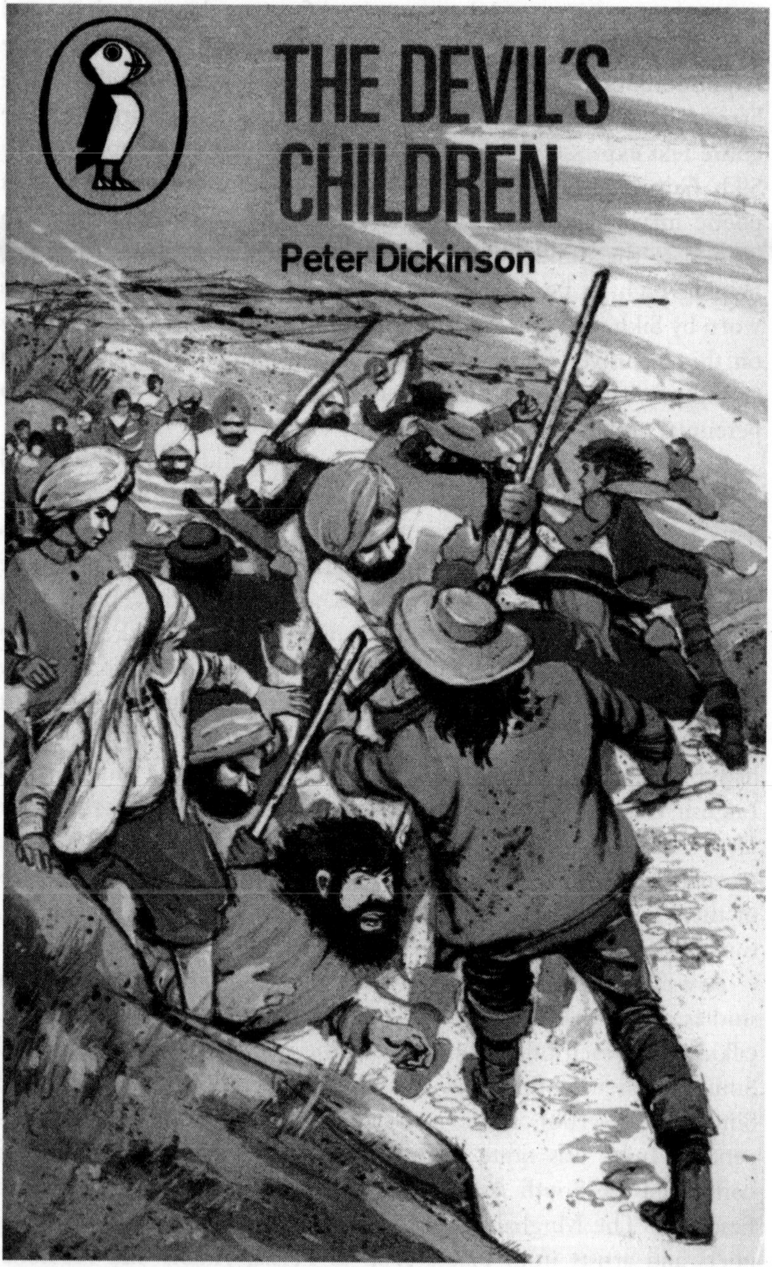

Figure 1: The front cover of The Devil's Children

history of European expansion and territorial invasion. The Portuguese had taken Goa, the Dutch were in Sri Lanka, the British were in Bengal and the French were in Pondicherry – all making their commercial incursions. The missionaries from different Christian denominations and countries were contacting the indigenous Hindus, Buddhists, Jains and Sikhs. From this religiously and culturally diverse landscape, the Sikh Guru implores that we engage with one another:

> *manas ki jat sabai ekai pahicanbo …*
> *ek hi sarup sabai ekai jot janbo* (Akal Ustat: 85)
> Recognize: humanity is the only caste…
> Know: we are all of the same body, the same light.

There is an urgency in his tone as he voices the two imperatives '*pahicanbo*' (recognize) and '*janbo*' (know). His people should know (*janbo*) that everybody has the same body (*ek hi sarup sabai*), and that they are formed of the same spiritual light (*ekai jot*). The Guru did not want his contemporaries to be afraid of one another; he did not want people with different colored eyes or complexions or accents merely to tolerate one another. Rather, he imposed a moral obligation that people must actively learn about others and recognize their fundamental humanity.

Indeed, an encounter with diversity brings a new understanding of others, as well as a renewed self-understanding. Dickinson's young protagonist, Nicky, who went to live with a group of Sikhs, soon learned about their customs and beliefs, and wished that the paranoid villagers around would also realize that the Sikhs were ordinary people like anybody else – 'bones and veins and muscles and fat'.[3] In this book I want to provide an accessible account of the history, doctrine, ethics, rituals, practices and art of the Sikhs, so that unnecessary phobias of the unknown *other* are overcome, and genuine conversations and mutual understanding can take place. Just as Nicky reached out to the Sikhs, in our own multireligious, multiethnic and multicultural village, we can speak to each other 'across language, across the generations, across every difference of race and birth and breeding' (*The Devil's Children*: 181).

My third aim is to recharge the Sikh community to live the liberating mode of existence intended by their Gurus. Beginning with the founder, the ten Sikh Gurus created a window of opportunity for men and women to break out of the imprisonment of age-old customs and taboos, but somehow their radical egalitarianism and broadmindedness has not been fully implemented. Patriarchal values dominate the interpretation of their message; and ancient feudal norms govern social behavior. The hallowed 'traditions' discarded by the Gurus are often ushered into Sikh praxis. Conventional codes, hierarchies and binaries fracture the enhanced personality envisioned by the Gurus. The empowering phenomenon of love at the core of Sikhism must not be suppressed into control or fear. The Gurus may not even have been aware of all the liberating implications of their words and actions, but they set them in motion, and Sikh men and women in the twenty-first century must keep that momentum going.

I also want to acknowledge that I was born and brought up in a Sikh home in the Punjab. Every morning I heard melodious recitations of Sikh scripture by my mother, and every night I saw my father work devotedly on Sikh scholarship. On Sunday mornings my parents' friends would visit, and our house would resound with animated discussions on Sikh politics and history. My larger home was the vibrant Punjabi University campus, where I was exposed to the social and cultural side of Sikhism during its many events and celebrations. I left home as a teenager, but my Sikh community always remained close to me. I am profoundly grateful to the many families and the Gurdwara congregations in North America and Europe who have hosted me, and inspired me with their warmth and love. Thus I have an 'insider's' perspective on the lived dimension of Sikhism.

At the same time, I have an 'outsider's' eye, as I grew up on American campuses from high school onwards (and was probably the only Sikh student in some of the towns I lived in). My immediate context is a broad-based US liberal arts college where Sikhism is just one of the Asian religions I teach along with Hinduism, Buddhism, Confucianism, Taoism, Zen, Shinto and Sufism. I also teach a course on South Asian women writers, and one on India and the Western imagination. This breadth enables me to grasp Sikh phenomena from a plurality of angles. During my career, Western, Eastern and West Asian feminist scholars have deepened my inquiry and honed my academic sensitivity. Female lenses are my key interpretative mechanism, and these were crafted in the feminist studies of religion. They provide me with a critical perspective to examine the subtle complexities of Sikhism.

Nevertheless, I do not profess to put on the hat of objectivity, as that is an impossible act. As the Australian feminist scholar Elizabeth Gross said: 'the conventional assumption that the researcher is a disembodied, rational, sexually indifferent subject – a mind unlocated in space, time or constitutive interrelationships with others, is a status normally attributed only to angels'.[4] Nor do I presume to have gathered all the aspects of five and a half centuries of Sikhism in this one volume! What has been selected here, and how it has been expressed, invariably bear my subjective imprint. Sikhism is not monolithic; like all religions, it is a diverse, dynamic and ever-accumulating process. *Sikhism: An Introduction* is just one glimpse into its kaleidoscopic patterns.

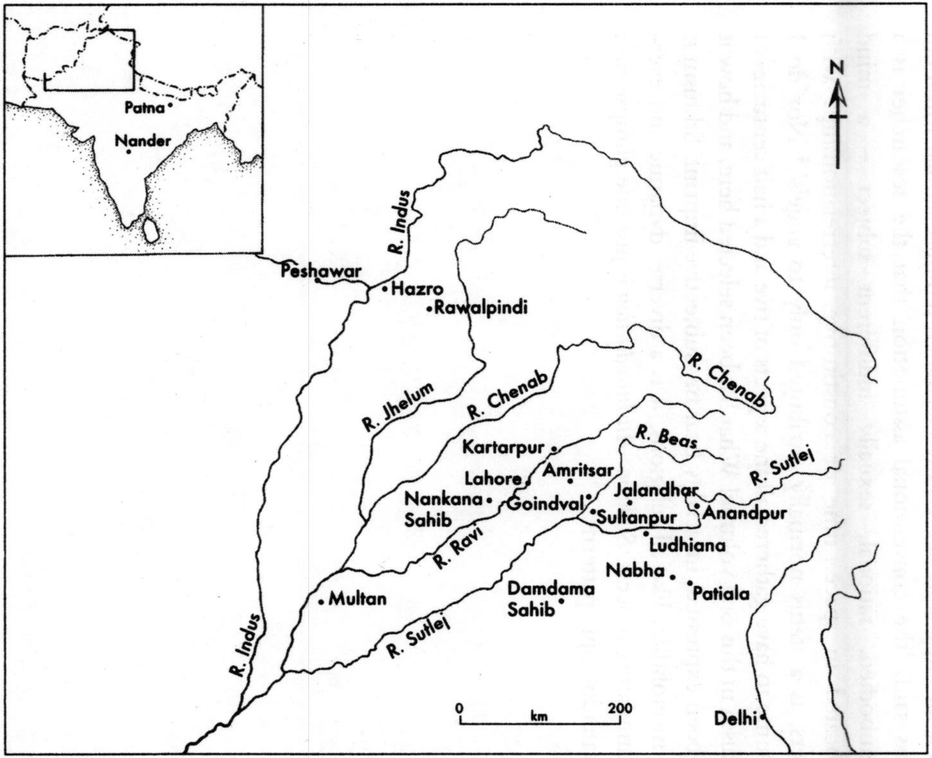

Map 1: Map of the Punjab, with inset map of India showing the location of Patna (birthplace of Guru Gobind Singh) and Nander (where he passed away)

Chapter I

Guru Nanak and the Origins of Sikhism

Sikhism began with the birth of Guru Nanak in 1469 at Talwandi, a village in north India, which is now in Pakistan. There is not much factual documentation on the founder Guru, but in spite of the lack of this, Guru Nanak's biography is strongly imprinted in the collective memory of Sikhs. There are three vital sources for his life: the Janamsakhi narratives; the ballads of Bhai Gurdas; and the Sikh scripture. Together they provide a vibrant portrait of his life and teachings. For the more than 23 million Sikhs across the globe,[1] Guru Nanak is the starting point of their heritage, as most begin their day by reciting his sublime poetry. Sikh homes and places of business display his images. Guru Nanak is typically represented as a haloed, white-bearded person wearing an outfit combining Hindu and Islamic styles; his eyes are rapt in divine contemplation, and his right palm is imprinted with the symbol of the singular Divine, *Ikk Oan Kar*. This chapter turns to the three traditional literary sources for an understanding of the person of Guru Nanak. (For his visual depiction, see Chapter VIII, on Sikh art.)

Janamsakhi Literature

Shortly after he passed away, Guru Nanak's followers wrote accounts of his birth and life. These are the first prose works in the Punjabi language, using the Gurmukhi script. They are called the Janamsakhi, from the Punjabi words *janam*, which means 'birth', and *sakhi*, which means 'story'. Through the years, they have been passed down in a variety of renditions such as the Bala, Miharban, Adi and Puratan. The dominant motif of the Janamsakhis is not chronological or geographical accuracy. As an eminent Sikh historian explains: 'These accounts were written by men of faith. They wrote for the faithful – of a theme, which had grown into their lives through the years as a real, vivid truth. Straightforward history was not their concern, nor was their description objective and conceptual.'[2]

The pattern of mythologizing is rooted in the Indian culture, and the Janamsakhi authors would have been familiar with ancient and medieval Indian literature. Narratives from epics like the Ramayana and the Mahabharata, and from the Puranas, have been told, remembered and retold for centuries. A mixture of mythology, history, philosophy and geography, these texts narrate events which actually happened; thus they are known in India as *Itihasa* (Sanskrit for 'history'). By the time that the Janamsakhis came into circulation, miraculous stories (*mu'jizat*) about Prophet Muhammad and about Muslim saints (*karamat*) had also become widespread in the Punjab through Sufi orders. The Janamsakhi writers were influenced by what was current in their milieu, and they took up the pattern in which great spiritual figures were understood and remembered.

Despite the personal loyalties and proclivities of their various authors, the Janamsakhis invariably underscore the importance and uniqueness of Guru Nanak's birth and life. In the language of myth and allegory, they depict the divine dispensation of Nanak, his concern for kindness, social cohesiveness, and his stress on divine unity and the consequent unity of humanity. Some of the stories incorporate verses from Guru Nanak's works to illuminate his theological and ethical teachings in a biographical framework. The quick and vigorous style of the Janamsakhis lent itself easily to oral circulation, and they became very popular. They continue to be read and told by both the young and the old. At night in many Sikh households, parents and grandparents read them as bedtime stories to young children. They have also been painted and brightly illustrated (which will be examined in Chapter VIII). The Janamsakhis provide Sikhs with their first literary and visual introduction to their heritage, and continue to nurture them for the rest of their lives.

They begin with the illustrious event of Nanak's birth to a Hindu Khatri couple. His father, Kalyan Chand, worked as an accountant for a local Muslim landlord; his mother Tripta was a pious woman. In their central concern and luminous descriptions, Nanak's birth narratives have a great deal in common with those of Christ, Buddha and Krishna (collected by Otto Rank in his study, *The Myth of the Birth of the Hero*).[3] The prophets told Buddha's father, King

Figure 2: Guru Nanak, the First Guru (B-40 Janamsakhi, 1733)

Suddhodhana, that his child would be a great king or a great ascetic. The three Wise Men followed a bright star to honor the baby Jesus, born in a stable in Bethlehem. And just as that stable was marked by the bright Star of Bethlehem, the humble mud hut in which Nanak was born was flooded with light at the moment of his birth. The gifted and wise in both the celestial and terrestrial regions rejoiced at the momentous event and bowed to the exalted spirit, which had adopted bodily form in fulfillment of the Divine Will. But unlike the 'virgin' births of Sakyamuni and Jesus, Nanak had a normal birth. The midwife Daultan attests to Mother Tripta's regular pregnancy and birth. That Tripta's body is entrusted to a Muslim Daultan symbolizes yet another significant fact: the respect and the close connection Nanak's family had with the adherents of Islam. The Janamsakhis show Tripta happily holding the baby in her arms, while Daultan proudly and excitedly reports that there were many children born under her care, but none so extraordinary as baby Nanak. Affirmation of the natural powers of conception, gestation and birth underlie their rejoicing.

The Janamsakhis continue to offer a substantial sketch of Nanak's life. When he grows up, Nanak becomes discontented with the existing norms. He is in conflict with his father, who wants his only son to succeed both financially and socially. The young Nanak does not like formal schooling. He has a contemplative personality and spends most of his time outside, tending the family's herd of cattle, conversing with wayfaring saints and Sufis, and devoting his time to solitude and inward communion. Nanak is close to his sister, Nanaki.[4] When he grew up, he went to live with Nanaki and her husband Jairam in Sultanpur, and worked at a local grocery shop. Later, his marriage was arranged with Sulakhni, and they had two sons, Sri Chand (b. 1494) and Lakhmi Das (b. 1497).

It was at Sultanpur that Nanak had a revelatory experience into the oneness of Reality (analyzed below). As the Janamsakhis recount, with his proclamation 'There is no Hindu, there is no Musalman', Nanak launched his religious mission. Thereafter he traveled extensively throughout India and beyond – spreading his message of Divine unity, which transcended the stereotypical 'Hindu' and 'Muslim' divisions of the time. During most of his travels, his Muslim companion Mardana played the *rabab* while Guru Nanak sang songs of intense love addressing the ultimate One in spoken Punjabi. The direct and simple style of Guru Nanak's teaching drew people from different religious and social backgrounds. Those who accepted him as their 'guru' and followed his teachings came to be known as Sikhs, a Punjabi word which means 'disciple' or 'seeker' (Sanskrit *shishya*; Pali *sekha*).

Guru Nanak eventually settled in Kartarpur, a village he founded by the banks of the River Ravi. A community of disciples grew around him there. Engaged in the ordinary occupations of life, they denied ascetic practices and affirmed a new sense of family. Their pattern of *seva* (voluntary service), *langar* (cooking and eating irrespective of caste, religion or sex) and *sangat* (congregation) created the blueprint for Sikh doctrine and practice. In his own lifetime, Nanak appointed his disciple Lahina as his successor, renaming him Angad ('my limb'). Guru Nanak died in Kartarpur in 1539.

This biographical framework is drawn up in miraculous detail. The Janamsakhis depict scenes in which dreadful and dangerous elements of nature either protect Nanak (such as the cobra offering his shade to a sleeping Nanak) or are controlled by him (with his outstretched palm, Nanak stops a huge rock that was hurled at him). They depict his divine configuration: at his death, the shroud is left without the body; flowers are found instead of Guru Nanak's body; and both Hindus and Muslims carry away the fragrant flowers – to cremate or bury according to their respective customs.

They repeatedly portray Guru Nanak denouncing formal ritual, often with great wit and irony. During his travels, Nanak visits Hardwar, the ancient site of pilgrimage on the River Ganges. When he saw some priests sprinkling water to the rising sun in the East, Nanak started sprinkling water to the West. The priests found his actions sacrilegious. So when they asked him who would benefit from his splashing water to the West, he questioned them in return. The priests responded that they were offering oblations to the spirits of their dead ancestors. Nanak then continues his procedure with even greater vigor. Through this dramatic sequence he makes the point that, if water sprinkled by priests could reach their dead ancestors, surely his would reach the fields down the road and help his crops.

This pedagogical pattern recurs frequently in the Janamsakhi narratives. Nanak twists and overturns the established ritual codes in a way that challenges people's innate assumptions, and orients them toward a new reality. The numerous miracles associated with him are not a means of amplifying his grandeur, but rather, they serve as lenses through which his audience can interrogate the inner workings of their own minds. When Nanak goes to Mecca, for example, he falls asleep with his feet towards the Ka'ba. The Qazi in charge gets upset because of the irreverence shown by the visitor. However, Nanak does not get ruffled. Rather than contradict him, he politely asks the Qazi to turn his feet in a direction he deemed proper. But as Nanak's feet are turned, so does the sacred Ka'ba. There is no need for readers to consider it a historical fact; the motion of circularity simply shatters rigid mental formulas. That the Divine exists in every direction and that internal religiosity cannot be expressed externally are effectively communicated. Narratives such as this dislocate conventional habits and linear structures of the readers, and whirl them into a vast interior horizon.[5]

In an oft-quoted account, Nanak refuses to participate in the *upanyana* initiation – the important thread (*janeu*) ceremony reserved for 'twice born' Hindu boys (from the upper three classes). The Janamsakhis point to a young Nanak disrupting this crucial rite of passage that had prevailed for centuries. His denial is framed within an elaborate setting arranged by his parents. A large number of relatives and friends are invited to their house. Pandit Hardyal, the revered family priest, officiates at the ceremonies. Pandit Hardyal is seated on a specially built platform purified by cow-dung plaster, and the boy Nanak is seated across, facing him. Pandit Hardyal lights lamps, lights fragrant incense, draws beautiful designs in flour-chalk and recites melodious mantras. When the priest proceeds to invest the initiate with the sacred thread (*janeu*), Nanak interrupts the ceremonies, questions him as to what he is doing with the yarn, and refuses to wear it. At this point, the narrative juxtaposes Nanak's criticism of the handspun thread with his ardent proposal for one that is emotionally and spiritually 'woven by the cotton of compassion, spun into the yarn of contentment, knotted by virtue, and twisted by truth'.[6] Rather than being draped externally, the *janeu* becomes an internal process. 'Such a thread', continues Nanak, 'will neither snap nor soil; neither get burnt nor lost'. Nanak's biography and poetry are thus blended together by the Janamsakhi author to illustrate his rejection of an exclusive rite of passage. A young Nanak interrupts a smooth ceremony in front of a large gathering in his father's house so that his contemporaries could envision a different type of 'thread', a different ritual, a whole different ideal. There are many such vignettes in which Nanak vividly dismantles the prevailing societal hegemonies of caste and class, and reinforces an egalitarian human dimension.

The Janamsakhis are particularly significant in introducing the earliest women mentioned in Sikhism. They may not fully develop their individual characters, and reveal them only in so far as they are related to the Guru. Yet even in their rudimentary presentations, the authors highlight the subtle awareness that the women possess. Mata Tripta is a wise woman who understands her son and can see into his unique personality – much more so than his father. The midwife Daultan is struck by the extraordinary qualities of the child she delivers. Like Mary Magdalene, who was the first woman to have witnessed the resurrection of Christ, sister Nanaki is the first person to recognize Nanak's enlightenment. Only Sulakhni's role is ambiguous, as if the authors did not quite know how to deal with her. As the wife of the founder of the Sikh religion, where was she? What was her relationship with her husband? How did she feel when he left her with their two sons and went on his long journeys?

The north Indian soil was rich with saints from various Hindu denominations, just as it was with the different orders of Sufism, Buddhist schools and Jain monks. With their holy presence, their devotional outpourings, and their message of love and charity, leaders and common folk from different religious backgrounds and ethnicities created a vibrant environment. The Janamsakhi literature depicts a pluralistic Nanak, who engages meaningfully with people of different faiths. Full of respect and with no acrimony, he discusses and discourses with them. There is the urge in him to know and get closer to 'others', so with his Muslim companion, he travels extensively. Nanak is seen in Hardwar, he is seen in Mecca, he is seen in the upper ranges of the Himalayas. He visits temples, mosques, viharas and khanaqahs; he attends a multitude of fairs and festivals. The basic commonness of humanity is what he carries to people of every faith. He invites all to be authentically themselves, and thus creates space for real and different religious commitments. When he meets Muslims, he adjures them to be faithful to the teaching of their faith; and when he meets Hindus, he urges them to abide by the tenets of their own tradition. With their practical sensibility and inherent wit, the Janamsakhi authors relay the pluralistic dynamism with which Nanak engages with the religious and cultural diversity of his times, and succeeds in establishing his own distinct faith.

Guru Nanak's Revelation

A profoundly simple yet highly nuanced narrative from the Puratan Janamsakhi celebrates Guru Nanak's revelatory experience of the singular Divine, configured as *Ikk Oan Kar*. On a closer analysis it highlights some unique aspects of Sikh origins, as well as the universal structures found in myths across cultures. This major event in Guru Nanak's life takes place in Sultanpur, where he was employed in a store owned by a local Muslim landlord. One day, Nanak did not return home after his usual morning bath in the River Bein. A wide search was made but there was no sign of him. His clothes were found by the river. Everyone thought he had drowned. The town was plunged into gloom. But Nanak reappeared on the third day. During this interval, the Janamsakhi recounts his direct communion with the Divine. This was his personal rite of passage, a symbolic birth that redefined Guru Nanak's social and spiritual identity. Having rejected the *Upanayana*, he goes through an entirely different rite of passage – conforming to the archetypal tripartite pattern of separation, liminality and reincorporation.

Separation

As Nanak goes to bathe in the river, he leaves behind his clothes – indicative of his previous set of codes and signs; he leaves behind his attendant – indicative of his home, family and society at large. He now possesses nothing. Nanak has stripped off his cultural conditions and divested himself of society's structures. He disappears in the Bein for three days. His Muslim employer summons the fishermen, has nets thrown into the river, and has his men search everywhere, but in vain. Nanak is nowhere to be found and Nanak's employer leaves dejected, thinking how good a minister Nanak was.

Betwixt and Between

In this 'interstructural situation', Nanak 'is at once no longer classified and not yet classified';[7] he is no longer the store employee, nor is he yet the Guru who will attract millions to a new world religion. Nanak has reached a dynamic threshold where the past borders are gone and future possibilities are yet to come. During the three days he is believed drowned, Nanak goes through a series of numinous events.

In the multilayered mythic account, Nanak is ushered into the divine presence and receives a cup of *amrit*: '*ehu amritu mere nam ka piala hai* – this *amrit* is the cup of my Name'.[8] Enclosed in the waters of the River Bein, Nanak receives the drink of immortality – *amrit* (literal meanings: *a* = not + *mrit* = death). He does not see; he only hears. The postmodern philosopher, Hans-Georg Gadamer, regards the phenomenon of hearing as being crucial to the building up of tradition: 'hearing takes in language and thus everything, not just the visible'.[9] The voice Nanak hears does not come from some high mountaintop; it comes from inside the river. To drink is a basic and primal function and need, and so the account validates a basic human process. The Divine command '*pio*' (drink) substantiates the human body with its capacity to drink, taste, grow and be nourished.

What Nanak received was *nam ka piala* – the cup of Name. *Nam* (the cognate of the English word 'name') is the identity of the transcendent One. This elemental process constitutes Nanak's introduction to the Divine: by sipping the universal drink, Nanak gets to *know* the Ultimate Reality. The immortal drink that Nanak receives is the sapiential experience of the transcendent One.

After being given the cup of *amrit*, Nanak is asked to go and instruct others. But there is also the implication in the Janamsakhi narrative that he is put through a test. Before he departs, Nanak is ordered to illustrate his method and technique: 'How does one praise my name? Recite!' Guru Nanak responds with a hymn that was his song – and proof – of praise. We find here a striking affinity between '*kahu*' ('recite' in Punjabi), the command that Nanak receives, and '*kun*' ('recite' in Arabic), the order given by God to the Prophet Muhammad through the Archangel Gabriel. While the Prophet Muhammad hears the Word in the caves of Mount Hira, Guru Nanak hears it in the River Bein. Neither was previously known for his poetic genius, but after passing through the spaces, both of them become the matrix for a voluminous and momentous and most artistic text – the holy Qu'ran and the Guru Granth, respectively.

Guru Nanak passes the test through poetic syntax and is accepted by the Divine. He recites a hymn, which demonstrates his psychic and spiritual power, as well as his artistic talent. Its final verse is:

> If I had a supply of bottomless ink, and could write with the
> speed of the wind;
> I would still not be able to measure your greatness,
> nor signify the glory of Your Name! (GG: 13)

Nanak becomes a poet. He explodes human language. He uses poignant similes, analogies and metaphors to describe that which is utterly ineffable. After Nanak's response the Voice spoke: 'Nanak, you discern My will.' The Janamsakhi thus attests to Nanak's success. Nanak then recites the Jap. Although the Janamsakhi does not produce the entire text of Nanak's hymn, it specifies that Nanak 'concluded the Jap – *japu sampuran kita*'. Recited at this particular point of his spiritual encounter, the Jap acknowledges Nanak's acceptance and gratitude. The Jap constitutes the core of Guru Nanak's metaphysics. It forms the opening hymn of Sikh scripture, and is recited daily by devout Sikhs.

In the third phase of his sacred liminality, Guru Nanak is given the dress of honor (the *sirpao*, more commonly known as *saropa*). As the Janamsakhi narrative continues:

> The Voice was heard again: 'Who is just in your eyes, Nanak, shall be so in mine. Whoever receives your grace shall abide in mine. My name is the supreme One; your name is the divine Guru.' Guru Nanak then bowed in gratitude and was given the dress of honor from the divine court. A sonorous melody in the Raga Dhanasari rang forth … Arati….

Nanak is initiated as the Guru. He is endowed with a new status and identity. The sacrum or the physical object that marks his special dispensation is the *sirpao*, a piece of material that goes from head (*sir*) to foot (*pao*). Since it is not tailored, it does not carry any male or female codifications, and could be worn by both sexes. On his conferral, the Guru rapturously recites Arati, a hymn in which he celebrates the transcendent light permeating every being. In the fecund waters of the river, Nanak recognizes the ontological basis of the universe, and is called on to share what has been revealed to him.

Reincorporation

After his radical experience, the protagonist returns to society as the Guru. In his new status and role, he has gained a new self-awareness.

Nanak's initiation does not establish his sexual status, and if at all, his rite of passage shatters the construction of a male identity. Though it was a son, brother and husband who entered the river, the mythic initiation endows him with his fundamental humanity. Located in the amniotic waters, he goes through the process of physical drinking, which gives him the metaphysical insight into the Divine. He responds in a sensuous, poetic outpouring, and is honored with gender-inclusive clothing from the Divine court. Unlike other initiation rites, there are no additions to or subtractions from the body: no tattoos, circumcision or scarring marked his transition. In Guru Nanak's case, his new identity is marked by the unity of *bana* (the material cloth) and *bani* (poetry); *sirpao* (dress) and *nam* (word).

As he reincorporates into society, 'antistructure' becomes the mode of existence. The first Sikh community that developed with Guru Nanak at Kartarpur fits in with the cultural anthropologist Victor Turner's description of 'antistructure', because the neat horizontal divisions and vertical hierarchies of society were broken down. The ancient fourfold class system with its rigid hierarchical codes, or the male–female gender divisions had no place in Nanak's new community. Three important institutions of Sikhism – *seva* (voluntary service), *langar* (community meal) and *sangat* (congregation) – evolved, in which men and women formerly from different castes, classes and religions played an equal part. Together they listened to and recited the sacred hymns, together they cooked and ate the *langar*, and together they formed a democratic congregation without priests or ordained ministers.

These institutions established in the first Sikh community at Kartarpur were a practical and existential consequence of Guru Nanak's epiphany recorded in the Janamsakhi. The mythic account may not have been factually true, but it has been essential to the historical development of the Sikh religion. The Tenth Sikh Guru's inauguration of the *amrit* initiation on Baisakhi Day 1699 is in fact a return to this primal moment of Sikhism. Years later, the 'beginning' of Sikhism embodied in the private, individual and mystical experience of the First Guru was transcreated by the Tenth as a public, social and institutional ritual in Anandpur. By initiating his Five Beloved with Amrit, the Tenth Guru extended the vigor of Nanak's *amrit* into perpetuity: he made the metahistoric drink an essential part of the psyche and practice of the Sikh community.[10]

Guru Nanak brought to life a 'Sikh' consciousness, which has continued to sustain the faith for the past five and a half centuries. His legacy is an enduring and integral part of daily life. Indeed, these Janamsakhis have enormous force as they continue to feed the individual and collective identity of the community. As Mircea Eliade rightly said, myths constitute sacred history, and hence are a 'true history', because they always deal with *realities*.

The Ballads of Bhai Gurdas

Bhai Gurdas was born in 1551, 12 years after Guru Nanak passed away, and died in 1636 at the age of 85. His long lifespan made him the contemporary of Guru Nanak's five successors – Guru Angad (Nanak 2) through Guru Hargobind (Nanak 6). Chronologically and geographically, Bhai Gurdas was very close to Guru Nanak and was himself an important figure in early Sikh history. His name Gurdas (*das* or servant of the Guru) is indicative of his parents' close association with the Gurus. His mother, Bibi Jivani, was appointed by the Third Guru to manage one of the Sikh districts.[11] His cousin, Bibi Bhani, was married to the Fourth Guru and gave birth to Guru Arjan (Nanak 5), who compiled the Sikh scripture and built the first Sikh shrine. The maternal uncle was chosen by Guru Arjan to transcribe the momentous sacred text. When the Akal Takht was built during the period of Guru Hargobind (Nanak 6), Bhai Gurdas was assigned to manage the premises. Guru Hargobind also selected Bhai Gurdas to teach his young son, Tegh Bahadur (the future Ninth Guru), classical texts and philosophies. Bhai Gurdas not only witnessed but also participated in the origins and crystallization of the Sikh faith in a vital way. Consequently, Sikhs rely on him as their foremost historian and theologian.

His literary works are revered as a 'key' (*kunji*) to the treasury of Sikh theology and history. His *Vars* (ballads) in Punjabi are especially popular, as Sikhs memorize and quote them with regard to belief and behavior. The genre of the *Var* is that of a heroic ode or ballad with several stanzas, and in these ballads, Bhai Gurdas presents Sikh ideals, morals and society in a simple, bold and urgent way. Many of the *Vars* have also been set to melodious rhythms and have become an important part of *kirtan*, the Sikh devotional music. Corresponding with the Janamsakhis, his *Var* 1 (Cantos 23–45) illuminates the person and role of the founder Guru.[12] Many of the Janamsakhi events and themes are eulogized by Bhai Gurdas in crisp linguistic textures and racy meters.

In his popular verse sung by Sikhs everywhere, the Guru is praised as the axial point between a human figure and the Divine Reality:

> As Guru Nanak appeared, mist lifted light filled the world
> Like the stars vanish and darkness recedes when the sun rises
> Like the deer scatter when the lion roars.
> Wherever the Baba set his foot, it became the seat of worship
> Seats sacred to the Siddhas now laud the name of Nanak.
> Every home has become a Dharamsal, resonant with sacred chant.
> Baba cultivated all the four corners and all the nine regions of the earth,
> Bestowing upon them the gift of True Name.
> In the age of darkness the holy Guru appeared. (I: 27)

Poetry and history fuse together to express the advent of the Sikh Guru. Bhai Gurdas creates a captivating contrast between the world prior to Guru Nanak and the one after his appearance. With the emergence of radiance, all kinds of density and opaqueness give way to clarity and transparency; the dark skies with twinkling stars burst into brilliance and effulgence. For Bhai Gurdas, just as the rising sun does not strike out the dark acrimoniously but delicately brings in light, so did Guru Nanak on the horizon of fifteenth-century north-west India.

He upholds the outlook of the Janamsakhis, and illustrates Guru Nanak as the starting-point of a new spiritual and ethical mode of being, and in his poetic eloquence, Bhai Gurdas describes the peaceful manner in which the founder Guru launched his new faith. The Guru does not impose his views on others. He does not reject the existing religious traditions, nor does he intend to replace them with his own. He validates the religious plurality of his day: 'Ram and Rahim occupy the same position – *ram rahim ikk thai khaloi*' (Bhai Gurdas, Var I: 33). Both the Hindu and Muslim religious ideals of his milieu are fully affirmed and given equal status.

The familiar Janamsakhi narratives acquire a poetic medium, for here again we see a pluralist Nanak actively reaching out to people of different faiths. He travels in four directions, he visits the sacred spaces of the many groups of Hindus, Muslims and Buddhists, and converses with them about their respective scriptures and philosophies. He leaves his footprints on distant lands, and his imprint on the hearts of people. In one such encounter, Bhai Gurdas pictures him going to Multan, an important Sufi centre. Nanak was received with a bowl full of milk, which signified that the region was already full to the brim with religious leaders, and that there would be no place for a newcomer like Nanak. How did Nanak react? Without any verbal, physical or philosophical tussle, 'the Baba produced a jasmine from underneath his arm and mixed it with milk in the bowl. It was like the River Ganga merging with the ocean' (I: 44). With the addition of Guru Nanak's 'jasmine', the milk did not spill out from the brimming bowl, but became more fragrant and colorful.[13]

In another pluralist venture, a young Nanak visits the Siddhas. He climbs up to Mount Sumer where the Siddhas with their leader Gorakhnath are known to reside after having obtained immortality through Hatha Yoga. As the Siddhas sit in a conclave:

> All the eighty-four adepts from Gorakh downward began to wonder in their hearts, who could have thus reached their realm.
> 'Listen, young seeker,' they spoke. 'What power do you possess which has brought you here?'
> 'I have but cherished the Supreme One; in love of the Supreme One have I sat meditating.'
> 'You must tell us at least your name, young seeker,' spoke the Siddhas again.
> 'My name,' said the Baba, 'is Nanak, revered Nathji; Repetition of the Divine Name is my sole sustenance.'
> The higher one ascends, the humbler one becomes. (I: 28)

Here Nanak is observed through the lens of the Siddhas, who spot a naive young fellow climbing up to their realm. Like modern scholars, they are curious about Nanak's religious heritage, and want to classify the newcomer into some neat category. From Guru Nanak's perspective, however, he is simply Nanak, whose identity is derived from the Supreme One: 'My name', said the Baba, 'is Nanak, revered Nathji; Repetition of the Divine Name my sole sustenance'. Politely and humbly, Nanak gives his name to their leader ('*nath*' means

Figure 3: Guru Nanak wearing an inscribed robe, late nineteenth century

master, and the suffix '*ji*' is an additional form of courtesy). Nanak has no historic lineage; his love for the True Name endows him with his individual personality and character. The True Name was Nanak's revelation of the singular Divine he personally experienced and expressed poetically. The medium of Divine revelation and the revelation thus come together, and throughout his text, Bhai Gurdas extols their convergence.

He conveys the mesmerizing quality of Guru Nanak's verse. When Guru Nanak travels to Baghdad with Mardana, his holy chant has an emotional impact: 'After the morning's devotions broke into holy chant/Hearing which people fell into a trance' (I: 35). Wherever he goes, men and women are transformed: 'Day by day his fame grew and he made the age of Kali reverberate with the Divine Name' (I: 45). People from different religious and social backgrounds started to follow Nanak because of the message he brought to them. In *Var* I: 38: 'from his lips flowed the holy Word which turned darkness into light'. Guru Nanak's oral gift is profoundly liberating, literally: *sati* (true), *sabad* (word), *mukat* (freedom), *karaia* (makes/brings). It dissolves doubts and fears, and opens up new possibilities.

Bhai Gurdas' entire focus is on the new religion launched by Guru Nanak. His way of life, with its stress on the Divine Name, becomes the paradigmatic mode of existence for his followers. Family and home are lauded; asceticism and otherworldly orientation are spurned. A new community with its own unique vision and practices is born. In fact, Bhai Gurdas offers a valuable snapshot of the daily routine of this earliest Sikh community: 'In the evening were recited *sodar* and *arati* and in the ambrosial hour, the *jap*' (I: 38). These hymns, subsequently collected in Sikh scripture, are also mentioned in the encounter with the Divine in our Janamsakhi account. To this day, Sikh homes and their formal places of worship maintain the routine of reciting Jap in the morning, and Sodar and Arati in the evening. From the start, Guru Nanak's word was the vital ingredient that fed Sikh identity.

Guru Nanak's installation of his successor is an important historical event, which is underscored in the Janamsakhis and the Guru Ganth as well. Bhai Gurdas conveys it compellingly:

> He promulgated in the world the authority of the Divine Order and created a community purged of the pollution [of selfish ego].
> While still in this world he installed Lahina as his successor, and bestowed upon him the umbrella of Guruship.
> Kindling another light with his light Guru Nanak changed his form
> None can describe the marvelous deed of the marvelous one.
> He changed his body into that of Angad, who reflected his own light. (I: 45)

Self-conscious about his mission, Guru Nanak at the close of his life installs his successor. Overlooking his own sons, his devout follower Lahina is made Angad (literally, limb of his own body). Light that is passed on from Guru Nanak to Lahina is like one flame kindling another (*joti jot milai kai*). Bhai Gurdas then goes on to narrate that Angad (Nanak 2) left Kartarpur and retired to the town of Khadur, where he passed the light he had received from Guru Nanak to Amar Das (Nanak 3) who then raised the town of Goindwal (I: 46). Bhai Gurdas sheds light on early Sikh chronology and its unique phenomenon of succession: beginning with Guru Nanak, the divine inheritance is maintained and passed from one Guru to the next. The foremost Sikh historian and theologian confirms the Janamskahi portrait of Guru Nanak as the intersection between a historical person and a timeless reality.

Sikh Scripture

In Sikh scripture, we encounter the Guru directly. The Fifth Sikh Guru collected Guru Nanak's 974 compositions when he compiled the Guru Granth in 1604. Indeed, Guru Nanak's verse forms the model for the entire scripture, with his Jap being the opening hymn.[14] In his extensive repertoire, Guru Nanak expresses his desire for the Infinite One. From his metaphysical poetry we gain a valuable insight into his personality. We get a feel for his self-understanding, and a perspective on the socio-political conditions of his period.

Historical Allusions

His Babur Vani compositions show that Guru Nanak lived in north-west India at the time of transition from the Afghan rule of Ibrahim Lodi to the Mughal rule of Babur (1483–1530). Guru Nanak's four hymns recorded in the Guru Granth (three in Rag Asa and the fourth in Rag Tilang) describe Babur's conquest of India as he comes down with his troops from Afghanistan. Guru Nanak's detailed and empathetic discourse is strong evidence of his geographical and temporal proximity to the events. These 'Babur Vani' compositions allude to Guru Nanak's multicultural period, in which the Hindu Puja and the Muslim Namaz took place side by side, and one in which Hindu women practiced *sati* and Muslim women observed the *purdah*. The vital way in which Guru Nanak responds to this particular moment in Indian history demonstrates that he was distressed by the fate of the last of the Delhi Sultans. Guru Nanak's spirituality is firmly based in his socio-political reality.

Angad is Appointed Guru

The founder Guru passing his succession to Guru Angad is also recorded in Sikh scripture. The composition of Satta and Balvand, two bards at the Sikh court, opens with praise of Guru Nanak as the initiator of a spiritual 'empire' (*raj*), a builder of a 'true' (*sac*) 'fort' (*kot*) with strong foundations:

> Nanak established his empire –
>   Building his true fort on firm foundations;
> He placed the canopy on Lahina's head,
>   As he praised the Divine, sipped ambrosia;
> He handed the strong sword made from
>   The instruction of spiritual wisdom.
> The Guru bowed to his disciple
>   During his own lifetime;
> He put the *tikka*
>   While still alive.
> Now Lahina succeeded Nanak –
>   He deserved it so
> It was the same light, it was the same manner,
>   It was the body that was changed;
> The immaculate canopy waves over him,
>   He has occupied the throne in the Guru's trade...
> (GG: 966–7)

In political language and royal tropes, the bards depict Nanak as a decisive figure who appoints his disciple as his successor during his own lifetime. The visionary Guru is keenly aware of his legacy, and ensures a new leadership for his evolving community. The transference to the next Guru is powerfully choreographed. Guru Nanak places the canopy (the cultural marker of honor) on his successor's head, he puts the *tikka* (ceremonial mark, another cultural trope for respect) on his forehead, and he bows respectfully to him. Nanak performs these acts in the accompaniment of Divine praise and drinking of ambrosial *amrit* – something he had done during his own revelatory experience in the River Bein. As noted above, Guru Nanak also passes the strong sword (*kharag jor*) to Guru Angad, a symbolic representation of the 'instruction of spiritual wisdom' (*mat gur atam dev di*). Later in Sikh history, one of the five symbols given by the Tenth Guru to his Sikhs is the sword. In consonance with Bhai Gurdas and the Janamsakhis (see Chapter VIII on Sikh art), this scriptural passage claims that Guru Nanak had made Lahina more than his successor: he had made him equal with himself. The poetic statements from Bhai Gurdas and the Guru Granth marvel as the First Guru is physically, intellectually and spiritually absorbed into the Second.

Self Identification

Guru Nanak calls himself a poet (*sairu/shair*), which comes from the Arabic word for poetry (*al-shi'r*). S. H. Nasr traces its root meaning to consciousness and knowledge.[15] Nanak's ideal of poetry is therefore very different from our word 'poetry', which means making. Rather than making or crafting, the poet Nanak is consumed by the intense awareness and love for the Divine: '*sasu masu sabhu jio tumara tu mai khara piara nanaku sairu eva kahatu hai sace parvadgara* – to you belong my breath, to you my flesh; says the poet Nanak, you the True One are my Beloved' (GG: 660). He frequently refers to himself as the Slave of the Divine. He admits: '*hau apahu bol na janada mai kahia sabhu hukmau jiu* – I do not know how to speak, I utter what you command me to' (GG: 763). The Guru who revels in calling himself a poet acknowledges the Divine as the source of his voice, his sensibility and his vision. As we may recall from the Janamsakhi narrative, it was through his poetic medium that he passed his test, and was charged with Guruship. Therefore, in its sublime language, Guru Nanak joins his subtle metaphysics with his ethical ideals and esthetic technique. His divinely inspired utterances appear at speed and take on beautiful, artistic forms. They are not contingent on any linguistic, grammatical or conceptual laws, and yet with a natural momentum, they flow out in perfect alliteration and rhyme, in lyrical assonance and consonance. Instead of the elite languages of Arabic, Persian and Sanskrit, Guru Nanak uses the vernacular Punjabi as the medium of communication. His verses create fascinating geometric patterns, verbal arabesques and dynamic somersaults, and reach a wide audience. The revealed word is exquisitely artistic. It brings thinking alive.

A Modern Thinker

Guru Nanak's communication style is in tune with modern academia, where the aim is to provoke thought. He does not preach. He does not give a belief system to follow. Instead, he questions, he learns, he shares, he invites people to be who they are. Without stipulating any rules or doctrines, the Guru artfully trains his readers to use their intellectual gifts and discover new tracks. For example, Stanza 21 of his Jap raises questions about primordial origins:

> What was the time, what was the hour,
> What was the date, what was the day,
> What was the season, what was the month,
> When creation was born?

Guru Nanak's questions are keen, and their pacing is quick. With such minute distinctions of time, hour, date, day, month, season, he incites readers to recollect their origins and really think about their place in the universe. His stimulating questions enter contemporary debates about the origins of our universe. When did it all begin? How did we evolve? The Guru mentions that, even in his time, scholars were offering their own answers. But he accepts no theories nor presumes any knowledge himself: 'The creator who designed this creation alone knows.' His response does not shut any doors; it merely makes people reflect more deeply about their reality.

His interrogative technique instills freedom and creativity in the minds of his readers and listeners. By raising questions, Nanak enables them to gain insights into their lives, to imagine unimaginable terrains, and to live their moral values. Here is another example: '*muho ki bolan bolia jisu sun dhare pyar* – what should our lips say that hearing it will win us divine love' (Jap: 4)? Priests and exegetes are made redundant, and instead, each person is instilled with the responsibility to hone their language. He makes us think seriously about what we say to our family members, peers and fellow workers. Enactment is a reflex of understanding. Poetically, the Guru trains people to speak a language that will usher love and not hate. Nanak is a teacher who teaches without teaching.

To conclude, the Janamsakhis, the ballads of Bhai Gurdas and Sikh scripture confirm that Guru Nanak brought a new message of Oneness to a multiethnic and multireligious medieval Indian society. Being a good human being takes precedence over being a good

'Hindu' or a good 'Muslim' (the basic religious categories of his time) was the message he communicated in his universal poetry, in vernacular language that crossed the boundaries of elite Sanskrit, Arabic or Persian. How to think, reflect, realize and feel the singular Divine was the foundation of his democratic institutions of *langar*, *sangat* and *seva*. Poetry and praxis constitute a reflexive process. A heightened experience of the Infinite is what his sublime verses convey. That is what his memory inspires.

Chapter II

Guru Arjan and the Crystallization of the Sikh Faith

The message and mission begun by Guru Nanak was carried through ten living Gurus. The Guru in Sikhism does not replace or incarnate the Divine in any way; rather, the Guru is a channel, a guide, who enlightens people to imbibe the love and nature of the Ultimate One. The transition of Guruship initiated by Guru Nanak was repeated successively until the installation of the scripture as the Guru eternal. The Ten Gurus of Sikhism are:

Guru Nanak (1469–1539)
Guru Angad (1539–52)
Guru Amar Das (1552–74)
Guru Ram Das (1574–81)
Guru Arjan (1581–1606)
Guru Hargobind (1606–44)
Guru Har Rai (1644–61)
Guru Har Kishen (1661–4)
Guru Tegh Bahadur (1664–75)
Guru Gobind Singh (1675–1708).

Each of the Ten played a crucial role in the development of the faith. The content of their instruction was the same; and the poetic method they utilized was also the same. They personified the same light. The same voice spoke through the Ten. The Tenth Guru, Guru Gobind Singh, ended the line of personal Gurus by passing on the succession of Guruship to the scriptural volume. Guru Arjan was the mid-point of the spiritual lineage between Guru Nanak and Guru Gobind Singh. He was the son of Bibi Bhani (daughter of Guru Amar Das, the Third Guru) and Guru Ram Das (the Fourth Guru).

Guru Angad (Nanak 2)

On his succession, Guru Angad (Nanak 2) helped the Sikh community to grow and spread for 13 years. He is known to have collected the hymns of Guru Nanak into a volume, which marked the beginning of written literature in Punjabi. Like his predecessor, the Second Guru valued the esthetic and epistemological power of Divine poetry: 'ambrosial word reveals the essence of existence; it comes with knowledge and contemplation – *amrit bani tat vakhani gian dhian vici ai*' (GG: 1243). The epilogue (*shalok*) to Guru Nanak's Jap, a popular item in Sikh liturgical prayers, is also attributed to Guru Angad. Its most memorable scene depicts the entire universe with its countless species playing in the 'lap of day and night, the male and female nurses – *divas rati dui dai daia khele sagal jagat*' (GG: 8). The various and complex creatures are freely and delightfully cradled on the maternal lap of night and day. Without rivalries or enmity, they are nestled together. The Jap hymn is a perfectly organic textual body: while Nanak's prologue with the *Ikk Oan Kar* directs readers towards the Infinite, Guru Angad's epilogue leaves them – humans and nature alike – playing happily together to the melodious movements of night and day. Guru Angad added his poetry to that of Guru Nanak's collection, and signed it with the name 'Nanak'. There are 62 couplets from the Second Guru in Sikh scripture.

After carrying on the office of Guru Nanak in Kartarpur, Guru Angad eventually moved to his native village of Khadur. His wife, Mata Khivi, is fondly remembered for her liberal direction of *langar*. With Mata Khivi's generous supervision and her plentiful supply of *kheer* (rice pudding), the tradition became a real feast rather than just a symbolic meal. Their daughter, Bibi Amaro, played an important role in the continuation of Guru Nanak's spiritual legacy, because it was from her lips that Amar Das (an uncle of Bibi Amaro's husband) heard Nanak's captivating verse. When he expressed his wish to meet the Guru, Bibi Amaro escorted Amar Das enthusiastically to her father, Guru Angad, in her native village. Though Amar Das was much senior in age, he became a devoted follower of the Second Guru, and eventually succeeded him to the Guruship.

Guru Amar Das (Nanak 3)

Guru Amar Das (Nanak 3) established the town of Goindval, which helped the community to expand further. In order to reach distant congregations, he created a well-knit organization by setting up 22 seats of authority (called *manjis*, literally charpoi or cot). Pious Sikhs were appointed as leaders. They taught Guru Nanak's message, looked after the congregation in their jurisdiction, and transmitted the disciples' offerings to Goindval. The Guru appointed women leaders as well. He paid special attention to the oppressed condition of women. The customs of *purdah* (veiling) and *sati* (dying on the funeral pyre of the husband) were denounced. During the traditional festivals of Baisakhi (Spring) and Divali (Autumn), the congregations were encouraged to visit Goindval, thus giving them a sense of developing their own 'Sikh' celebrations. Guru Amar Das had built a large well with 84 steps in Goindval to provide drinking water for the residents, and for the Sikhs it began to serve as a special place associated with their compassionate Guru.

The Third Guru had great reverence for sacred poetry, and made important contributions to the codification of the canon. He collected the compositions of his predecessors and some of the saints of his time. His own verse is charged with profound beauty. In fact, all Sikh rites and ceremonies conclude with the congregation reciting together sections of his composition 'Anand' (meaning 'bliss'). 'Anand' has also been incorporated into the evening prayer, so at the end of the day Sikh men and women enter into its joyous expanse. Its opening stanza is:

> *anand bhaia meri mae*
> *satguru mai paia*
> *satgur ta paia sahaj seti*
> *man vajian vadhaian*
> My Mother! I am in bliss,
> for I have found my true Guru;
> My true Guru I found so easily,
> my mind rings with felicitations!

The Guru is in bliss as he has found the true enlightener within himself. Readers enter with him a sphere where there are no divisions, no defense mechanisms. Here is freedom; here is ecstasy. Beautiful music wafts, and the mind reverberates with melodious rhythms. There are 907 such lyrical hymns of Guru Amar Das included in the Guru Granth, which help us imagine total unity and experience polymorphous delights. Before he died in 1574, Guru Amar Das chose his daughter's husband as his successor.

Guru Ram Das (Nanak 4)

Guru Ram Das (Nanak 4) continued to compose sacred poetry and foster the self-consciousness of the community. He instituted simple ceremonies and rites for birth, marriage and death, which promoted a distinct identity for the Sikhs. His composition 'Lavan' now serves as the basis for the Sikh wedding ceremony. *Lavan* (circling) describes marriage as a rite of passage into deeper and deeper circles of existence. The journey begins with active work in the world and adoration of the Divine Name. The second verse describes the mind, which recognizes the singular One within all that is seen and heard. The Divine is encountered everywhere and the 'unstruck sound' (*anahad sabad*) is heard within the depths of the self. In the third circle, that feeling surges, and the self becomes fully absorbed in the Divine Love. As the fourth round commences, '*an din har liv lai* – night and day we contemplate the Divine', rapture takes over the entire self and unites the individual with the Infinite. Marriage is thus both literal and metaphorical. On the literal level it is a union of two people; and on the metaphorical level it is a union of the microcosm with the macrocosm. Fully in tune with the Divine, husband and wife begin to live sensuously in this world.

The Fourth Guru introduced the office of the Masand to the earlier Manji system. These Masands were community leaders who served as honored liaisons between the local congregations and the Guru in the center. They led the congregation in prayers, guided them doctrinally, and often led them to the Guru's presence. Guru Ram Das is remembered most notably for the founding of Amritsar, which was important for the development of Sikhism. The town was originally known as Ramdaspur, named after the Fourth Guru, and since it was located near the Delhi–Kabul trade route, it prospered quickly. Even during Guru Ram Das' time, it became the focal point for Sikhs to gather during the spring and autumn festivals, and with

Guru Arjan, Guru Ram Das' son and successor, Amritsar became the religious capital of the Sikhs.

Guru Arjan (Nanak 5)

The first 11 years of Guru Arjan's life were spent with his parents, Bibi Bhani and Guru Ram Das at the home of his maternal grandfather, Guru Amar Das, at Goindval. In this town located on the imperial highway between Delhi and Lahore, young Arjan learnt several languages – Gurmukhi from Bhai Buddha, Sanskrit from Pandits Keso and Gopal, and Persian from the local Muslim schools. He spent the next seven years in Ramdaspur and Lahore. In Ramdaspur, Guru Arjan received training in classical ragas from both resident and visiting musicians. He married Ganga Devi. In his young adulthood phase, he also spent time in Lahore, where he set up the morning and evening patterns of Sikh worship among the congregations. He made the most of the vibrant atmosphere of Lahore by visiting Sufi centers and interacting with people of different faiths. In 1581, Guru Ram Das chose Arjan to succeed him as the Fifth Guru, which generated much hostility from Guru Arjan's eldest brother. However, with his boundless creativity, the Guru proved that he was the rightful heir.

During his Guruship, Sikhism acquired strong scriptural, doctrinal and organizational foundations, and Sikh philanthropy and social commitment expanded beyond the welfare of the community. Guru Arjan initiated new construction projects and completed the building of sacred pools at Amritsar, Santokhsar and Ramsar, begun by his father. When a famine hit the Punjab, the Guru traveled from village to village, helping people to sink wells and undertake other works for the general good of the public. As a result, many more people were brought into the Sikh fold. Guru Arjan also established new Sikh centers and founded the new town of Taran Taran. He encouraged agriculture and trade, and organized a system of financial support for the Sikh religion. During this period, Sikhs traded in Afghanistan, Persia and Turkey.

The powerful Mughal Empire provided Guru Arjan's historical and political backdrop, and Emperor Akbar, with his liberal religious vision, was at the helm. The Muslim ruler brought people together for inter-religious discussions and produced a new 'Divine Faith'

(*Din-i-Ilahi*). Interestingly, just when Persian was becoming the lingua franca of the Mughal administration, the regional language of Punjabi on the north-western periphery of the Indian peninsula was being crystallized by Guru Arjan. The Sikh Guru compiled the Granth, the first anthology in the Punjabi language, and to enshrine it, he constructed the Harmandar (the Golden Temple of modern times). During Emperor Akbar's tolerant regime, Guru Arjan articulated a distinct Sikh identity that was clearly different from Hinduism and Islam: 'I do not make the Hajj nor any Hindu pilgrimage, I serve the One and no other. I neither perform Hindu worship nor do I offer Muslim prayers, I have taken the formless One into my heart. I am neither Hindu nor Muslim' (GG: 1136). Guru Arjan's compilation of the Granth and building of the Harmandar (origin of the Golden Temple) were both vital elements in the construction of Sikh psyche and Sikh identity.

Guru Granth

When Guru Angad (Nanak 2) inherited the Guruship, he composed poetry in the metaphysical vein of his predecessor and developed the Gurmukhi script used by Guru Nanak during his apprenticeship in storehouses. Evolved from his *lande/mahajani* business shorthand, Gurmukhi eventually became the script for the Guru Granth.

As the succession of Guruship passed on, so did the word of one Guru to the next. Each valued and nurtured the literary inheritance from his predecessor, and adding his own compositions to the collection, he would pass on the poetic legacy to the next. The different Gurus in the Guru Granth all use the pseudonym 'Nanak'. Guru Nanak was cherished as the founder of something new and different, and they felt that they were simply continuing his message. In 1603, Guru Arjan began to compile the Granth, which required sustained labor as well as rigorous intellectual discipline. He took up this arduous task for two reasons. First, he realized that his community (*panth*) needed a text (*granth*) that would concretize the Sikh world view. The fellowship of Sikhs had increased numerically and spread geographically, and they needed a central canon for their spiritual and moral life. It thus became urgent that the revelation coming from Guru Nanak and his successors be canonized. Second, there was the problem of 'counterfeit' works. Since the Fourth Guru

Figure 4: Guru Granth and Kirtan performance at the Golden Temple

had bypassed his sons and appointed Arjan as his successor, the eldest son, Pirthi Chand, became estranged from him. Pirthi and his gifted son Meharban began to compose sacred poetry under the name of Nanak. It was with a view to fixing the seal on the sacred Word and preserving it for posterity that Guru Arjan began to codify his Sikh literary legacy into an authorized volume.[1]

With his extraordinary mystical insight, Guru Arjan began the momentous task, calling on Bhai Gurdas to help him. Messages were sent to Sikhs to gather the hymns of the preceding Gurus. Two collections were in the family of Guru Amar Das' son, Baba Mohan, in Goindval, but he refused to part with them. Guru Arjan had to go to Goindval himself, and when he finally got the collections, they were accorded the utmost respect. The volumes (or *pothis* as they were called) were placed on a palanquin decorated with precious stones and carried by the Sikhs on their shoulders. The mode of travel for the *pothis* would be no different from that of royalty in Guru Arjan's culture. The power of sublime poetry was felt so intensely that the Guru refused to ride his horse and walked behind barefoot.

He chose a picturesque spot on the outskirts of Amritsar for the compilation process. Today, a shrine called Ramsar marks this site.

Figure 5: Golden Temple with Nishan Sahib (the Sikh flag)

There was a vast amount of poetic material, and selections had to be made from the works of the preceding four Gurus, as well as his own. Guru Arjan was a superb poet with an expansive repertoire. Furthermore, whatever was in harmony with the Sikh Gurus, even if it was the verses of the Hindu or Muslim saints, was also to be included. Finally, what was genuine had to be sifted from what was spurious. With his extraordinary literary finesse, Guru Arjan was able to carry out meticulously the work of compiler and editor. Bhai Gurdas was the calligrapher. Gurmukhi was the script used for transcription.

The Guru's framework did not mark boundaries between Sikh, Hindu or Muslim: the spiritual language was common to them all. Whatever resonated philosophically and artistically with the vision of the founding Guru, he included it in the Granth. But Guru Arjan did not model the Sikh canon on either Muslim or Hindu scriptures, nor did he include passages from either of their revered scriptures. Against a divisive backdrop in which God was either *Ram* or *Rahim*, the worship was either *namaz* or *puja*, the place of worship *mandir* or *masjid*, and the language of scripture either Sanskrit or Arabic, Guru Arjan brought together voices that expressed a common spiritual quest. What governed his choices was not a syncretism or synthesis of concepts and doctrines from prevailing religious traditions, but rather his penetrating insight into the Divine. Like his predecessors, Guru Arjan believed that knowledge of the Transcendent is attained neither through servitude to a God of the Hindu pantheon (*sevai gosain*), nor through worship of Allah (*sevai allah*). It is received through an active recognition of, and participation in, the Divine Will (*hukam*):

> Some address Ram, some Khuda,
> Some worship Gosain, some Allah ...
> Says Nanak, those who recognize the Divine Will
> It is they who know the secret of the Transcendent One.
> (GG: 885)

Guru Arjan was a prolific poet and reiterated Nanak's metaphysical formulation, *Ikk Oan Kar*, literally 'One Being Is', in vivid imagery, and from a variety of perspectives. The Granth contains 2,218 hymns by him, including his popular *Sukhmani*, 'the Pearl of Peace'.

Once the compositions were selected, Guru Arjan arranged them in the order of their musical patterns. Apart from a few hymns, the entire collection is organized into 31 sections, with each section containing poems in one musical measure (*raga*, which means both 'color' and 'musical mode' in Sanskrit). Guru Arjan also utilized folk music patterns with elemental beats, as well as regional Bhakti and Kafi forms with their own primal rhythms, and various other musical styles extending all the way from Afghanistan to the south of the Indian peninsula. In the standard version of the Guru Granth, the Ragas appear in a specific order: Sri Raga, Majh, Gauri, Asa, Gujri, Devgandhari, Bihagara, Wadahans, Sorath, Dhanasri, Jaitsri, Todi, Bairari, Tilang, Suhi, Bilaval, Gaund, Ramkali, Nut-Narayan, Mali-Gaura, Maru, Tukhari, Kedara, Bhairo, Basant, Sarang, Malar, Kanra, Kalyan, Prabhat and Jaijawanti. Each Raga has a season prescribed for its singing, it has a prescribed time of the day, an emotional mood, and a particular cultural climate as each measure evolved in a specific region. Each measure has its particular characteristics, its timing and season. For example, the first is Sri, the word itself meaning 'supreme'. It is one of the parent measures from which the others are derived. This Raga is compared to the philosopher's stone which, supreme among other stones, transforms baser metals into gold. It is

Figure 6: Nishan Sahib (the Sikh flag) on the Golden Temple

sung in the evening, when darkness takes over. In content too, it expresses the darkness of ignorance and superstition into which Guru Nanak's society was sunk. Seasonally, the Sri Raga is associated with extreme heat and cold, indicating an intensity of emotion. The poets in this measure express their ardent yearning for the Divine.

Within each of the sections, Guru Arjan arranged the compositions in a definite scheme. First came the works by the Gurus in the order of their succession. As we have seen, all the Gurus signed their compositions with the name of Nanak, to show that they were continuing his legacy. To avoid any confusion, the Guru distinguished each one at the outset by the use of numerals. He wrote Mahalla 1 if the composition belonged to the first Guru, Mahalla 2 if it was by the second Guru, and so on. The word Mahalla means 'body', and it underscores that the Gurus are a corporeal and spiritual continuation. The compositions of the Gurus were followed by those of Bhaktas and Sufis. A list of names of the contributors and the numbers of their hymns follows:

Guru Nanak: 974 hymns
Guru Angad: 62 couplets
Guru Amar Das: 907 hymns
Guru Ram Das: 679 hymns
Guru Arjan: 2,218 hymns
Guru Tegh Bahadur, the Ninth Guru: 59 hymns and 56 couplets (these were added by his son, Guru Gobind Singh, the Tenth Guru).

Bhaktas and Sufis:
Kabir: 292 hymns
Farid: 4 hymns and 130 couplets
Namdev: 60 hymns
Ravidas: 41 hymns
Jaidev: 2 hymns
Beni: 3 hymns
Trilochan: 4 hymns
Parmananda: 1 hymn
Sadhana: 1 hymn
Ramananda: 1 hymn
Dhanna: 4 hymns
Pipa: 1 hymn
Sain: 1 hymn
Bhikhan: 2 hymns
Sur Das: one line
Sundar: 1 hymn

Mardana: 3 couplets
Satta and Balvand: 1 hymn
Bhatts: 123 *swayyas*.

After sustained physical and intellectual labor, the Granth materialized, and the joy of the Sikhs was boundless. They celebrated with great jubilation. Later Sikh history compares the festivities with those of a wedding. Huge quantities of *Karahprashad*, the Sikh sacrament made up of equal quantities of sugar, butter, water and flour, were distributed. Sikhs came to see the most sacred volume and were thrilled by the sight. This sacred volume prepared at Ramsar was carried with great pomp to the newly constructed Harmandar. Bhai Buddha, the elderly and venerable Sikh devotee, carried it on his head, while Guru Arjan walked behind holding the whisk over it in homage. Musicians played hymns from the sacred text.

On 16 August 1604, the Granth was ceremonially installed in the inner sanctuary of the Golden Temple. Sikhs had gathered from different regions, and as they together experienced the melodious message of their Gurus, the distinction between self and other blurred, fostering the spirit of *communitas*. On that historic day, Guru Arjan stood in attendance as Bhai Buddha opened the Granth to obtain the Divine message:

santa ke karaj ap khaloia hari kam karavanu aia ram
dharati suhavi tal suhava vicu amrit jal chaia ram
amrit jalu chaia puran saju karaia sagal manorath pure
jai jai kar bhaia jagu antar lathe sagal visure
puran purakh acut abinasi jasu ved purani gaia … (GG: 783)
The One stood by the devotees to fulfill their divine task
rendered help
Beautiful is this spot, beautiful this pool
filled with ambrosial waters.
Ambrosial waters flow, the task is accomplished
all desires have been fulfilled.
Joy pervades the world, suffering has ended
Complete, Pure, Eternal,
Exalted in song by the Vedas and Puranas…

This 'first' *vak* (or *hukam*) in the public memory of the Sikhs celebrates the Divine as the source of all actions and accomplishments. It expresses a rapturous exaltation, illustrating Rudolf Otto's famous dictum: *mysterium, tremendum et fascinans*.[2] Though not deified in the architectural setting of the Harmandar with its pool and four doors, the Divine is felt very closely, and through the intensity of experience, wide temporal and spatial horizons open up. The unique Sikh moment creates a continuity with the past, for it acknowledges precisely that which has been exalted from time immemorial: 'the Vedas and the Puranas have sung your glory'. Paradoxically, the joy felt within the precincts of the newly constructed Harmandar extends beyond its walls 'into the whole world': '*jag antar!*' Guru Arjan's intersection of the Granth and the Harmandar forged a renewed relationship with people across the ages and across the globe.

At dusk, the Granth was closed and wrapped in silks, and taken to a specially built chamber. There it was placed on a pedestal while Guru Arjan slept on the floor by its side out of reverence. Early next morning it was taken out in state to the Harmandar and after the *sohila* hymn was recited by the congregation in the evening, brought back to rest in the room designated for it by the Guru. This pattern is followed by the Sikhs to this day, except that the Guru Granth is now taken to the Akal Takht.

The Construction of the Harmandar

Like the Granth (sacred text), which was conceived by the first Guru, gestated with his successors, and finally delivered by Guru Arjan, the Harmandar (sacred place) also goes back along the spiritual line.[3] Guru Amar Das, the Third Guru, conceived the idea for a specific place for Sikh worship. His successor, Guru Ram Das, began the excavation of the pool in 1577, and Guru Arjan completed the famous shrine in the middle of the pool in 1601. The Gurus knew that mental, psychic and spiritual landscapes are grounded in the places people inhabit; indeed, the way they orient themselves to the world, the way they remember their history, the way they transform social reality, and even the way they imagine and conceive and define themselves are all contingent on geographical locations. For the consolidation of the Sikh community, 'place' was extremely important.

Guru Arjan was a brilliant poet and a brilliant architect who linked his three-dimensional structure with intangible sound to reproduce '*taha baikunthu jah kirtanu tera*: that place is paradise where we recite your praise' (GG: 749). Throughout the scripture, he reiterates the union of beautiful paradisal topography with sonorous sublime rhythms: '*tah baikunthu jah namu uchrahi* – paradise is where your name is recited' (GG: 890); '*jasu japat kai baikunth vas* – singing divine praise many live in paradise' (GG: 236); and '*jahan kirtanu sadhsangati rasu tah saghan bas falanad* – where the community relishes divine praise, that place is auspicious, full of fragrance, fruit and joy' (GG: 1204). Sensuous fragrances, tastes, enjoyments are all the result of Divine praise resounding in the company of good people. Through his artistic genius, Guru Arjan physically combined metaphysical poetry and transcendent space so that his society could gather together and recreate 'paradise' on earth.

The Guru-architect's structural plans and the designs for the Harmandar merge with the philosophical message and the literary patterns of the Granth he so meticulously compiled. The Book created by Guru Arjan is primarily the expression of the essential Sikh principle: *Ikk Oan Kar*. The Infinite One recorded at the opening of the Granth and reiterated throughout its 1,430 pages is represented architecturally in the layout of the complex. He built the Gurdwara in the center of a pool that his father had begun. Emerging from the shimmering waters, Guru Arjan's structure appears to stand without any solid borders or boundaries. The view of the building merging with glittering water in the radiant sunlight sweeps the visitor into a sensory swirl. Here the Sikhs visually encounter Guru Nanak's perception of the Infinite One.

Entry into the complex involves a downward angle. The physical descent is an architectural device to ensure that the precincts are entered with a sense of humility. Guru Nanak said: '*haumai marai gur sabad pae* – getting rid of ego, we receive the Word' (GG: 228). In order to absorb the Divine, the self has to be emptied of the selfish, egotistical 'me'. The Fifth Guru reiterated the pathogenic effects of egocentricity. In his own words: '*taj abhiman bhai nirvair* – by getting rid of arrogance we become devoid of hatred' (GG: 183). Again, he says: '*taj haumai gur gian bhajo* – get rid of ego, contemplate Divine knowledge' (GG: 241). Arrogance and egocentricity are constricting. They are the poison which fills the arteries with hostility towards others, and the mind with inertia and ignorance. The physical movement of going down the steps mentally prepares devotees to greet the Infinite One.

The four doors of the Harmandar translate architecturally his ethical injunction enshrined in the Guru Granth: '*khatri brahmin sud vais updesu cahu varna kau sajha* – Kashatriya, Brahmin, Sudra and Vaishya, all four classes have the same mandate' (GG: 747). His word for class is '*varna*', meaning 'complexion'. The four doors in his sacred structure welcome people from different classes and complexions. They shatter age-old oppressive social and racial hegemonies. Walking through the doors, Sikhs can see and feel what Guru Nanak meant in his Jap: '*ai panthi sagal jamati* – accept all humans as your equals, and let them be your only sect' (Jap: 28).

While sharing many features with mosques and temples, the Harmandar is an entirely different space. The utter feeling of submission to an omnipotent creator felt in the mosque is taken over by the feeling of elation in the Gurdwara. Fundamental aspects of mosques such as the *mihrab* (prayer niche), *minbar* (pulpit) and the tombs of saints (especially popular in Sufi sacred spaces), have no place in Sikhism. Nor is there anything particularly potent about the topology of the Harmandar in the traditional Indian sense. Unlike Hindu temples, which are built at very specific places – 'where the gods are seen at play' – the site for the Harmandar was not chosen for any specific reason. The idea for the pool within which Guru Arjan built the shrine goes back to the time of the Third Guru, Amar Das, when Goindval was the Sikh center.

The Gurdwara is not constructed using traditional diagramatic plans either. Guru Arjan did not use the highly elaborate Hindu science of architecture with its technical blueprints that secure a deity on to the site. As the renowned art historian Stella Kramrich observes: 'Wherever a Hindu temple stands, whatever age witnessed its growth, and to whatever size, as house, body and substance for God (the Essence) to dwell in, it is built in principle on the same plan, the Vastupurushamandala.'[4] Since the Mandala is the ritual, diagrammatic form of the universal essence (*purusha*), which carries its bodily existence (*vastu*), each temple building becomes the substantial form of God. However, the Sikh shrine does not attempt to install the Divine into its structure. Its landscape is not deified in any sense. The Gurdwara is simply a door (*dwara*) towards enlightenment (*guru*).

Having completed and lined the pool begun by his father, Guru Arjan wanted to set a building within it. He may have imagined the construction as a 'lotus' sitting serenely on the waters, or even as a 'ship' sailing across the ocean, as Michael Ondaatje describes the Harmandar in his contemporary novel, *The English Patient*:

> Singing is at the centre of worship. You hear the song, you smell fruit from the temple gardens – pomegranates, oranges. The temple is a haven in the flux of life, accessible to all. It is the ship that crossed the ocean of ignorance.[5]

Guru Arjan's architectural model rises above provincialism and narrowness into a vaster and more profound perspective. It is not 'syncretic' by any means.

Across from the Harmandar, the Sixth Guru built a platform to carry out his political duties, which later developed into the Akal Takht (the throne of the Timeless One). Whereas the Harmandar forms the center for Sikh spirituality, the Akal Takht is the center for secular affairs. Later patrons, including Maharaja Ranjit Singh, employed Muslim, Hindu and Sikh craftsmen to build on and embellish the unique Sikh ideals cherished by the Gurus. Today, the Harmandar – the Golden Temple – is a very popular spot. As you walk through the rooms on marble floors, you see the sanctuary rising gently from the waters, and your ears ring with the scriptural verse: '*kaul tun hain kavia tun hain ape vekhi vigasu* – You are the lotus, you are the water-lily, you yourself watch and rejoice' (GG: 23). In its precincts, the Divine is closely felt in myriads of ways.

The Golden Temple complex has the capacity to recharge visitors, and enable them to recognize the Infinite One. The weaving, circulating and colorful text of the *granth* is visible on its floors, walls and ceilings. The black and white marble slabs upon which one walks are repeated rhythmically. So are the stylized flowers and birds, vines and fruits, arabesques and lattice-work on the walls. The structure itself repeats its arches and domes, pillars and kiosks, windows and storeys. Among the unending repetitions one walks upon, touches on the walls, sees on the building, melodious words are heard. The rhythmic repetitions create a dynamic movement for the senses and imagination. Together they impel one onwards. Any feeling of unease gives way to harmony; doubts and dualities begin to dissolve; and the ignorant psyche is inspired to discover its essential spark. Through its finite structures, the Harmandar creates an energetic movement toward the Infinite Transcendent. The undulating aural rhythms of the Guru Granth reproduced in the visual patterns of the Harmandar reveal the wide range of human experience. Clearly, Sikh art is not representation; it is a revelation. In this revelatory process, constricting barriers are broken down, and we are ushered into our innermost recesses. The interlacing designs that are heard or read merge with those that are seen, establishing in turn mental and spiritual connections – among Sikh, Hindu and Muslim; brown, black and white.

Guru Arjan's Martyrdom

With the death of Emperor Akbar in 1605, the liberal political-social scene changed for the Sikhs. The new regime of Emperor Jahangir (reigned 1605–27) was influenced by Sheikh Ahmad of Sirhind, who aspired to reverse Akbar's broad and open-minded religious policy.[6] Guru Arjan's thriving success posed an immediate problem for the new Emperor. His hostility towards the Sikh Guru is expressed in his memoir *Tuzuk-i-Jahangiri*: 'he had captured many of the simple-hearted of the Hindus, and even of the ignorant and foolish followers of Islam … They called him *Guru*, and from all sides stupid people crowded to worship and manifest compete faith in him … Many times it occurred to me to put a stop to this vain affair or to bring him into the assembly of the people of Islam.'[7] Guru Arjan incurred still more of the Mughal Emperor's wrath for his alleged support of Khusrau – Jahangir's recalcitrant son – who tried to claim his father's throne.

Emperor Jahangir's memoir testifies that Guru Arjan was put to death under his imperial orders: 'I ordered them to produce him and handed over his houses, dwelling places and children to Murtaza Khan, and having confiscated his property commanded that he should be put to death.'[8] In a letter written from Lahore on 25 September 1606, the Jesuit Father Jerome Xavier reported the 'many injuries, pains and insults' inflicted on Guru Arjan.[9] In the Sikh collective memory, their Guru was cruelly executed in Lahore. For several days he was subjected to severe physical torment: he was seated on red-hot iron plates while burning sand was poured over him; he was doused in hot oil, and was cast into the River Ravi.

Rapt in mediation, the Guru died peacefully on 30 May 1606. Though his body was not recovered from the river, a Gurdwara enshrines the spot where the Guru entered the water. Every year, Sikhs commemorate his martyrdom by distributing a cool drink of milk and water. The soothing drink honors the agony Guru Arjan endured for the sake of their faith.

With his meticulous compilation of the Granth, Guru Arjan gave the Sikhs an authoritative volume, which not only became their spiritual and religious guide, but also shaped the intellectual and cultural environment of their community for generations to come. With his personal response to the Granth, he provided new patterns for worship and ceremonies. With his construction of the Harmandar he gave them a new venue for spiritual and social practice; the Sikhs now had their own pilgrim spot, their own Mecca. And by giving up his life, he created another vital layer to the self-consciousness of the Sikh people. But before he left this world, as Bhai Gurdas reports: 'Arjan changed his body; he gave it the form of Hargobind' (Var I: 48).

Chapter III

Guru Gobind Singh and the Cultivation of Sikh Identity

The Fifth Guru's martyrdom generated a strong impulse of resistance, and inaugurated a new era of martial élan. In response to his father's ordeal, Guru Hargobind (Nanak 6) wore warrior dress, alongside the rosary and other saintly emblems, for his succession ceremonies. He put on two swords – one he called the sword of *piri*, and the other the sword of *miri*. Both these terms had come to India with Islam: '*piri*', from *pir*, denotes a religious teacher; '*miri*', from *amir*, means a commander of the faithful. The Sixth Guru's overt act of combining them marked an important development in the evolution of the Sikh community. The symbolic sword given by Guru Nanak to his successor Angad had now taken on a physical shape, investing the Guru with both spiritual and secular authority.

Guru Hargobind raised a small band of armed Sikhs, and sent out messages that disciples in the future must come with gifts of horses and weapons. He enjoined them to bear arms to defend themselves and others who were righteous. He introduced the martial symbols of the kettledrum and the pennant. The booming kettledrum used in the retinue of his troops to build up their heroism is today popularly heard during the recitation of *ardas* in Gurdwaras. Likewise, *nishan sahib*, the flag hoisted as a mark (*nishan*) of Sikh sites, is also traced back to Guru Hargobind Singh's political sensibility. To defend the town of Amritsar, in 1609 he built a fortress called Loh Garh (Iron Fort). As a seat of temporal authority, he laid the platform for the Akal Takht (the Throne of the Timeless One), directly facing the Harmandar. The Guru sat here regally and conducted the secular affairs of his community. Bhai Gurdas, who tutored the Guru when he was young, described him as '*vadda jodha bahu parupkari* – great warrior, very philanthropic' (Var I: 48). An expert huntsman, the Guru ended up fighting several battles against Mughal officials, but in his later years he moved to the Shivalik hills, where he spent his final years. Away from political scrutiny, he founded the town of Kiratpur on the eastern bank of the River Sutlej. He had five sons and one daughter, Bibi Viro. Before he passed away he appointed his grandson, Har Rai, as his successor. The Seventh Guru is remembered for his tender sensitivity, which is abundantly portrayed in Sikh paintings (see Chapter VIII). Guru Har Rai appointed his young son, Har Kishen, as the Eighth Guru, but unfortunately the child contracted smallpox and died when he was only eight years old. The succession then passed to his contemplative great uncle, Tegh Bahadur (Guru Hargobind and Mata Nanaki's youngest son).

The martial atmosphere introduced into Sikhism by Guru Hargobind came into full play after the martyrdom of Guru Tegh Bahadur (Nanak 9). The Sikh Guru had challenged the policy of the Mughal ruler of converting Hindus by force. For his defense of religious freedom he was executed in public in Chandni Chowk, near the Red Fort in Delhi on 11 November 1675. His son and successor, Guru Gobind Singh, provides the *raison d'être* for his supreme sacrifice: 'he protected the frontal mark and sacred thread – *tilak janjhu rakha prabh taka*' (*Bicitra Natak* 5: 13). Guru Tegh Bahadur was not a votary of either *tilak* (mark on the forehead) or *janeu* (sacred thread worn by upper caste male Hindus), yet the Ninth Sikh Guru staked his life for the rights of those who believed in them. The defense of these two religious symbols signified the right of each individual to practice his or her religion freely. Guru Gobind Singh's admiration for his father's tremendous courage continues to flow out in verses of haunting beauty in his autobiographical *Bicitra Natak*: '*seesu deeya paru see na ucari* – he gave up his head, but did not utter a sigh' (5: 13); and in the next verse: '*seesu deeya paru siraru na deeya* – he gave up his head but not his faith' (5: 14). Again: '*teghbahadure see kria kari na kinhun ani* – a deed like Tegh Bahadur's none has dared to do' (5: 15).

Guru Tegh Bahadur himself composed poignant couplets. They are included in Sikh scripture, and are recited during its ceremonial conclusion. Liberation (*mukti/moksha*) for the Guru is living in equanimity – basically feeling the same One every minute, and in every material: 'For whom praise is the same as blame, and gold is the same as iron, says Nanak know that person is free – *ustati nindia nahi jihi kanchan loh saman/kahu nanak suni re mana mukati tahi tai jan*' (GG: 1427).

Figure 7: Guru Gobind Singh, the Tenth Guru

After his father's execution, Guru Gobind Singh provided vigorous leadership to the Sikhs. Emperor Aurangzeb (1658–1707) was the ruler. Unlike his grandfather, Akbar, who abolished the Jizya and introduced an inter-religious *Din-i-ilahi* (Divine Faith), or his brother, Dara Shikoh, who sponsored the translation of several Upanishads into Persian, Aurangzeb tried to make India into an exclusively Muslim country. He issued repressive edicts against non-Muslims. The Jizya, a tax that non-Muslims had to pay for permission to live in an Islamic state, was reimposed. It was a way of forcing those who could not afford to pay the tax to embrace Islam.[1] He sponsored the codification of Islamic laws called the Fatawa-i-Alamgiri, and founded Muslim colleges to promote the study of Sharia. Those who did not practice Islam, including Guru Gobind Singh and his Sikh community, became victims of Aurangzeb's orthodoxy. Even Shia Muslims and some Sufi orders bore the brunt of his Islamization process. All 'Hindus', with the exception of Rajputs, were prohibited from riding in palanquins, or on elephants or thoroughbred horses. They were also prohibited from carrying arms.

Guru Gobind Singh was born during this repressive regime, to Mata Gujari and Guru Tegh Bahadur in the town of Patna, in Bihar, in 1666. His father at that time had traveled east to visit holy spots and undertake works of charity. Patna, known in ancient times as Pataliputra, was once the famous capital of the great Buddhist King Ashoka (273–232 BCE). Lord Buddha is said to have visited it. From a thriving Buddhist center, Pataliputra became the imperial capital of the powerful Hindu dynasty of the Guptas (fourth to sixth centuries CE). The Islamic presence was added when a mosque was built in 1510 by Ala ud-Din Husain Shah of Bengal. In 1541, Sher Shah built a fort, and Emperor Akbar conquered the city for the Mughals in 1574. English and Dutch East Indian companies established factories in 1640 and 1666, respectively. Guru Gobind Singh spent his formative years in this vibrant metropolis, which bustled with Hindus, Muslims, Buddhists, Jains, Parsis and Christians. Centuries of religious and cultural diversity must have been absorbed by the young Gobind. With his birth, Patna acquired significance for the Sikhs. Takht Sri Harmandir Sahib commemorates Guru Gobind Singh's birth. This shrine in the old quarter of Patna was originally the mansion of Salis Rai Johri, a follower of Guru Nanak. To show his devotion to the Sikh faith, he converted his home into an inn, free for travelers and pilgrims. Guru Tegh Bahadur stayed there when he visited Patna. Later, a magnificent Gurdwara was built above the inn, and the building has become famous as one of the Five Seats (*Takhts*) of Sikhism.

Among the many stories told about Guru Gobind Singh's childhood, there is one about a queen named Mania who was very sad because she had no child. She often saw the little Guru, who was only four years old at that time, and wished she had a boy of her own. The Guru felt sorry for her and told her he would be like a son to her. They became friends and Mania would give him corn. To this day corn is served in the *langar* at Patna Sahib as a celebration of the friendship between little Gobind and Queen Mania.

When he was seven years old, the family moved to Anandpur in the Shivalik hills. Anandpur, literally 'the city of bliss', was founded by Guru Gobind Singh's father, Guru Tegh Bahadur. It is set picturesquely on the lower spurs of the Shivalik range in the Ropar district of the Punjab. The high mountain peaks of Naina Devi rise behind, about seven miles away. The River Sutlej flows past the hills of Anandpur. It was here that the nine-year-old received the head of his executed father, which was brought to him from Delhi by Sikh devotees. But young Gobind showed remarkable courage. On Baisakhi day, 29 March 1676, he had the Guruship conferred on him. With support from his mother, Gujari, he quickly transformed the devastating and immobilizing impact of the execution of his father into creativity and action. In a spiritually and physically energetic atmosphere, the Divine was remembered, heroic poetry was recited, elemental music was performed and mock battles took place. Such activities obliterated the horrific memories and diverted the Sikhs from thoughts of retaliation. Anandpur began to resound with holy hymns and heroic ballads, the galloping of horses, martial exercises, a variety of sports, and with the beating of Guru Gobind Singh's drum of victory. But the neighboring hill kingdoms were threatened by these symbols of political power, and consequently, the Guru and his followers had to fight several battles.

The Guru continued with his study of the languages of Braj and Persian, and, as some scholars report, the study of Sanskrit and Arabic as well. He was married to Mata Jitoji in 1677, and to Mata Sundari in 1684, and had four sons with them: Ajit Singh, Jujhar Singh, Jorawar Singh and Fateh Singh. He married his third wife, Mata Sahib Devan, in Anandpur in 1700.

Like his predecessors, Guru Gobind Singh was a superb poet. Through his poetry he expressed themes of love and equality, and a strictly ethical and moral code of conduct. Deprecating idolatry and superstitious beliefs and practices, he evoked the Singular Divine. Poetry also became the medium to impart a new orientation to his subjugated community. He introduced vigorous meters and rhythms to revitalize his people, and created novel images and paradoxes to stretch their imaginations. He drew on themes from ancient Indian epics and mythology to evoke martial fervor.

Guru Gobind Singh was a great patron of the arts. The town of Paunta (from *pav*, the foot of his horse implanted on the soil), which he founded on the banks of the River Jumna, became the center of a spiritual and cultural regeneration. The Guru held poetry symposia and distributed awards. Many poets from different religious backgrounds gathered at scenic Paunta, and 52 of them, including Sainapat, Alam, Lakhan and Amrit Rai were permanently employed there. Several Sanskrit and Persian classics were translated by the poets, who were rewarded handsomely for their work. Later in his life, the Guru made Damdama an important center of scholarly activities. Situated near Bhatinda in the Punjab, Damdama came to be known as the 'Guru's Kashi' – the Sikh equivalent of the ancient Hindu center of learning and literature. He spent several months in Damdama pursuing his literary aspirations among men from different social strata. Under his direction, the final recension of the Guru Granth was prepared here by Bhai Mani Singh. Since much of the poetry written by Guru Gobind Singh and his court poets was lost during his evacuation from Anandpur in 1705, Bhai Mani Singh spent years collecting what materials he could salvage, and from these he produced the first recension of the Dasam Granth. It is 1,428 pages long, so it is almost the same size as the Guru Granth (1,430 pages). The Guru Granth, also known as the Adi Granth (First Book), is the sacred scripture of the Sikhs, but some parts of the Dasam Granth are also used in Sikh prayers. The authorship and authenticity of a large proportion of this work is questionable. Most of the Dasam Granth is in the Braj language, but the entire work is printed in the Gurmukhi script.

The Dasam Granth remains controversial among scholars, and elicits a range of responses from devotees. Compositions such as the *Jaap*, *Akal Ustat*, *Bicitra Natak*, *Candi Caritra*, *Candi di Var*, *Sabd Hazare* and *Gian Prabodh* are generally accepted as Guru Gobind Singh's compositions, and these are revered by the Sikhs. A large proportion of the Dasam Granth (about 1,185 pages) is devoted to stories, many of them based on Indian myth, and others dealing with amorous intrigues.[2] Most people believe that these sections were written by the poets of the Guru's entourage. They are therefore neglected, but the *Benati Chaupai* from this section is one of the daily Sikh prayers.

The Dasam Granth opens with the *Jaap*. Analogous to Guru Nanak's Jap (first hymn in the Guru Granth), Guru Gobind Singh's Jaap carries forward Nanak's message of the One Reality at breathtaking speed. Many Sikhs recite it every morning. It is also one of the hymns recited as part of the Sikh initiation ceremony. Through dynamic metaphors and rhythms, the Jaap exalts the animating and life-generating One who flows through and interconnects the myriad creatures: 'salutations to You in every country, in every garb' (Jaap:

66). Like Nanak's Jap, Guru Gobind Singh's Jaap celebrates the presence of the Transcendent within the glorious diversity of the cosmos: 'You are in water, You are on land' (Jaap: 62); 'You are the sustainer of the earth' (Jaap: 173).

The Jaap is followed by *Akal Ustat* (Praise of the Timeless One), which occupies 28 pages of the Dasam Granth. It proclaims the unity of humanity:

> Hindus and Muslims are one…
> The Hindu temple and the Muslim mosque are the same…
> All humanity is one.

Mahatma Gandhi popularized these verses in his famous prayer, 'Ishvara and Allah are your names, temple and mosque are your homes'.[3] When India was bleeding from the wounds of partition in the twentieth century, the Mahatma tried to bring peace and harmony by reviving Guru Gobind Singh's vision.

The *Bicitra Natak* (Wondrous Drama) follows the Akal Ustat, and consists of 38 pages. This poetic autobiography is a magical mixture of biographical facts and literary imagination. It is the only autobiographical work by any of the Sikh Gurus.[4]

The three *Durga-Candi* poems come next and retell the story of Durga's titanic battles against the demons from the Devi Mahatmaya. With all his artistic zeal, the Guru amplifies the warrior role of the ancient Hindu heroine. His similes are highly appealing because of their unexpected simplicity and humor. Many of the parallels come from the familiar crafts and trades of carpenters, oil extractors, dyers and confectioners. Soldiers in chariots, elephants and horses are hurled down by her – like a confectioner dunking *varras* (delicious Punjabi sweet balls of confectionery)!

Khalsa Mahima (Praise of the Khalsa), which comes later in the Dasam Granth, is a favorite hymn among Sikhs. It celebrates the democratic Khalsa community created by Guru Gobind Singh: 'the Khalsa is my special form … the Khalsa is my body and breath'.

Following the principle of the earlier Gurus, he too appropriates love as the highest form of action. Without love, religious practices are ineffective. Guru Gobind Singh's devotional compositions reiterate Sikh ideals and ethics. As noted in the Introduction to this book, their tone is forceful and their imperatives are clear:

Recognize the single caste of humanity
Know that we are all of the same body, the same light. (Akal Ustat: 85)

The Tenth Guru's verse continues to have great resonance for our global society. Difference should not stand in the way of getting to know one another: 'Different vestures from different countries may make us different. But we have the same eyes, the same ears, the same body, the same voice' (Akal Ustat: 86).

Inauguration of the Khalsa

Guru Nanak's vision of affirming and celebrating the Oneness of Ultimate Reality, and the oneness of humanity, was concretized by Guru Gobind Singh. On Baisakhi day 1699, he inaugurated the Khalsa: the Order of the Pure.[5] In front of a large congregation, he performed a dramatic act: he asked for the lives of five devotees and acted as if he had killed them. Though historical documentation may be lacking, the event is deeply etched in Sikh minds and hearts. As the leading historian, Hew McLeod, says perceptively:

> It matters little whether five volunteers were actually summoned or whether five goats were actually slain. The overriding fact is that in its essential outline the story is firmly believed and that this belief has unquestionably contributed to the subsequent shaping of conventional Sikh attitudes.[6]

It is memories that construct all identity, and Baisakhi 1699 is indeed critical to the shaping of Sikh identity. The genesis of the Sikh personality, name, birthplace, religious rites and prayers – in other words, what they do and wear and how they view themselves – can all be traced to Guru Gobind Singh's Baisakhi of 1699.

As the narrative goes, for the celebration of the annual spring festival of Baisakhi 1699 in Anandpur, Guru Gobind Singh ordered especially elaborate preparations. Sikhs came in large numbers. The air in Anandpur was tense with anticipation. Finally, Guru Gobind Singh came before the large assembly. Holding an unsheathed sword in hand, he asked: 'Is there a complete Sikh present here, who would offer their head to the Guru?' His strange demand numbed the audience. Nobody moved, nobody uttered a word. Guru Gobind

Singh repeated his words. Confusion began to turn into fear. When the Guru repeated the call for the third time, Daya Ram, a member of the congregation, arose and offered himself. He walked behind the Guru into a tent. The audience heard a loud thud and saw a flow of blood. The Guru emerged alone from the tent, his sword dripping with fresh blood. He then demanded the head of a second Sikh. This was more than many could endure. People started to leave. Some of them went to complain to the Guru's mother. Soon, however, a second person, named Dharam Das, stood up to offer himself to the Guru's sword. He too was taken into the tent and the Guru returned with his sword dripping with more fresh blood and demanded yet a third head. The pattern repeated itself five times. The other three devotees who offered themselves were Muhkam, Himmat and Sahib Chand. After the fifth time, the Guru led them – all hale and hearty – back to the assembly. Instead of the five men, five goats had been beheaded.

The Baisakhi event comes across as an analogue of the founding event in the Hebrew Bible – God's testing of Abraham by asking him to sacrifice his beloved son Isaac. The role of Guru Gobind Singh's sword is similar to the knife that Abraham carries to the land of Moriah to kill his beloved Isaac. Abraham's knife is called *ma'achelet,* from the root *achol,* to eat, and according to the Midrash Rabbah: 'everything that Israel eats in this world is by virtue of that knife'.[7] Guru Gobind Singh's sword has been nurturing the Sikhs emotionally and spiritually for generations. His was not drama for drama's sake, nor a selfish test; rather, it was a profound culmination of years of deep reflection and commitment to his moral vision. Guru Gobind Singh's creative choreography was intended to strengthen his devotees with their own inner power. Though only five from the congregation went through the process, the entire Baisakhi 1699 gathering was intensely involved in it. Something new came into the world of Sikhism. The Guru's *aqedah* had psychological significance for both the individual Sikh and the community at large. By putting them through the death crisis, Guru Gobind Singh gave his Sikhs a new attitude toward life and living. It was the moment when he made them aware of their self-determination and love. The *aqedah* was his way of bringing them into consciousness – instilling inner confidence so that they would grow and develop both morally and spiritually.

Figure 8: Celebrating the 300th anniversary of the enthronement of the Guru Granth Sahib at Nander in 2008. Seen in the photo: Member of the Indian Parliament Sardar Tarlochan Singh; Ambassador of Sikh Dharma Sardar Satpal Singh Khalsa; and Mr G. S. Bawa from the SGPC member body

The five courageous Sikhs who responded successively to Guru Gobind Singh's call became his Five Beloved (*Panj Pyare*). The Guru fed them the immortal (*amrit*) elixir, and with that initiated them into the new order of the Khalsa. In this popularly known *khande ki pahul* (initiation through the double-edged sword), the Guru churned water in an iron bowl with his double-edged sword (*khanda*) while chanting sacred verses. His wife, Jitoji, came forward and put some sugar-puffs into the vessel. Sweetness through the feminine hand was thus mingled with the alchemy of iron. The present-day custom of preparing the *amrit* elixir with the double-edged sword to the accompaniment of five hymns (Guru Nanak's *Jap*, Guru Gobind Singh's *Jaap*, *Swaiyyas*, *Chaupai*, and Guru Amar Das' *Anand*), is believed to have begun on that day with Guru Gobind Singh's initiation of his Five Beloved. This event marked Guru Gobind Singh's plan to found a new fellowship, which would be strong and courageous to resist any form of tyranny and oppression.

The Five Beloved had come to Anandpur from different regions of India and belonged to different social classes. But they drank from the same bowl, the *amrit*, prepared by the Guru and his wife. This marked a radical departure in traditional Indian culture, where even the shadow of a lower caste person was considered to pollute food or drink. Through the *amrit* drink, the five were bonded together into a new relationship with no more social, religious or cultural differences. With each sip, ancient norms upholding segregation and the hierarchies of caste and creed were washed away. Their drinking together defined their new birth and equal membership in the family of the Khalsa. Just as sharing a mother's milk welds her offspring into a family, so sipping the Guru's *amrit* welded the Five Beloved into the Khalsa family for ever. Through *khande ki pahul*, the Guru produced a new morality and eliminated the immemorial custom that people had to fulfill the specific roles assigned to them at birth. By vehemently rejecting biological castes and their assigned codes, Guru Gobind Singh opened up a window for his community to throw out all social disparities. That the Guru did not only intend to erase the hegemony of the high caste Brahmin over the untouchable Shudra, but also that of man over woman, has yet to be acknowledged by the Sikh community.

The five who received the *amrit* from Guru Gobind Singh were also given the surname of Singh, meaning lion, and were ever after to wear the emblems of the Khalsa popularly known as 'the Five Ks'. These were *kesha* or long hair and beard; *kangha*, a comb tucked into the *kesha* to keep it tidy, in contrast with the recluses who kept it matted as a token of their having renounced the world; *kara*, a steel bracelet; *kacha*, short breeches worn by the soldiers of that time; and *kirpan*, a sword. Their rebirth into the new order meant the annihilation of their previous family ties, of their confinement to a hereditary occupation, of all their earlier beliefs, and of the rituals they had so far observed. They were enjoined to help the weak and fight the oppressor. They were to have faith in the One, and were to consider all human beings equal, irrespective of caste and religion. Guru Gobind Singh spoke to them:

> I wish you all to embrace one creed and follow one path, rising above all differences of religion as now practiced. Let the four Hindu castes, who have different duties laid down for them in their scriptures, abandon them altogether, and adopting the way of mutual help and cooperation, mix freely with one another. Do not follow the old scriptures. Let none pay homage to the Ganges and other places of pilgrimage which are considered to be holy in the Hindu religion, or worship the Hindu deities such as Rama, Krishna, Brahma and Durga, etc., but all should cherish faith in the teachings of Guru

> Nanak and his successors. Let each of the four castes receive my Baptism of the double-edged sword, eat out of the same vessel, and feel no aloofness from, or contempt for one another.[8]

The *amrit* initiation was open to both men and women. Women were also to wear the five emblems of the Khalsa. As men received the surname Singh, women received the surname Kaur, signifying princess, though once again, the exact historical origins of this tradition are obscure.[9] Single or married, Sikh women retain the last name Kaur. Thus the patriarchal structure of society is modified. Men and women no longer trace their lineage or occupation to the 'father'. 'Singh' and 'Kaur' became equal partners in the new family of Sikhism.

Khande ki pahul was the transforming ritual that breathed new life and gave freedom to all recipients. The Khalsa was Guru Gobind Singh's collective and democratic institution, one in which all the members were royalty – *equally* Singhs and Kaurs. After initiating his Five Beloved, the Guru took *amrit* from them to become their equal. This too is quite a radical performance: the disciples initiating the Guru! They are given confidence and responsibility to lead; not be led. His hymn of praise celebrates their mutuality: 'the Khalsa is my special form (*khalsa mero roop hai khas*), the Khalsa is my chief limb (*khalsa mero mukh hae anga*), the Khalsa is my body and breath (*khalsa mero pind paran*), the Khalsa is my life of life (*khalsa meri jan ki jan*)'. The liberating new mode of selfhood generated by Guru Gobind Singh for the gathering in 1699 was meant to be for future generations as well.

There is a typological relation between Jap, the first hymn in Sikh scripture and the Tenth Guru's Baisakhi performance. Stanza 16 of Guru Nanak's Jap introduces the Five ('*Panch*'):

> The Panch are accepted, and the Panch lead on
> The Panch receive honors in the Court,
> The Panch shine splendidly in the Royal Gate,
> The Panch meditate on the one and only Guru. (Jap: 16)

The *Panch* are role models for divine love; they receive honors, they shine resplendently, and they meditate on the singular One. This Nanakian passage forms a script for the dramatic emergence of the Five Beloved – who, drenched in their love for their Guru, gave themselves to his sword. In turn they become leaders of their community, showing the entire Baisakhi gathering the Sikh path to liberation launched by Nanak himself. Like Nanak's *Panch*, the *Panj* are treated with the utmost respect and dignity. They are not chosen as such; they volunteer themselves, and they prove themselves in their infinite love. By feeding them the *amrit* churned with the poetic praises of the Divine coming down from his predecessors, Guru Gobind Singh provides his Five Beloved (*Panj Pyare*) with an immediate taste and recognition of That One. In effect, the drama enacted out on the Baisakhi stage in 1699 was penned by the First Sikh Guru.

Even the Five Ks can be traced farther back. As I explored in a previous work, the Five Ks worn by Sikh men and women are foreshadowed in their scripture.[10] They all commence with the letter *k*, but they all end up in and with the infinite One, for each of them is a symbolic reminder of multivalent spiritual associations. For example, the *kara* (bracelet) around the wrist is the sign par excellence of *krita nasa* – an annihilation of hereditary occupations that determine one's place in society. In the scripture, Guru Nanak recalls the Divine as the creator of the bracelet: '*kari kar karta kangan pahirai in bidhi citu dharei* – she wears the bracelet created by the Creator, so consciousness is held steadily' (GG: 359). Thus the transcendent is pulled into the daily rhythms of life. The ordinary articles from Guru Gobind Singh's culture – something so simple and common as a comb, a bracelet, long hair, particular underclothes, a sword – had extraordinary personal meaning for the Tenth Guru because they were laden with spirituality in a text he grew up on. That he would endow it with Guruship in the final hour of his life (to which we shall turn next) manifests the profound motivational significance that the sublime word had for him. As the Five Ks unite artistically and philosophically with the Granth, they link Guru Nanak to Guru Gobind Singh as a single historical horizon.

The Tenth Guru produced a perfect valence between *bana*, the items that Sikhs physically wear, and *bani*, the poetry that Sikhs recite. It was in a period of intense social and political oppression that he created the Khalsa and gave them their external identifications. The Five Ks promote self-cultivation: they are concerned with shaping an ethical citizen situated within an active social, political and religious world. Like the robe that the first Sikh Guru received from the Divine during his mystical experience in the River Bein, the Five Ks were given to the Khalsa as symbols of self-respect and respect for one another. Each of these physical items is made up of spiritual elements.

The Granth is Appointed the Guru Eternal

After Aurangzeb's death in March 1707, the Guru traveled with the new Mughal Emperor Bahadur Shah to the Deccan. At some point he broke his journey and camped at Nander, a small town on the banks of the River Godavari. Here the Guru was stabbed, under the orders of the Nawab of Sirhind, who was jealous about the new Emperor's conciliatory attitude towards the Sikh Guru. When the news reached Bahadur Shah, he sent expert surgeons, including an Englishman, but unfortunately the stitched up wounds tore open, and Guru Gobind Singh passed away on 6 October 1708 (according to the Bhatt Vahi tradition). Shortly before this, he made the scripture the Guru Eternal.

The passing of Guruship to the sacred book was another momentous accomplishment. In a manner reminiscent of Guru Nanak's appointment of Angad as his successor, Guru Gobind Singh placed a five paise coin and a coconut before the Granth, and bowed his head in veneration. He said to the gathered community that it was his commandment that in future they acknowledge the Granth in his place. Amid political and religious turmoil, amid wars and battles, the physical presence of the Granth sustained, nurtured and centered the Gurus and their devotees. So crucial was the sacred word for Guru Gobind Singh that he made the Granth the Guru for ever. A contemporary Sikh document, *Bhatt Vahi Talauda Parganah* Jind, describes the event in detail:

> Guru Gobind Singh, the Tenth Prophet, son of Guru Tegh Bahadur, grandson of Guru Hargobind, great-grandson of Guru Arjan, of the family of Guru Ram Das, Surajbansi Gosal clan, Sodhi Khatri, resident of Anandpur, Parganah Kahlur, now at Nander, in the Godavari country, in the Deccan, asked Bhai Daya Singh, on Buddhvar [Wednesday] Katik chauth, shukla pakkh, samvat 1765 [6 October 1708] to fetch Sri Granth Sahib. In obedience to his orders, Daya Singh brought the Granth Sahib. The Guru placed before it five paise and a coconut and bowed his head before it. He said to the congregation, 'It is my commandment: own Sri Granth Ji in my

Figure 9: Sikh children in St Patrick's Day Parade in Dublin

> place. Whosoever acknowledges it thus will obtain her/his reward. The Guru will rescue that Sikh. Know this as the truth.'[11]

The Guru did not pass on the Guruship to any of his disciples; he passed it to the Guru Granth in perpetuity. Sikhs were not to perceive Guru in any other form. The Word alone was to be the Guru Eternal. The Guru Granth is thus revered as both the physical body of the Gurus and the metaphysical body of their poetry.

The physicality of the Book was stressed emphatically by Mata Sundari, wife of Guru Gobind Singh. After his death, Sikhs looked to her for guidance. She appointed Bhai Mani Singh to manage the sacred shrines at Amritsar and commissioned him to collect the writings of Guru Gobind Singh. Edicts issued under her seal and authority (*hukamnamas*) were sent out to Sikh congregations. When schismatic groups tried to claim succession to the Guruship, with the aim of setting up their own leaders, Mata Sundari boldly rejected any such move. In a strong voice she issued the following pronouncement:

> Khalsaji, you must have faith in none other except the Timeless One. Go only to the Ten Gurus in search of the word. 'Nanak is their slave

> who obtain their goal by searching the Word.' 'The Guru is lodged in the Word. That One Itself merged with the Guru who revealed the Word.' The Word is the life of all life: through it we meet with the ultimate One.[12]

Clearly, the attributes and properties of the physical Guru are embodied in the Word; the 'Guru is lodged in the Word – *guru ka nivas sabad vich hai*'. So the Word is not a formless 'logos' but 'the life of all life – *jian andar ji sabad hai*'. At a politically and socially unstable time for Sikhs, Mata Sundari drew their attention toward life and living. She reaffirmed the Book as a concrete reality of the Timeless One (*akal*). Containing the Divine–human encounter of their Ten Gurus, Sikhs were in future to derive their guidance and inspiration from the Guru Granth. There would be no other Guru. The reality of the Ten was embodied in their verse. However, Mata Sundari exhorts that the 'Word' has to be actively searched (*khoj*). Sikhs cannot passively accept the Guru = Granth identity. Each person has to see, hear, touch, feel, imagine their way dynamically through the sacred verses of their Gurus to gain their own access to and intimacy with the Timeless One.

On a similar note, Nand Lal, a celebrated poet in Guru Gobind Singh's entourage, also emphasizes the physicality of the Guru Granth. In his poetic testimony recorded in Sanskrit, the Tenth Guru during his final hours urged his followers to continue to relate to the Granth as with a breathing Guru:

> The Granth indeed is the Guru:
> This is what you should see; this is what you should honor;
> this is what should be the focus of your discourses.[13]

The Granth was the Guru, and so it was to be seen, honored and engaged with by Sikhs for perpetuity. The relational quality is deemed to be vital. The Granth is not a distant 'object' venerated from afar, or a text to be merely recited; it is cherished as the living Guru from whom Sikhs solicit advice and with whom they share their anxieties and joys.

The Guru Granth gives birth to generations of Sikhs, hones them esthetically, and sustains them emotionally, socially and spiritually. As the Guru Granth itself proclaims: 'Know the Book as the site of the ultimate One – *pothi parmesur ka than*' (GG: 1226). The revelation of the Gurus connects the Sikhs with the Divine. During moments of personal or corporate piety, Sikhs intimately partake in the Gurus' presence. By appointing the Granth as the Guru, the Tenth Sikh Prophet made their historical and spiritual past eternally present for the Sikhs. Professor Harbans Singh commemorates his phenomenal accomplishment:

> This was a most significant development in the history of the community. The finality of the Holy Book was a fact rich in religious and social implications. The Guru Granth became Guru and received divine honours. It was owned as the medium of the revelation descended through the Gurus. It was for Sikhs the perpetual authority, spiritual as well as historical. They lived their religion in response to it. Through it, they were able to observe their faith more fully, more vividly. It was central to all that subsequently happened in Sikh life. It was the source of their verbal tradition and it shaped their intellectual and cultural environment. It moulded the Sikh concept of life. From it the community's ideals, institutions and rituals derived their meaning. Its role in ensuring the community's integration and permanence and in determining the course of its history has been crucial.[14]

In his intricate mechanism, Guru Gobind Singh brought together the three distinct categories that scholars attribute to metaphors: 'ontological', 'orientational' and 'structural'.[15] The metaphysical book of poetry, personified as the actual breathing Guru, is an 'ontological' metaphor: Guru Gobind Singh's entire past is sustained in the text; the abstract is made concrete. It qualifies as an 'orientational metaphor' because it gives a spatial direction to the Sikhs: the scripture was to be the center of their personal, social and religious life. And since the *poetry* of the Gurus is understood and expressed in terms of their *body*, it emerges as the perfect 'structural metaphor'. Through these combined forces, Guru Gobind Singh created a unique phenomenon in the history of religion. Indeed, the Hebrew Bible, the Vedas, the New Testament, the holy Qu'ran, are absolutely significant in their respective traditions, yet they do not embody the Jewish Prophets, or the Rishis, or the Evangelists, or the Prophet Muhammad. In the Sikh case, Guru Gobind Singh ended personal Guruship, and passed his historical and spiritual legacy to the sacred Book. It has since acquired the status of a juristic person, and is even accepted as such by the Supreme Court of India.[16] All Sikh ceremonies, rituals and rites of passage take place in the presence of their scriptural Guru. Daily, Sikhs commemorate the shared identity of the Guru Granth and the manifest bodies (*deh*) of their Gurus as they recite in unison:

> *guru granth ji manio pragat guran ki deh*
> *ja ka hirda sudh hai khoj sabad mahi leh*
> Know Guru Granth as the manifest body of the Gurus;
> Those whose hearts are pure, they discover it in the Word.

The Guru Granth is the physical body that bonds the Sikhs metaphysically with the Divine One, historically with their ten Gurus, and socially with their community. By attributing the Granth as the person of the historical Gurus, the Tenth intended to allow his Sikhs to imagine unprecedented ways of being in the world. His semantic innovation shatters the tyrannical division between body and mind, temporal and eternal, language and reality; it opens up a space for Sikh men and women to experience the sacred and the sensuous in their daily lives.

Chapter IV

Sikh Metaphysics, Ethics and Esthetics

The Sikh religion is based entirely on Guru Nanak's revelation, '*Ikk Oan Kar* – One Being Is'. The Guru Granth opens with this premise, and its 1,430 pages of sublime poetry reiterate the expansiveness and unity of the Divine. Sikh metaphysical doctrines, ethical practices and esthetic experience derive from it.

Sikh Metaphysics

Doctrine of Oneness

In a historical and geographical context where God was voiced either as Ram or Rahim, and people were caught in conflict over 'monotheistic' and 'polytheistic' notions, Guru Nanak innovatively pronounced ੴ (*Ikk Oan Kar*, One Being Is). Here, three modes of knowledge have been used to signify the Divine – numerical, alphabetical and geometrical. The prime number '1' is recognized by people of every language and culture. It is followed by the alpha of the Gurmukhi script, also a sign for *Oan* ('being'; Sanskrit *Aum*). It is completed by the sign for *Kar* (Is), a geometrical arc reaching away into space. While the former two constitute the beginning of the mathematical and verbal languages, the arc is without beginning or end. The existence of the One gestures motion and movement – an opening to countless possibilities.

Guru Nanak's successors followed his example and the Guru Granth is replete with expressions of the singular Divine reality:

sahibu mera eko hai
eko hai bhai eko hai (GG: 350)
My sovereign is One,
One It is, yes One only!

ekam ekankaru nirala
amaru ajoni jati na jala (GG: 838)
One, One Being exists uniquely –
Eternal, unborn, without any caste or limitation.

ham kichu nahi ekai ohi
agai pachai ekai soi (GG: 391)
We are nothing, only That One is
Ahead or behind, it's That One!

gahir gabhiru athahu aparu aganatu tun
nanak vartai ikku ikko ikk tun (GG: 966)
Deep, fathomless, infinite, boundless, inestimable are You,
O' Nanak, only You, One alone, sustains us all.

har ikko data vartada
duja avar na koe (GG: 36)
The One Giver pervades all;
There is no other!

ghar ikko bahar ikko
than thanantar aap (GG: 45)
The One is within, the One is without;
That One is in every place and interspace!

ape pati kalam api upari lekhu bhi tun
eko kahiai nanaka duja kahe ku (GG: 1291)
You Yourself are the slate, You the pen, and You are the writing upon it as well,
Says Nanak, proclaim but the One, why call any other?

Numerous verses in the Guru Granth continue to assert the singularity and unity of the Divine. Clearly, this mathematical One is formless. It is beyond causality. It is all space and time, and yet also transcends infinitely beyond. In the Sikh intuition of pure Oneness, there are no borders, no images (male or female), no concepts, no designation whatsoever. As such, it constitutes a significant repatterning of prevalent theological structures. Guru Nanak states categorically that the One cannot be imaged or shaped in any exclusive form: '*thapia na jae kita na hoe* – that One cannot be imaged; that One cannot be installed' (Jap: 5). There is only the One; none other.

The Sikh monotheistic vision is different from that of the West. As a continuation of the Abrahamic traditions, Islam penetrated India with the concept of the 'One God', which conflicted with the polyphonic imagination of the diverse schools of the Hindus, Buddhists and Jains. In the Sikh belief, there is no opposition between the One and the many, nor is there any dualism between unity and plurality. The Guru Granth claims: '*ikkasu te hoio ananta nanak ekasu mahi samae jio* – from the One issue myriads and into the One they are ultimately assimilated' (GG: 131). Unity becomes plurality, and plurality eventually becomes unity. The Kantian dictum about totality being plurality regarded as unity echoes the same truth. It is not an exclusivist monotheism, but rather an inclusive Oneness of Being that the Guru Granth reiterates over and over: 'Always, always you alone are the One Reality – *sada sada tun eku hai*' (GG: 139). Persian terminology is used to emphasize the unity of being: '*asti ek digari kui ek tui ek tui* – only the One is, who else could there be? Only you, you only' (GG: 144). Again: '*hindu turk ka sahib ek* – Hindus and Muslims share the One sovereign' (GG: 1158). (The term 'Turk' referred to all Muslims in this period.) Since everything is a manifestation of that One being, every manifestation would be a part of it. No god, no body and no thing is excluded from this all-pervasive being. The arc of *Oan* flying off launches the imagination to intuit the unintuitable One, and everybody is welcome to perceive that One in their own way. Blotting out conventional icons and images that created divisions and animosities, the mathematical One embraces the Tao, Yahweh, Ram, Allah, Parvati … this numerical symbol has the potential to end conflicts over *my god/your god*.

Creation

Though Sikhism raises questions about the Creation, it does not offer any fixed answers or theories about when the cosmos came to be. Importantly, it recognizes the visible world as an expression of that One. In fact, Guru Nanak denotes *Ikk Oan Kar* as 'True Name' (*sat nam*). Without positing any ontological, epistemological, moral or teleological proofs, he celebrates the Absolute (*sat*) as an ever-present identity (*nam*). Likewise, Guru Arjan says: '*ap sat kia sabh sat tis prabh te sagal utpat* – Itself Truth, creates but Truth; all creation comes from that One' (GG: 294). Sikhism regards the phenomenal world as the fullness and reality of the Divine.

Frequently, the Arabic term *qudrat* (in the sense of what is created or natural) is used as a disclosure for the One. In the following passage, various phenomena manifest the Divine. Physical matter – including earth, sky and nether regions; the psychological states of joy, love and fear; the religious texts of Hindus and Muslims; practical activities such as eating, drinking and dressing up – characterize that formless One in unison:

qudrat disai qudrat suniai qudrat bhau sukh saru
qudrat patali akasi qudrat sarab akaru
qudrat veda purana kateba qudrat sarab vicaru
qudrat khana pina painanu qudrat sarab piaru (GG: 464)
What we see is the One's *qudrat*,
What we hear is the One's *qudrat*,
Qudrat is at the core of happiness and fear,
The skies, the nether regions and all that is visible is the One's *qudrat*
The Vedas, the Puranas, the Qu'ran, indeed all thought is *qudrat*,
Eating, drinking, dressing up is *qudrat*, so is all love *qudrat*!

In this philosophically intricate passage, the entire cosmos is merely the nature of that One, our first principle. It is the original force, the sole reality. As such, there can be nothing beside the One and nothing outside of the One. While disclosing a harmonious bond between matter, thought, emotion and action, the passage spells out an inclusivist approach towards other faiths. Hindu and Muslim scriptures (*veda purana kateba*) and all modes of reflection (*sarab vicaru*) are celebrated as a revelation of the One Indivisible Reality. The One does not impose *a* scripture or specify *a* mode of thought; but rather, its very being consists in the many. Diversity of scriptures and ideologies is fully affirmed and profoundly respected. And as the finale asserts, existential activites, eating, drinking and dressing up, are bound together with the ontological principle.

Divine Illumination

Ultimately, the infinite One dwells in the individual itself: '*sabh mai joti joti hai soi* – there is a light in all and that light is that One' (GG: 13). The utterly transcendent is intimately within. Since the formless One informs each and every form, everybody is equal; every person has the same ontological status. However, the dialectic between the finite and the infinite, the particular and the universal, the physical and the metaphysical, is maintained constantly. This Sikh view differs from Plato's theories, where pure ideas are divorced and distanced from the everyday phenomena that we see and touch. For Plato, only the is-ness, the essence, the formlessness of the rose is real; the particular roses – those that can be seen, smelled and touched – are mutable, temporary and unreal. For the Sikh Gurus, in contrast, the universal highlights the particular. Form is Formless, and vice versa. It is important that the dialectic is ever alive; otherwise, Guru Nanak's vision of the One would be misinterpreted. The Divine is not understood as actually residing within, or encapsulated inside a form, for then it would only become substantialized and reified. The One is everywhere without being contained in anything as such. Clearly, it is not a pantheistic view. The One is never reduced to any particular form; it is transcendent, and transcendent it illuminates every shape and form. Sikh scripture consistently maintains a fluid connection between the particular and the universal, and the entire world pulsates with divine potentiality, every atom vibrating with ultimate possibility.

An Interior Metaphysic

The Oneness articulated by Guru Nanak is neither a monistic principle nor a conceptual doctrine; it is an interior metaphysic. It is intriguing that, from the rich variety of Sanskrit, Persian and Arabic terms at his disposal, he should have used *Oan* to articulate that One. *Oan* is the primal vocalic syllable of the Indian languages. *Oan* is the Punjabi equivalent of the Sanskrit word for being – *Aum* or *Om*. *Aum* is expounded on with much intellectual sophistication in Hindu scriptures. In the Mandukya Upanishad it is explained as a four-tier psychological journey.[1] The fourfold Mandukya analysis begins with the first stage, 'A', the realm of consciousness in which there is an awareness of the world existing out there. It is basically a stage in which the subject is contrasted with the objects, the self versus others. The second, 'U', stage is the psychological state of the semi-conscious, where absolute categories start to break down. The logical world begins to dissolve and there is an expansion of the self. One could, for example, be in different places at the same time. The third stage, that of 'M', is the deep sleep state, the state of utter unconsciousness, but here one does not experience anything. It is a state of utter oblivion. The final stage, the fourth one in which the A, the U and the M are fused together, is the experience of totality. This is the unity of which one is deeply aware, a unity one fully enjoys, a unity where the self is totally cognizant of its becoming Oneness itself. Guru Nanak's usage of *Oan* in the Sikh primal statement manifests the theological and spiritual nexus of the Sikh religion: the Ultimate is an inner, subjective experience of infinity on earth rather than an objective knowledge of a God out there.

By frequently juxtaposing the Absolute and Infinite One to the second person *tun* (a familiar form of the word 'you', like the French *tu*), Sikh scripture offers an intimate relationship between the individual and the Divine that is very much like the 'I–Thou' encounter of the famous Jewish philosopher, Martin Buber. According to Buber, the 'I–Thou' relationship is one of subject to subject. This relationship governed by mutuality and reciprocity is opposed to the 'I–It' relationship, where the other exists merely as an object or a thing. When the individual is in an 'I–Thou' relationship with God, then this universal relationship flows into all other relations.[2] Certainly, when there is only One Divine, human beings become aware of each other not as separate or isolated atoms but as having a unity of being. A personal 'I' reaches out to all; and *others* are regarded as a Thou – not as foreigners or aliens. Feelings of respect, commitment and responsibility extend toward fellow beings. In the Guru Granth, the metaphysical *ikk* (One) maintains a subjectivity and an existential quality. There is a personal encounter with that One, which in turn validates an authentic human situation. Sikh mystical vision has social implications.

Diversity in Unity

Guru Nanak was keenly aware of religious diversity. He believed that the Subject was the same, but that it could be comprehended and taught in different styles. With his liberal attitude, he wanted people to see through the external differences of various methods into the universal matrix. Respect for the diversity of teachers and schools of thought rings audibly in his verse: '*gur gur eko ves anek* – the Guru is the same but the forms are many' (GG: 12). There is also a gender balance, for the teachers are acknowledged as being both male and female: '*gur isar gur gorakh barmah gur parbati mai* – the Guru is Shiva, Guru is Vishnu, Guru is Brahma; the Guru is Parvati, Laxmi and Sarasvati' (Jap: 5).[3] Respect and reverence for the faith and belief of people from different backgrounds is sustained throughout Sikh scripture.

Translating the One

It is critical that we do not put Guru Nanak's truly unique configuration of *Ikk Oan Kar* into any pre-existing molds. The standard translation 'There is One God' does not quite express the vastness, the plenitude or the intimacy bursting forth in the original. Instead of an opening into limitless possibilities as envisioned by the founder Sikh Guru, scholars and translators have selected, structured and shaped *Ikk Oan Kar* into a male god. As the feminist philosopher Mary Daly has warned, the term 'god' is a reified 'noun' that is static and laden with Jewish and Christian patriarchal assumptions. 'God', with its 'Father–Lord' connotations, has negative effects on society as it produces unhealthy perspectives on our experience with the Divine, and unhealthy relationships among ourselves. Transcending languages, cultures and religions, Guru Nanak's primary numeral One with its soaring geometric arc is a universal modality. In any interpretation or translation, we must retain the Oneness of the numeral One, and I would say 'Be-ing' (recommended by Mary Daly in a Western context) works out quite well as an English equivalent. In this dynamic verb, the One can be accessed by anybody in any region of the world, and the Guru's intention is preserved. Guru Nanak's powerful inspiration must not be reduced to any exclusionary concept or any intimidating male symbol.

Sikh Ethics

The goal of Sikh moral life is union with the Divine. This union liberates the individual from the cycle of birth and death. When individuals merge with the spaceless and timeless One, they become infinite themselves. Thus confinements are shattered and the person never returns to any finite form. However, this freedom (*moksha* or *mukti*) is attained while participating vibrantly in daily life. Sikh ethics emphasize the following principles.

Orthopraxy

Guru Nanak's statement – *Ikk Oan Kar Sat Nam* (One Being Is Truth its Name) – is soon followed by his question 'How to become Truth? How to break the walls of falsity?' (GG: 1). There is a quick shift from the focus on the metaphysical Divine to the individual; from the timeless Creator to life lived truthfully here and now; from the metaphysical ideal to practical daily affairs. Orthopraxy takes precedence over orthodoxy, for a truthful mode of existence is deemed to be higher than the conception of Truth: 'Higher than everything is Truth but higher still is True living' (GG: 62). How are we to live 'truthfully' in our complex world? Sikhism mandates that people actively search for ways of living truthfully among family, friends and community. It charges people to figure out their essential nature and to live in accordance with it.

So often we ignore our true self, and get caught up in artificialities and appearances, which only bring tension, anxiety, unhappiness and frustration. The Sikh Gurus urge people to see beyond superficial blemishes and wrinkles, to the intrinsic reality. When there is Truth within, it radiates on the face. Guru Arjan vividly describes the actions of people who live with the recognition of Truth: 'Truth is in their hearts, Truth is on their lips, Truth is in their sight, Truth their form, Truth is their way, Truth their revelation. They who discern the Divine as Truth, says Nanak, they themselves merge with Truth' (GG: 283). The Sikh Gurus are similar to liberation theologians who claim that Truth is something that is *done*. The goal of Truth becomes the path itself. And so ethics and religion integrate into a singular venture, a life fully lived with the knowledge and experience of the Divine.

Social Equality

Since everybody possesses the same spiritual ingredient, everybody on earth is the same. The crucial pan-Indian term *dharam* (used for religion, virtue, duty, propriety, morality, cosmic order and law) acquires a whole new meaning in Sikhism. Though *dharam* retains its Sanskrit etymology (from the root *dhr*, to sustain, uphold, support –

Figure 10: Opening page of the Guru Granth from an illuminated manuscript, circa 1859

shared with *dharti* or earth), it does not carry any of the conventional regulations. Dharam in Sikhism does not prescribe the customary fourfold division of Indian society into Brahmins, Kshatriyas, Vaishyas and Shudras, nor does it institute a division of the stages of life into that of *brahmacarin*, *grahastha*, *vanaprastha* and *sanyasin* (*varna-ashrama-dharma*). In contrast to the fourfold societal hierarchy and its corresponding privileges, duties and responsibilities, Sikh scripture stipulates one and the same *dharam* for people of every class, race, faith and age. Guru Nanak categorically says that there is only one *dharam*: '*eko dharam*' (GG: 1188). The mutually exclusive scripts that were forced on people simply on the basis of their biological birth were obliterated. Everyone is equally impelled to perform their ethical duty throughout their entire life. The Guru Granth firmly proclaims that all four classes possess one and the same mandate: '*khatri brahman sud vais, updes cahu varna ko sajha* – be they Kshatriyas, Brahmins, Shudras or Vaishyas, the injunction is shared by people of all complexions' (GG: 747). This message has great relevance for our own time because the four classes are based on complexion (*varna* literally means color or complexion), and though 'castes' may seem a thing of the past, color and race are vitally important issues that contemporary society needs to face. The divine mandate is shared not just by people of the four castes but includes people of all complexions. Rejecting distinctions and restrictions, the Guru Granth declares that *dharam* succeeds 'when the entire earth becomes equal' – literally, one color: '*sristi sabh ikk varan hoi*' (GG: 663).

Spiritual Journey

The opening hymn of the Guru Granth launches readers and reciters into deeper and deeper intensity through the realms of *Dharam*, *Gyan*, *Saram*, *Karam* and *Sach* – Duty, Knowledge, Esthetics, Action and Truth.[4] The maps and charts of this spiritual journey are drafted totally on the longitudes and latitudes of planet earth (*dharat*). Its starting point is Dharam Khand – living as moral agents on earth. The universal and egalitarian structure of Dharam Khand is expressed in its very constitution:

> *rati ruti thiti var*
> *pavan pani agni patal*
> *tisu vici dharati thapi rakhi dharamsal* (GG: 7)
> Amidst nights, seasons, solar and lunar days
> Amidst air, water, fire and netherworld
> The earth is placed, the place for righteous action.

The foremost duty for humans is to coexist harmoniously and ethically with all beings on earth. On this earth are 'colorful beings and lifestyles, infinite are their names and infinite their forms' (GG: 7). Plurality and multiplicity are fully accepted, but everyone is interconnected. So there is no implication of any disjunctions or divisions of gender, race or class. The earth as the *Dharamsal* provides everybody with an equal opportunity to act ethically and purposefully. No action is singled out or reserved for anyone in particular. But whatever is done has an effect. The universal injunction plays out: as you sow, so shall you reap. In Sikhism, the sense of morality is developed in and within the world. There is nothing on earth that is bad or polluted: 'the earth is not false; water is not false – *jhuth na dharti jhut na pani*' (GG: 1240).

With the whole earth designated as *Dharamsal*, all parts of the world are equally important. Morality is not fostered in some distant cave or a faraway forest; rather, it is practiced in the immediate world of family and profession. Another scriptural verse reaffirms the earth as the stage for righteous action: '*karma bhumi mahi boahu namu* – in the field of actions sow the seed of devotion' (GG: 176). The earth, referred to as *dharti* or *bhumi*, first offers existence itself and then the opportunity to engage in moral and ethical action. In an alliteration of '*ds*', Guru Nanak reiterates: '*dharat upai dhari dharamsal* – the earth was created to establish the home of Dharam' (GG: 1033). In yet another explanation: 'for the sake of good people the earth is embellished – *gurmukh dharti sachai saji*' (GG: 941). Such scriptural statements reveal moral responsibility. The earth is beautiful, and human beings are created to do good. Everybody across the globe is *equally* responsible: we must all work together to construct a better world for all of us, and for our future generations. The Kashatriya is not obligated to take up arms for justice, nor the White Man to carry *his burden*. Such social hegemonies and racial dominance play no part in Sikhism.

Therefore, rather than 'turning around from facing the world to face God', or a commitment to 'worldlessness', Sikh ethics is marked by turning fully into the world. Spurning asceticism and renunciation, the Guru Granth proclaims: 'spiritual liberation is attained in the midst of laughing, playing, dressing up and eating – *hasandia khelandia painandia khavandia viche hovai mukt*' (GG: 522). Whereas in many religious traditions such human activities would be denigrated, Sikhism values them profoundly, and posits a cheerful attitude toward life and living. The world is a good place. Human life is precious 'like a diamond' (*hire jaisa*). The temporal world is a part of the Infinite One and partakes of its characteristics. The journey through the five stages is not an ascension into some higher regions beyond our lives and our world; rather, it is based on drawing the Divine into the human situation. It is in our everyday existence that we develop our moral, intellectual, esthetic and spiritual capacities, and experience the Ultimate One. Thus we live in the truest sense, living freely and expansively as life would be in *Sach Khand*, the Realm of Truth.

Rejection of Vice

Sikhism lists five psychological propensities as being harmful to the human race: *kam*, *krodha*, *lobh*, *moh* and *ahankar* – lust, anger, greed, attachment and pride. These are viewed as thieves and robbers residing within, who steal the precious morality with which humans are equally endowed (GG: 600). Lust, anger, greed, attachment and pride put a person out of joint; each of these emotions hurts a person psychologically and physiologically. Each of them also puts social cohesion and integration in jeopardy. They rob the individual of the underlying unity of humanity and brutally destroy social relations. From the Granthian perspective, then, the individual and the society are interrelated, and the psychological balance of an individual constitutes the good of society at large.

Sikhism also instructs that religion should not be confused with economic, political and territorial issues. Very often we transfer our deep psychological conflicts on to external differences. Religious difference is an easy target for our own psychological sickness, and therefore inner propensities become misplaced and dislocated as religious conflicts. The Hindu–Muslim conflict confronting the society of the Gurus is carried on into modern times, now as Jewish versus Palestinian, Sikh versus Hindu, Catholic versus Protestant, Hutu versus Tutsi, Sunni versus Shi'a, and so on. But what we are really doing is avoiding facing up to our personal vices. Individual lust, anger, greed, attachment and arrogance are fabricated into a dangerous rhetoric that arouses exclusivism and sectarianism.

In his hymn entitled *Babur Vani*, Guru Nanak offers a timeless insight. At the terrible hour of Babur's attack on Hindustan, the Guru was deeply pained by the violence inflicted on South Asians. Nevertheless, he saw through it all and commented: '*jaru vandi devai bhai* – it is wealth that divides brothers' (GG: 417). Guru Nanak knew his attack on the Muslim Lodis was his psychological problem – Babur's lust for power, territory and wealth. Essentially, we are one family, with one progenitor. The cause of conflict is greed – dividing brother from brother, the Muslim Babur from the Muslim Lodis – not one religion from another. The Gurus transcended the exterior and outward form of Hinduism and Islam; they saw the common bond of humanity. From different angles, the Guru Granth makes us look into ourselves and examine our maladies, our sibling rivalries and our jealousies.

Getting Rid of Haumai

The root cause of the five vices is *haumai*, literally, 'I–Myself'. *Haumai* is the selfish investment of oneself with pride and arrogance. By constantly centering on 'I', 'me' and 'mine', the self is circumscribed as a particular person, wrenched from his/her universal root. In the Jap it is compared to a wall: just as a wall forms a barrier, so does *haumai*. By building up the selfish ego, the individual is divided from the One Reality. Duality (*dubida*) comes into play. The selfish ego asserts itself in opposition to others. The divine spark within is veiled. The singular harmony is not experienced. Such an existence is measured through competition, malice, ill-will towards others, and a craving for power. Blind towards others, the individual lives for himself or herself alone. The selfish person is called *manmukh*, 'turned towards the *me*', in contrast to one who actualizes the Divine Oneness, and is called *gurmukh*, 'turned toward the Guru'.

Virtue

How are the five thieves caught? How is the wall of selfishness broken? Prescribed religious practices such as pilgrimages, fasts and asceticism are of no avail. 'One removes vice with virtue, for virtue is our only true friend and sibling' specifies the Granth (GG: 595). Metaphors that integrate us with family and friends are used to express the importance of living virtuously. Vice can be got rid of by keeping a rhythm of natural daily routine and leading a life of balance and poise. To this end the Guru Granth promotes *sunia, mania, manu kita bhau*.

This triple formula is applicable to all cultures and religions. *Sunia* literally signifies hearing, and means listening to the Divine One. It is the first step toward awakening to the transcendent Core of the universe. Hearing is the sense that connects the conscious and the unconscious realms most directly. According to the Guru Granth, listening to the melodious Name of the Divine, we fathom the oceans of virtue. Stanzas 8–11 of the Japji explain the vital role of listening. Through listening, one gains the faculties of all the gods, one gains knowledge of all the continents, one acquires the import of all the ancient texts, one learns all the techniques of meditation, one masters the experience of all the sages of Hinduism and Islam (and by implication, all religions), and through listening, all suffering and anxiety are annulled. The refrain in these stanzas acknowledges that the devotees who hear the Name of the True One enjoy eternal bliss.

Mania means remembering the One, keeping the One constantly in our mind. This process is not purely intellectual as it has connotations of trust and faith. It is the second step, for it is only after something is heard that it can enter the mind. By keeping the Divine in our mind, we do not succumb to vice. We liberate ourselves from the constant bondage of birth and death. Importantly, we also reach out to others and assist in liberating our family and friends.

Manu kita bhau means to be full of love for the Divine. This state of devotion is the third step, one that goes beyond hearing the One, and keeping that One in mind. For those who attain this state, 'every thread of their being is drenched in love'. There is an abundance of words for love in Sikh scripture – *pyar*, *muhabbat*, *ishq rang*, *rasa*. Indeed, love is passionate; love is transformative. It takes lovers to depths of richness and fullness where there is freedom from all kinds of limitations of the self. But it is a gift that 'comes with the knowledge of the Infinite One' (GG: 61). Hence love and knowledge, emotion and cognition, are intrinsically connected in Sikhism. In fact, the same term *man* is used for both 'heart' and 'mind'. Love is consistently applauded as the supreme virtue:

> Those who hear, appropriate, and nurture love in their hearts,
> They cleanse themselves by bathing at the sacred fount, which is within. (GG: 4)

> Pure, pure, utterly pure are they, says Nanak, who recite the Name with love. (GG: 279)

Without love, ablutions, charities, studies and rituals are utterly worthless. They only prevent people from relating to the surrounding beauty and diversity.

Scriptures across religions draw attention to the emotion of love. In the Gospels, Jesus says: 'The greatest commandment of all is this – love your God with all your soul, mind and strength, and love your neighbor as yourself.' In the holy Qu'ran, Allah expresses love for humanity through the analogy of the jugular vein: 'We are closer to him than his jugular vein' (50:16). In the Bhagavad Gita, Lord Krishna reveals a new way of reaching the Divine as he conjoins *bhakti* (love) with the traditional paths of *jnana* (knowledge) and *karma* (action). Yet, in spite of it, all across the globe human beings are trapped in hate and conflict. Those who claim to lead normal lives find themselves utterly devoid of this emotion. Sikh scripture strongly urges us to assess our loss: '*andar khali prem binu dhai dheri tanu char* – without love inside, we are but dust and ash' (GG: 62). This love is not a selfish obsession; it is a realization of that infinite One which produces positive energy within the individual, who then reaches out from one body to another and to everything around. Divine passion leads to compassion for all the beings in the world. According to the Guru Granth, the enlightened are 'those who view everyone equally, like the air touching king and beggar alike' (GG: 272). Love takes the person beyond semantic categories such as Hindu or Muslim, black or white, Brahmin or Shudra, male or female, rich or poor. It inspires hard work for the well-being of our collective community.

The Sikh Ethical Code

The *Sikh Rahit Maryada* is the authoritative statement of Sikh conduct, published in 1950. The *Sikh Rahit Maryad*a defines a Sikh as a person who has belief in the Timeless Being (*Akal Purakh*), without allegiance to any gods or goddesses. A Sikh should regard only the Ten Gurus and their teachings as the medium for liberation. A Sikh should not practice caste, untouchability, magical rites or superstitions. The Sikh code specifically prohibits the following four acts:

1. Cutting or trimming hair, for both men and women.
2. Eating of meat cut through the slow purification rite (*halal*). [Sikhs may eat meat but only that from an animal slaughtered in one stroke (*jhatka*).]
3. Adultery.
4. Use of narcotics.

Sikhs should not take intoxicants and narcotics, such as hemp, opium, spirits or tobacco, as they harm the mind.

In the case of a violation of these imperatives, the person may appear before any religious congregation of the Sikhs, seek their punishment, perform it cheerfully and be reinitiated into Khalsahood.

Sikh Esthetics

The Sikh Gurus fostered *esthetics* as the approach to knowledge and spirituality. The opposite of anesthetic (the deadening of senses), esthetics is the heightening of hearing, seeing, touching, smelling, tasting. In short, esthetics is feeling and experiencing the Divine immediately and intensely.

The method was inaugurated by the founder Guru himself: 'Only the relisher of fragrance can recognize the flower – *rasia hovai musk ka tab phul pachanai*' (GG: 725). The complex process of recognition (*pachanai*) requires a physical act as well as a cognitive realization. Therefore, a heightened sensuous experience becomes necessary for metaphysical knowledge. In another passage he states explicitly: '*akhi qudrat kani bani mukh akhan sach nam* – eyes must see the divine nature, ears must hear the divine word, lips must speak the true name' (GG: 1168). Through his esthetic discourse, the first Sikh Guru tried to awaken his followers and revitalize their senses, psyche, imagination and spirit. His entire teaching was through the medium of poetry. As we saw in chapter 1, Guru Nanak identified himself as a poet: '*sasu masu sabhu jio tumara tu mai khara piara nanaku sairu eva kahatu hai sace parvadgara* – to you belong my breath, to you my flesh; says the poet Nanak, you the True One are my Beloved' (GG: 660).

A heightened sensuous experience is a requirement for metaphysical knowledge. Consequently, the human body is important. The physical is celebrated. Most often, however, religion and esthetics are pitted against each other. Whereas religion is deemed a 'spiritual' enterprise, the esthetic is denigrated as something merely 'sensuous'. Scholars tend to divide philosophy into logic, ethics and esthetics, the goals of which are separately the true, the good and the beautiful.[5] However, as we discover in Guru Nanak's case, the esthetic experience of an individual is absolutely crucial for ethical development. By honing the senses, knowledge of the infinite One is attained, which frees people from debilitating binary structures. With a sense of that One, the selfish 'I' or 'me' dissolves, resulting in moral actions, thought and speech.

At the very outset, Guru Nanak enunciates esthetics integral to the development of consciousness. It is in the realm of esthetics (*Saram Khand*) that 'we sharpen consciousness, wisdom, mind and discrimination – *tithai ghariai surati mati mani buddhi*' (Jap: 36). In this dynamic sphere, wisdom (*mati*), along with consciousness (*surati*), mind (*man*) and the power of discrimination (*buddhi*), is refined. *Ghariai*, from the infinitive *gharana*, literally means to sharpen or chisel. However blunt our mental, psychological, intellectual and reasoning faculties, they are developed and keenly chiseled in this realm of art and beauty. The honing that takes place in *Saram Khand* leads us to the mystical and divine experience: '*tithai ghariai sura siddha ki suddh* – here the consciousness is sharpened to that of the gods and mystics', continues Guru Nanak (Jap: 36). The Sikh Guru's perspective finds a remarkable parallel in the thoughts of twentieth-century Western artist Wassily Kandinsky:

> Art is not vague production, transitory and isolated, but a power which must be directed to the improvement and refinement of the human soul – to, in fact, the raising of the spiritual triangle.
>
> *Concerning the Spiritual in Art*[6]

The Fifth Guru crystallized the esthetic mode. He gathered together sublime poetry spanning religions, centuries, languages and regions. With his artistic genius he amplified the esthetic impulse by utilizing the *raga* system. He ensured that the text of love and devotion was to be approached with reverent wonder; it could not be pried into with mere intellect. The revealed Word (*bani*), empowered by the *ragas*, in turn serves as a melodious instrument for stimulating the senses and the mind into intuiting the Infinite One. The ears hear the Divine Word. The tongue tastes its deliciousness. Every pore of the body bathes in its passionate color. The Gurus constantly acknowledge the esthetic power of *bani*. So intense is its beauty that, on hearing it, mind and body are invigorated ('*sun sun man tan haria*', GG: 781). Once drenched in its passion, its color never leaves or fades (GG: 427). Guru Arjan equates this immutable experience with ambrosia, and qualifies it as delicious ('*amrit bani amio rasa*', GG: 963). For the Guru, an esthetic tasting was important: 'My tongue tastes the ambrosial word – *amrit bani rasna chakhai*', he divulges (GG: 395).

The compiler intended his community to gain supreme enjoyment from the literary volume, and in his epilogue (*mundavani*) to the Granth we clearly hear his objective:

> *thal vicu tinu vastu paio*
> *sat santokh vicaru…*
> *je ko khavai je ko bhuncai*
> *tis ka hoe udharo*
> in the platter lie three things:
> Truth, contentment, contemplation…
> they who eat, they who relish
> are liberated.

Guru Arjan here uses the analogy of a platter. The holy volume is a *thal* (large metal dish) on which are placed Truth, Contentment and Contemplation. The identity of knowledge and food lodged in the epilogue of the Guru Granth is prefigured in its opening hymn: '*bhugati gianu daia bhandarani* – knowledge is the banquet, compassion the hostess' (Jap: 29). Knowledge is a delectable banquet. The sumptuous array of dishes indicated by Guru Nanak is specified by Guru Arjan as Truth, Contentment and Contemplation. The epistemological value of these dishes is not conceived intellectually or argued logically; it is swallowed and digested by the body. But mere 'eating' (*khavai*) is not enough; the esthetic heightening, 'savoring' (*bhuncai*) is crucial for the esthete par excellence.

Food is a biological necessity, keeping every body from shriveling up and dying. So is knowledge. By equating it with food, the Sikh Gurus make knowledge essential for all – not just for Plato's philosopher-king or the Brahmins of Vedic India. The cognitive and digestive activities are not relegated to either male or female domains, nor set apart from other activities. Knowledge is eaten, and just like food, it is necessary for human growth and fulfillment. Eating is a most creative act: we take something from the external world and turn it into ourselves. A tiny morsel makes a circuit in the body, and through the bloodstream becomes a cell, a muscle, a neuron, a thought, an emotion, an embrace. The poets of the Guru Granth repeatedly wish the Divine to be remembered in every 'morsel of food – *sas gras*' (GG: 961), making the alimentary canal elementary to spiritual progress.

It was this platter of Truth, Contentment and Contemplation that the Tenth Guru offered as the eternal Guru. Its words are to be fully absorbed, literally made a part of the bloodstream. Literature, like all art, has profound influence on shaping world views, attitudes and behavior. In order to bring about a moral transformation in their discordant society, the Gurus wanted to reach into the very consciousness of the masses. Their verse offers a sumptuous variety of images, symbols and metaphors that have the potential to help readers realize the countless resources of our common humanity. The literary devices integrate the intellectual faculties with the esthetic, axiological and emotional self. Absorbing them fosters morality. For the Gurus, the esthetic experience of ambrosial poetry was the only avenue to real change. It would make the inner circuits and impact external conduct. As we shall explore in Chapter 5, hearing and reciting their universal hymns constitutes the core of Sikh practice. Even for us today, only when we get a real feel for that *oneness* we all share will we be able to implement our social, political, economic and environmental policies. If we align ourselves with that One, we shall take constructive steps toward equality, healthcare, education and caring for the environment. The esthetic experience is neither antithetical to the metaphysical doctrine of Oneness, nor antithetical to moral behavior; rather, it is the mechanism for ethical and spiritual growth.

Chapter V

Worship, Ceremonies and Rites of Passage

As discussed in the opening chapter, Guru Nanak rejected conventional beliefs and practices that centered on external authorities and outward response. Numerous passages in the Guru Granth condemn the emphasis on external practice, whether it be from any Hindu, Muslim, Buddhist, Jain or Yogic tradition. Inward reflection on the Divine takes precedence over, for example, sacrificing a horse, giving one's weight in gold to charity, offering sweet rice at Gaya, bathing at the confluence of the rivers, living on the banks of the Ganges at Varanasi, reciting the four Vedas by heart, performing religious rituals, or expounding on Shiva and Shakti (GG: 873). Accordingly, the true practice of Islam consists of making mercy the mosque, devotion the prayer-mat, honest living the holy Qu'ran, good action the Ka'ba, and modesty the rite of circumcision (GG: 140). Idolatry, worship of fire, making pilgrimages, depending on horoscopes, keeping fasts, withdrawing from life, and notions of purity and pollution are utterly abandoned. Dietary taboos find no place: 'idiots fight over the fetish of meat, without either knowledge or reflection – *mas mas kar murakh jaghare gian dhian nahin janai*' (GG: 1289). Since the entire Creation is a part of that One, all space and time are equally holy: 'only the stupid and idiots rely on dates and days – *thiti var seveh mugadh gavar*' (GG: 843). From its very genesis, Sikhism condemned the division between sacred and profane, and posited interior reflection on the singular Divine as the sole religious practice.

Consequently, the medium that would inspire such interiority has become the center of Sikh life. Guru Granth, the transcendent Word, is the presiding agent for all ceremonies and rites of passage. Whether in Gurdwaras or privately at home, the volume embodying the universal divine passion of Sikh Gurus, Muslim Sufis and Hindu Bhagats is treated with the highest respect and veneration. It is always draped in silks and brocades (called *rumala*), placed on quilted mats and supported by cushions. A canopy hangs over it for protection, and a flywhisk is waved over it by an attendant. Such cultural symbols as the whisk and the canopy for royalty are used in Sikhism to express the sovereign status of the scriptural Guru. Men and women remove their shoes and cover their heads before they come in its presence.

Gurdwara

The Sikh place of public worship is called a Gurdwara – a door or threshold (*dwara*) to the Guru. These can be either historic Gurdwaras, which are constructed to mark important events in Sikh history, or community Gurdwaras, built to meet religious and social needs. A typical Gurdwara is open all day, with devotees coming and going whenever they wish. Religious activity consists of simply seeing the Guru Granth or listening to it being read, interpreted or sung, and these can be done either individually or with the rest of the congregation. So a sense of freedom permeates the Gurdwaras. Some of them serve community meals on a regular basis and have room for pilgrims to stay over. Thus Gurdwaras become more than places of worship: they are the source of assistance, food, shelter and fellowship. Architecturally, they are designed on the open and inclusive pattern of the Harmandar (see chapter 2 for details). Since the Guru Granth is the focal point to which everyone has equal access, there are no images or icons, nor is there any central chamber from which any male or female is excluded.

Besides the Harmandar, there are five popular pilgrimage sites, called the five *takhts* (five seats). The Akal Takht in Amritsar faces the Golden Temple and is regarded as the supreme seat of religious and temporal authority. The other four are associated with the Tenth Guru: Patna Sahib in Bihar, where he was born; Keshgarh, in Anandpur, where he created the Khalsa; Hazur Sahib in Nander, where he breathed his last; and Damdama, near Bhatinda, where he took rest – it later developed into a center of Sikh learning. Sikhs try to visit the five takhts at least once in their lifetime. Even if they cannot make the pilgrimage in person, devotees send money for scriptural readings, for the community kitchen, for the general upkeep of the shrine, and for gifts such as the *rumalas*.

Other places marking the birth of the Gurus or the sites they visited have also accrued great historical value. In the former princely state of Patiala, for example, Dukhniwaran Sahib Gurdwara, and Bahadurgarh on its outskirts, are reminders of the Ninth Guru's visit. They are important attractions for Sikhs from all over the world. A dip in the pool of Gurudwara Dukhniwaran Sahib is believed to cure all suffering – *dukhniwaran* literally means the end of suffering (*dukh*). Similarly, there is a Gurudwara in the old fort in Bhatinda. Incidentally, it was in this fort that Empress Razia Sultana, the first woman ruler of India, was imprisoned before her execution. The Gurdwara stands at the top of the fort, marking the place where Guru Gobind Singh fought with an enemy. The Sis Ganj Gurdwara in Delhi, where the Ninth Guru was executed, is another vital site. These Gurdwaras bring the past alive for Sikhs. Even diasporic Sikhs, when they return home to India, try to visit their historical shrines, taking their children with them.

A mini-Gurdwara at home – a room enshrining the Guru Granth – is the wish of most Sikh families.

Worship

One of the first acts of worship consists of *matha tekna* (bowing) to the Guru Granth, or *darshan karana* (seeing) it. As a sign of humility and submission, devotees perform *matha tekna* by going down on both knees and bowing low until their forehead (*matha*) touches the ground in front of the scripture. Many make offerings of money or flowers. *Darshan* is the pan-Indian religious process in which the devotees go to see and be seen by their Divine source, but in the Sikh instance, the visual reception of their scripture is fused with the aural. Catching a glimpse of their text, listening to it, or reading, singing or just sitting in its presence constitute 'taking *darshan*'.

At home or in Gurdwaras, the Guru Granth is opened daily at dawn and adorned in robes. This ceremony of opening the holy book is called *prakash*, 'making the light manifest'. It is a ritual enactment of the Guru being enthroned and ready to receive the public, and radiate its luminosity. The *hukam* (order) or *vak* (reading) of the day is obtained by opening the Book at random, and reading the passage at the top of the left-hand page, which is understood as the message for the day. Meant for the entire congregation, the *hukam* at a Gurdwara is displayed on a board so that visitors during the course of the day can read it and interpret it for themselves. For any major decision or undertaking, Sikhs individually and collectively solicit the *hukam* for guidance. It is their Guru's direct channel of communication with them. In contemporary global society, Sikhs can access their Guru's directive electronically from their most celebrated shrine, the Golden Temple. With the recent televising of its morning and evening ceremonies, Sikh devotees are beginning to participate in their tradition in a new way. The televising is also having an impact on public worship, as more and more Gurdwaras try to follow the standard routine at the Harmandar.

In the evening, the Guru Granth is ceremoniously closed. This closing ritual is called *sukhasan*, the position (*asan*) of rest or comfort (*sukh*) for the night. The sukhasan performance parallels the morning *prakash*, and the two create the daily framework for congregations to attend to their sacred Book. In Gurdwaras, these ceremonies are elaborate. In the Golden Temple, for example, the Guru Granth is taken in a gold and silver palanquin (*palki*) to a special chamber for its nightly rest. Chanting Guru Nanak's hymn 'Arati', the large procession of devotees (and visitors) carries the palanquin from the Harmandar to the Akal Takht. This short transit can take a long time as worshippers try to pay homage by shouldering the palanquin. The accompanying hymn conjures *arati*, the beautiful traditional mode of worship, in which devotees encircle a platter decorated with lamps, incense, flowers and fruit set around their favorite deities. But Guru Nanak transforms it into a cosmic choreography of the planets: the spacious and ethereal skies serve as the platter (*thal*), on which the sun, moon and twinkling starry lamps perform *arati* around the infinite One. Such a synthesis of sounds and scenes during the evening ceremony evokes universal harmony and joy.

The infinite sky offered by Guru Nanak as the cosmic platter was reconfigured by his Fifth Guru successor; as discussed in Chapter IV, Guru Arjan changed it into a Granth that contained the dishes of Truth, Contentment and Contemplation. Subsequently, this wholesome text was appointed Guru Eternal by the Tenth Guru, so that generations of Sikhs could be fed its nutritional elements. Their Gurus' enchantment with the sacred poetry has been institutionalized into Sikh practices and rites. The Guru Granth is read at all rites of passage, at any family celebration – a new house, new job, birthdays, engagements, and during all times of uncertainty and difficulty, such as sickness or death. Usually, the reading at these events is *akhand*, a 48-hour, nonstop reading of its 1,430 portfolio pages, during which several readers take turns.[1] Any Sikh, male or female, who can read Gurmukhi script may read the Guru Granth. Sikhs engage with their text through *path* (recitation), *kirtan* (singing) and *ardas* (supplication).

The Five Daily Prayers

The daily spiritual routine (*nitnem*) consists of a recitation (*path*) of hymns from the various Gurus. Every morning and evening, Sikh sacred spaces and homes (and even cars and trucks!) resonate with the melodious sounds of their daily hymns. Children hear them from the lips of their parents, who could be involved in the daily chores of cooking, combing hair and watering plants. Some adults hear them on CDs and satellite TV. The Jap, Jaap, Swayyai, Rahiras and Kirtan Sohila constitute the daily repertoire. There is no rigid timing for any of the five, but they fall into two parts: the Jap, Jaap and Swayyai are three prayers for the morning; while Rahiras and Kirtan Sohila are for the evening.

Jap is Guru Nanak's composition. This first prayer in the Guru Granth presents the fundamental philosophical and ethical beliefs of the Sikhs. It is recited at the break of day, when the mind is fresh and the atmosphere serene. Described as the ambrosial hour in the Jap, pre-dawn is considered most conducive to grasping the Divine word. Reading, reciting or hearing the Jap enables Sikhs to conceive the Formless Reality and instills faith in them to have a deeper communion with the Infinite One.

Jaap (with a long a) and Swayyai are the compositions of the Tenth Guru. They are from Guru Gobind Singh's Dasam Granth, which was mentioned in Chapter III and is very controversial. While the Guru Granth is at the center of Sikh worship, the poetry of the Tenth Guru is also held in high esteem by Sikhs, and so the Jaap – along with the Swayyai – form part of their daily prayers. Jaap is Guru Gobind Singh's poetic obeisance to the Transcendent One. In 199 couplets, it is a breathtaking profusion of divine attributes that flashed onto Guru Gobind Singh's artistic consciousness. Interestingly, Guru Gobind Singh stops after couplet 199, which signifies that there is no culminating point. The never-ending words saluting the Infinite Reality are dynamic, their rhythm is rapid, and so this morning prayer of the Sikhs becomes an important esthetic medium for contemplating the One brought forth in Guru Nanak's Jap.

The *Swayyai* are in quatrains. The ten Swayyai that have been included in the Sikhs' daily prayers underscore devotion as the essence of religion. They reject all forms of external worship, and cast Guru Nanak's message of internal love in an undulating rhythm. These Swayyai are also recited during the administration of *amrit*, the initiation ceremony of the Khalsa.

Rahiras is part of the evening service. It includes hymns from Guru Nanak, Guru Ram Das and Guru Arjan. Guru Gobind Singh's Chaupai Benati (supplication in quatrains) also forms a part of this evening prayer. The Rahiras concludes with the first five stanzas and the final one of Guru Amar Das's Anand (Bliss). Summer and winter, the Sikhs recite Rahiras just as day and night come together during the reflective period of dusk. Through the Rahiras, the Sikhs pay homage to the Transcendent Reality, they sing praises of Divine Magnificence, they seek the protection and succor of the omnipotent Creator, and they express their joy on hearing the melodious Word within their inner self.

Kirtan Sohila, meaning 'the hymn of praise', is the finale to the evening prayers. It is recited just before going to bed, as the holy book is closed and carried ceremoniously to rest. It is also recited at cremation ceremonies, linking the end of the day with the end of life.

Kirtan Sohila consists of five hymns. The first three are by Guru Nanak, followed by one each from Guru Ram Das and Guru Arjan. They have great philosophical and artistic value. The first hymn visualizes the union of the individual self with the Divine. The second underscores the singularity of the Divine, despite the endless diversity of scriptures, teachers and philosophies. The third is Nanak's Arati, which imagines the entire cosmos offering a harmonious worship to that One. The fourth hymn in this nightly prayer, by Guru Ram Das, explains the importance of the Divine Name, through which suffering and transmigration are annuled. The fifth hymn, by Guru Arjan, celebrates life on earth: everybody must avail themselves of this wonderful opportunity to serve others and to win Divine merit. The transcendent mystery is revealed within the body, and so the enlightened enjoy the bliss and freedom of immortality.

Though it is not part of the daily routine, Guru Arjan's hymn *Sukhmani* is also regularly recited. *Sukh* means peace and *mani* could mean either pearl or mind (from the word *man*), so the title can be translated as Pearl of Peace or Mind of Peace. This rather long hymn extols the importance of Name. Sikh tradition maintains that Guru Arjan composed it under the ber tree, which can still be seen beside the sacred pool of Ramsar in Amritsar.

The Sukhmani is especially popular among women. Groups get together on a weekly or monthly basis in a private house or in a Gurdwara to read it together. On such occasions, several copies of the Sukhmani are made available for the congregation. Someone begins to read out a section, and anyone who wishes may join at the end to lead in the reading of the next section. The final couplets in each segment are read by the entire group. The Sukhmani *path* is being incorporated into kitty parties: instead of playing cards and other games at these parties, women jointly read the Sukhmani, which brings peace to reader and listener alike.

Rituals

Kirtan is the basic Sikh ritual: the singing of scriptural verses. Harmonium and *tabla* (a set of drums) are the most common accompanying musical instruments. As the verses of infinite love mingle with the music, they sink deep into the unconscious, to awaken cosmic awareness. The Fifth Guru put most of the scripture into classical and regional melodies precisely to evoke the essential *rasa* (flavor or taste) of the Guru's word. According to the Gurus, wherever divine *praise* is recited, that place is paradise itself.

Ardas (from the Persian *arz-dasht*, a written petition) is recited as a solo by a leading member of the congregation. The entire gathering stands up with hands folded together and heads bent in reverence before the Granth. The congregation joins in at certain points, exclaiming 'Wahe Guru!' (wonderful Guru). *Ardas* has powerful associations, which remain constant for all occasions. These include remembering the Divine One, the ten Gurus, their merging with the Guru Granth, and events of Sikh heroism, devotion and martyrdom. Toward the end of the *ardas*, a special request is made for the specific purpose for which the congregation came together. The *ardas* invariably ends with a supplication for the prosperity and happiness of all humanity.

Bhog, which literally means pleasure, is the joyous culmination of every Sikh event. Thus it is similar to the Christian Eucharist, which also means rejoicing. *Bhog* involves reading the concluding pages of the Guru Granth, and culminates in the distribution of *Karahprashad*.

Karahprashad is the sweet sacrament consisting of equal portions of butter, flour, sugar and water. These ingredients are stirred vigorously on a stove so they remain moist and sticky. During the preparation of *karahprashad*, men and women keep their heads covered, their feet bare, and recite the verses of the Gurus. When the *karahprashad* is ready, it is put into a large, flat dish and placed on the right side of the Guru Granth. As the finale of worship, the warm and aromatic sacrament is distributed to the entire congregation, who receive it in cupped palms – with both hands joined together.

Sikh Institutions

Seva is voluntary manual labor in the service of the community. Seva means a deed of love and selfless service for fellow human beings. Seva is presented as the highest ideal in Sikh ethics. By *seva* one cultivates humility. By *seva* one overcomes the obsession with egotistic self and extends beyond individuality. Seva is an essential condition of spiritual discipline. According to Guru Nanak, 'by practicing deeds of humble and devoted service alone does one earn a seat in the next world' (GG: 26). Serving others with a cheerful attitude is deeply cherished, and *seva* has become an essential part of Sikh life. It may take the form of attending to the Holy Book, or sweeping and dusting the shrines, or preparing and serving food, or looking after and even cleaning the shoes of worshippers. A visitor to any Sikh shrine cannot but marvel at the zeal with which young and old, rich and poor alike take it upon themselves to perform different jobs. Seva also entails serving the community at large by building schools, hospitals and charity homes. Service to others goes beyond serving fellow Sikhs. There is an episode extolling *seva* towards friend and enemy alike, which is deeply imprinted in the collective Sikh memory. In a battle, some soldiers of Guru Gobind Singh saw a Sikh named Ghanaya giving water to the enemy. They went to the Guru

Figure 11: Preparing langar *at the Golden Temple*

with their complaint. Ghanaya was called and questioned. Ghanaya's response was that he had not helped the enemy: as he went around the battlefield, he saw no friend or foe but only the Guru's face.

Langar, the community kitchen, asserts the social equality and familyhood of humanity. This fundamental Sikh institution started by Guru Nanak involves the process of preparing meals together as well as eating together. The term denotes both the meal and the place where it is prepared and served. The food served at *langar* is vegetarian. Both men and women, irrespective of race, caste or religion, involve themselves in one task or another – chopping vegetables, kneading dough, rolling it out and fluffing it, and cleaning utensils. And without any consideration of caste or rank, they sit in rows and partake of the meal. In fact, we all experience a certain intimacy with people with whom we dine. Thanksgiving and Christmas dinners, Seders and Id celebrations are shared with people closest to us. Guru Nanak's establishment of *langar* is a fundamental step towards bonding humanity together, regardless of the differences in race, gender, caste and class. The *langar* as an instrument of social transformation continued to gain in importance during the time of the successive Gurus. In Guru Angad's day, his wife, Mata Khivi, was compared with 'a thickly-leafed tree' that provides shade for everyone, because she used to serve rich food in the *langar* (GG: 967). Guru Amar Das insisted that visitors should first enjoy the *langar* meal with others before meeting him: 'first *pangat* (the row in which all sit together to partake of the *langar* meal) and then meeting with the Guru' (GG: 967). In Sikh life, eating and serving in the *langar* have always been considered meritorious. In modern times, a visitor to the Punjab can be left astounded by this Sikh institution. During certain celebrations, such as the birthdays of their Gurus, *langar* is even served on the highways! Young and old together stop speeding buses, cars, trucks or slow-going bullock-carts, rickshaws and pedestrians, and enthusiastically serve them hot tea and meals. Every few yards, people standing in rows block traffic or tree trunks are laid across the road, and the meals are offered to travelers.

Sangat refers to any Sikh gathering or local community. It highlights three important elements of the Sikh religion. First, the importance of the community. Rather than individuality and isolation, comradeship and company with others is prized. According to a popular Sikh saying: 'One disciple is a single Sikh, two form a holy association, but where there are five present, there is the Ultimate Reality Itself.' Guru Nanak paved the way for an active and fruitful engagement with the community, implying a full acceptance and celebration of this very world. Second, *sangat* (like *langar*) is open to all, thus liberating the members from social, religious and gender restrictions. In Sikh congregations, members sit together on the floor, singing hymns, listening to expositions of the holy text, reciting verses and making supplications. Third, sangats provide spiritual and moral inspiration. According to Guru Nanak: 'Through *sangat*, one obtains the treasure of the Divine Name ... Just as iron rubbed against the philosopher's stone turns into gold, so does dark ignorance transform into brilliant light in company of the good' (GG: 1244). Participation with others is a catalyst for moral and spiritual development.

Celebrations

Every moment is sacred for the Sikhs, and daily routine is imbued with the religious. As we noted, Sikh scripture does not view one hour as being more auspicious than another. As a result, there is no reliance on horoscopes for matrimony or the start of important ventures. The founder Guru rejected astrological charts: 'We remain busy counting and determining auspicious days, but we do not know that the One Reality is above and beyond such considerations' (GG: 904).

Nevertheless, certain days of the month and of the year have an added element of festivity for the Sikhs, so their calendar is full of celebrations. But there is a categorical distinction between Gurparabs, the religious celebrations commemorating major events in Sikh history, and the regional cultural festivals. Since the Punjab has been predominantly an agrarian society, Sikh commemorations and celebrations are marked by the agricultural cycle and seasonal moods. The Sikh calendar combines both solar and lunar characteristics. Therefore, *sangrand*, Sanskrit *sankranti*, (the first day of the zodiac sign) and *masia* (the darkest night of the month) are special for them. Both historic moments and the eternally returning seasons are celebrated exuberantly.

Gurpurabs (literally the *purab* or day of the Guru) commemorate the birthdays and death anniversaries of their ten Gurus, important historical events, and the martyrdom of their heroes. All over the world, Sikhs joyously celebrate the birth of Guru Nanak, the installation of the Guru Granth in the Harmandar, and the birth of the Khalsa.

Gurpurab celebrations include huge Sikh processions with colorful floats carrying the Guru Granth and depicting different aspects of Sikh life. Scriptural hymns are recited. Langar is served in huge quantities. Wherever the procession goes, people come out of their homes; they cover their heads and take off their shoes, and pay homage to the Guru Granth. Important Sikh scholars are invited to Gurdwaras to deliver lectures. Great displays of treasure are exhibited at the Golden Temple and other historic shrines. There are uninterrupted readings of the Guru Granth followed by *bhog* ceremonies everywhere. Prayers are said and *karahprashad* distributed. Even in their homes, people have readings of the Guru Granth and recitation of Kirtan. Abroad, Sikhs celebrate these occasions with great rejoicing and festivity. They get away from their busy schedules and immerse themselves in their religious past. Gurdwaras in Toronto, San Francisco, New York and Washington invite musicians and lecturers from India during the Gurpurabs and have extra lavish

Figure 12: A scene from a local street in Amritsar

langars and celebrations. Often, they combine the religious ceremonies with intellectual and cultural events. They have seminars organized around Sikh themes, in which both Sikhs and others can participate. And they have cultural evenings when they organize plays, poetry readings, and performances of folk music and dance, from their heritage. Special customs are related to certain Gurpurabs. For the anniversary of Guru Arjan's martyrdom, cold milk mixed with water is served in bazaars and neighborhoods in India, which is very welcome in the hot period of May/June. Guru Arjan is remembered for being tortured to death by having scalding water and hot sand poured over him. The martyrdom of the young sons of Guru Gobind Singh is commemorated with great devotion in Fatehgarh Sahib, near Sirhind in the Punjab. Zorawar Singh and Fateh Singh heroically chose to be buried alive in a brick wall rather than give up their Sikh faith. Thousands gather each December in the Sirhind area, and are inspired by the courage of the young martyrs. Farmers bring out wheat, grain, milk and vegetables, and everyone shares enthusiastically in cooking, serving and cleaning. Even on waysides, devotees stop fast-moving cars and buses, and offer tea and many other treats to travelers.

Baisakhi, which is also the first day of the Sikh calendar, commemorates Guru Gobind Singh's creation of the Khalsa in 1699. It has become a vital social, political and religious occasion. The city of Amritsar, however, is the special center for this occasion. From far and near, Sikhs visit the Golden Temple on this day. The voices of specially trained singers and musicians fill the air. The entire complex is full of devotees bathing in the waters, listening to exegetes and musicians, preparing and eating *langar*, making special offerings, or reverentially walking around the promenade.

Outside the Golden Temple complex too, it is a lively scene. Since it is the last opportunity to relax before beginning the harvest, the large farming element in the society makes the most of this time. An animal fair is held, where goats, buffaloes, camels and other animals are bought and sold.

The saddest Baisakhi festival was in 1919. At that period Indians were not allowed by British administrators to gather due to fear that they might conspire against the Raj. But many went ahead and gathered in an enclosure called Jallian Wallah Bagh, which is very close to the Golden Temple. Under General Dyer, the British army fired on the assembly and hundreds of innocent civilians were killed. In commemoration of Baisakhi 1919, political rallies take place at Jallian Wallah Bagh.

Important academic functions also take place on Baisakhi. New books are released and scholars receive their awards. New members are initiated into the Khalsa community. At Gurdwaras, new Sikh flags are hoisted to replace the old ones. Overall, the New Year's Day is regarded as auspicious for all kinds of new beginnings and new undertakings.

Gurpurabs enable the Sikhs to participate in something that is different from the everyday. Psychologically, these events offer them a relaxation from their hard work; and socially, they enliven and strengthen the foundations of the community. Through them, Sikhs share their heritage and are in turn empowered. Like their Gurdwaras, their Gurpurabs open up an entry into a timeless dimension where Sikhs experience the esthetic and spiritual core of their religion. Sacred space and sacred time are not after all two different and separate entities; rather, they converge into the singular experience of the sacred, which is beyond all space and time.

Cultural Festivals

Sikhs also celebrate cultural festivals, and as they participate enthusiastically in ancient Punjabi festivals, they give a new – specifically Sikh – meaning to them.

Divali, short for *deepavali*, literally means a string of lighted lamps. When winter sets in and the days get shorter, there is a need for warmth and light. A festival of lights in some form seems to be a universal practice. Thus, around the time of Christmas and Hanukkah in the West, Divali is celebrated in India. For the Hindus it is a major festival welcoming the visit of Goddess Lakshmi, the goddess of wealth and prosperity. It also commemorates the return of King Rama and his beautiful queen Sita to their kingdom of Ayodhya after 14 years of exile. In Sikhism, it is Bandi Chhor Divas, the day when the Sixth Guru was released from Gwalior Fort after being imprisoned by Mughal officers under Emperor Jahangir.

At the Golden Temple, Divali is celebrated with great rejoicing for three days. The central shrine in the middle of the pool, the entire walkway and the adjoining building are brilliantly illuminated. Electric lights and earthenware lamps filled with oil decorate the building, and candles and lamps are also set afloat in the pool. And as the lights on the temple are reflected in the water, they merge splendidly with the floating lamps. Fireworks explode to light up the night sky. Special singers and musicians are invited to perform *kirtan* for the occasion. Lectures are delivered and heroic ballads recited. Devotees from far and wide come to make obeisance. They offer gifts of cash, flowers, *karahprashad*, rice, butter, milk and flour. The precious possessions and jewelry of the Golden Temple are displayed. Crowds come to view the golden gates, the golden canopy with its bejeweled peacock, pearl tassels, golden fans and the flywhisk made up of millions of hair-like fibers from sandalwood.

People's houses too are decorated with earthenware lamps and candles. Gifts are exchanged between families and friends. Sweets are distributed. Houses are whitewashed and painted. The celebration of Divali reveals that across cultures and continents, lights symbolize peace and joy.

Lori is celebrated in the winter months, when the evenings are short and cold. Bonfires are made, reminiscent of the Celtic festival of Samhain. For the Lori bonfires, men, women and children throw sesame seeds and peanuts into the fire. Children go around the neighborhood collecting money and sweets. A daughter's family sends gifts and money for their son-in-law and his family.

Basant is a spring festival celebrated with great joy. As the lovely mustard seeds blossom in the Punjab and the butterflies flutter in the air, so do the hearts of the people. As though in emulation of the bright yellow mustard-seed fields, people wear yellow, eat yellow rice and are joyful. The rooftops in the villages and towns are full of youngsters flying kites. There are competitions to see who can fly their kite the highest, but part of the fun is to sabotage your opponent's kite. The boys stick ground glass to the strings of their kites to make them razor sharp so they can cut down the other flying kites.

Holi is a traditional spring festival of the Hindus, celebrating the playful presence of their dark God, Lord Krishna. The festival occurs just as the winter mellows into warm spring and emotions too become full of life and vitality. The celebration of Holi allows their joyful expression. People throw brightly colored paint and dye at one another; they drink, gamble and make merry. The scenes in the bazaars, parks and streets is one of vibrant colors. People – friends and strangers alike – are sprayed, splashed and smeared with yellows, greens, reds and blues. Social segregations dissolve in the holistic panorama of magnificent colors.

This traditional spring festival was given a Sikh coloring by Guru Gobind Singh. He started the Hola Mohalla in Anandpur, which was a three-day festival during which the Sikhs were trained as soldiers. Though it corresponded with the same period as Holi, the emphasis of this new festival was on physical training and not on merrymaking. There were contests in horsemanship, wrestling and archery; mock-battles and military exercises. But the peaceful arts were also encouraged and competitions of music and poetry took place. The festival is still celebrated with great vigor at Anandpur. A large fair is held annually and many events take place, including singing, discussions and competitions using physical skill.

Tian is the festival for young girls. The evenings that follow a hot day in the plains of the Punjab can be most refreshing. Tian takes place in August and is celebrated by Punjabi women during those delightful evenings. They receive new clothes and new jewels. Glass bangles of every color are put on their arms. Girls and women share their gifts with one another and enjoy one another's company. Together with their friends, sisters and sisters-in-law, they go to the local fairs. Riding high on swings is a big part of the ritual celebrations. Tian affords women a break from their regular routine, and for those who cannot often leave their home, tian is a much-awaited festival.

Rakhri is also celebrated around mid-August. A *rakhri* is a bright band, which is tied around a brother's right wrist by his sister as a reminder that he is her protector. Sweets are shared and the brother gives her money, clothes or jewelry. In many Sikh homes, *ardas* is said before the tying of the *rakhri* and *karahprashad* is distributed afterwards.

Gidda and Bhangra

Socially and culturally, Gidda and Bhangra are popular performances during Sikh celebrations. Gidda is choreographed by women in gentle and lithe movements. Together they celebrate nature and her bountiful gifts through the seasons of spring, summer, monsoon, autumn and winter. Amid sparkling agrarian scenes, Gidda captures simple activities: how they milk cows, cook mustard seeds, do needlework, fan in the summer, buy glass bangles, churn milk in the morning, carry water in earthenware pitchers sturdily balanced on their heads, and help with ploughing and harvesting. Bhangra is traditionally performed by a group of men. It dates back to the fourteenth century, originating in West Punjab (now a part of Pakistan). But in modern times, Bhangra has become extremely popular with both Sikh men and women. Dressed in bright colors, the group dances in an elemental rhythm to the beat of a large drum and everybody joins in the songs celebrating Punjabi village life. With the migration of Sikh communities to the West, this Punjabi folk dance has become the latest rage with young music lovers in Britain, Europe and North America. The modern form of Bhangra combines North Indian folk music with contemporary styles, including reggae and Western pop. In the post-colonial and diasporic reality, Bhangra, with its complex cultural webs, has become a crucial marker of Sikh memory and identity.

Rites of Passage

The term 'rites of passage' was coined by Arnold van Gennep in 1907 for rituals marking the individual's journey through the different stages of the life cycle. People across centuries and cultures participate in these rites in different ways. According to the anthropologist

Barbara Meyerhoff, the rites share an inherent universal pattern, which joins nature and culture, continuity and change, private psyche and social values.[2] In Sikhism there are four rites of passage: name-giving, *amrit* initiation, marriage and death.

The *name-giving* ritual can be extremely simple or elaborate, but basically it involves naming a child in consultation with the holy Book. While the spine of the Guru Granth rests on the cushions, a reader (a family member if the rite is conducted in the home, or an official reader if it is at the Gurdwara) holds the Guru Granth closed with both hands and then gently lets it open at random. The child is given a name that begins with the first letter appearing at the top of the left-hand page where the Guru Granth opens. Sikhs do not have different names for boys and girls. The addition of the name Kaur (for girls) or Singh (for boys) indicates the gender of the child. The child also receives its first *kara*, or steel bracelet. The recitation of *kirtan* (hymns of praise), readings from the Guru Granth, recitation of *ardas* (the daily prayer) and the partaking of *langar* are the central activities, just as they for all Sikh rites of passage.

Amrit initiation replays the memorable event of Baisakhi 1699 (discussed in detail in Chapter III). That day, the Tenth Guru and his wife prepared the *amrit* drink (a mixture of water, sugar, iron and sacred verse), and five men from different castes, in front of a large Baisakhi gathering, drank from the same bowl. Their drinking together was a bold gesture of wiping out divisions of caste, class and hereditary profession. They were also given a new name as a mark of their new identity.

This pattern is followed in contemporary practice. *Amrit* initiation may take place anywhere, but the Guru Granth and a reader must be present. Any five Sikhs who are already members of the Khalsa can prepare and administer the ceremony. The initiated drink *amrit* from their cupped hands and sprinkle some on their eyes and hair. They also sip *amrit* from the same bowl, and together recite Guru Nanak's Mul Mantra, remembering the One Singular Reality. The initiation marks their new birth in the Khalsa family: they are now children of Guru Gobind Singh and his wife Mata Sahib Kaur. The initiated are to maintain the philosophical principles enshrined in the Guru Granth, and their physical identity by wearing *kesha* (long hair), *kangha* (comb to keep the hair tidy), *kirpan* (sword), *kara* (bracelet) and *kacha* (underwear).

In this initiation rite, no particular age is prescribed. It may be as soon as a boy or a girl is old enough to be able to read the scripture and comprehend the articles of the Sikh faith. Or it may be later in life – some people even wait until their own children are grown up. The initiation is open to all. According to the Sikh Ethical Code (the Rahit Maryada): 'Any man or woman of whatever nationality, race, or social standing, who is prepared to accept the rules governing the Sikh community, has the right to receive *amrit* initiation.'

Anand Karaj (*anand* = bliss; *karaj* = event) is the Sikh rite of marriage. No words or gestures are exchanged directly between the bride and groom, nor any legal formalities performed between their families. Though there can be many cultural accretions, *anand karaj* is the sole religious Sikh wedding ceremony. It takes place either in a Gurdwara or in the home of the bride, with everyone seated on the floor facing the holy volume. The father of the bride hands one end of a scarf (about two meters in length) to the groom, and the other to his daughter. Instead of the exchange of wedding bands as in the West, the Sikh couple is bonded together through this auspiciously colored scarf (pink, saffron or red). Each holding one end of the scarf, the groom and the bride then walk around the sacred book four times. The four circuits by the couple correspond to the four *lavan* (circles) passages read by the official reader of the Guru Granth.[3] As each scriptural verse is recited and sung, the couple reverentially walk around the Guru Granth in a clockwise direction. The bride follows the groom. The relatives escort them around to show their support for the couple. After each circle, the bride and groom touch their foreheads to the ground, and rejoin the congregation by seating themselves on the floor. During the fourth round, the bride and groom are showered with petals by the entire congregation as a symbol of rejoicing. Bowing together to the scriptural Guru marks their acceptance of each other. They are solely – and equally – bound to the sacred word rather than to any legal or social authority. The scriptural *lavan* launches the couple together in their spiritual passage. Dr Owen Cole is quite right in his comment: 'Lavan presents a reversal of the *varnashramdharma* process by affirming that the path to *moksha* is one of deepening love, not increasing asceticism.'[4] The wedding rite concludes with Amar Das' rapturous hymn, *anand* (bliss – the name of the wedding ceremony itself).

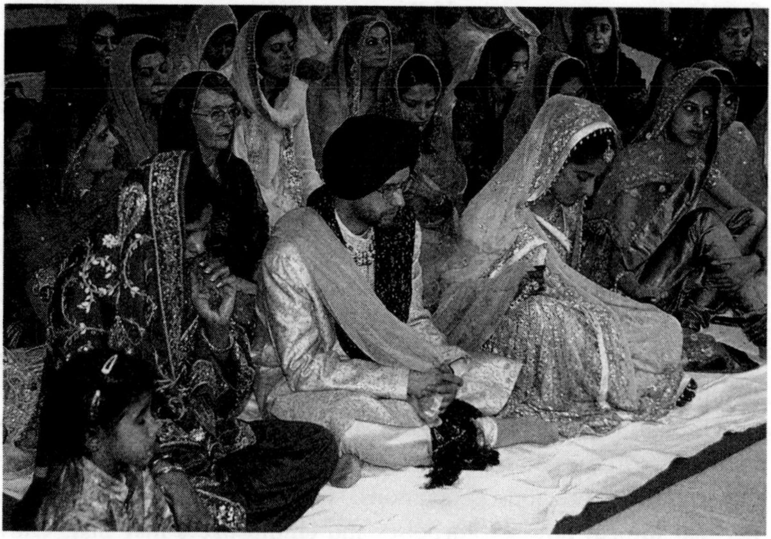

Figure 13: Sikh wedding: bride and groom in the presence of the Guru Granth

Life and death are regarded as natural processes, and just as each day the sun must set, so must all people depart. When a person dies, his or her body is bathed and dressed in clean clothes. Non-widows are dressed in bridal clothes. The body is carried on a stretcher by the closest male relatives and friends of the family to the funeral ground (which is usually on the periphery of the village or town). There it is placed on the top of a platform of firewood, and the eldest son (or closest male relative) lights the fire. The evening hymn Kirtan Sohila is recited at that point. Following the Kirtan Sohila, *ardas* is offered, seeking blessings for the departed person. When the party returns from the cremation ground, the mourners wash themselves, and *karahprashad* is distributed. This joyous action might appear incongruous, but it says symbolically that grief must end and normal life return once more.

On the fourth day, a few family members and/or close friends return to the cremation ground to collect the ashes and bones (called *phul* – literally, flowers), which are then placed in the flowing waters of a river or stream. Thus the body returns to the elements it is made up of: the fire of the person merges with the crematory flames; their breath with the air; their body with the body of the earth; and their bones and ashes immersed in running water signify the return of the fourth element to water itself. The town of Kiratpur, on the banks of the Sutlej in the Punjab, is the revered site for the final immersion.

At the home of the deceased, the scriptural Guru takes on a central role. During its continuous reading, family and friends keep congregating. They wear white, black and earth colors, brighter colors being reserved for weddings and other festive occasions. No words are exchanged. By sitting silently together they share their grief and loss. The bereaved family and the community derive solace from hearing the Guru's word, and sitting in its presence. A *bhog* ceremony takes place on the tenth day, with the *antam ardas* (the final *ardas*) recited on behalf of the deceased. At the death anniversary, the family serves *langar* to the community.

Through their celebrations and commemorations, Sikhs share the joys and sorrows of their community members, and link to the experience of previous generations. The capacity to celebrate is a peculiar human power: 'Porpoises and chimpanzees may play. Only man celebrates.'[5] In our multinational world that element of real verve is waning. The force of commercialization conspicuous at Christmas, for example, is actually far more pervasive. As in all religions, the performance of rituals and ceremonies is becoming a status symbol in Sikhism. Simple rites have become highly elaborate, and sometimes in the case of marriage and dowry, downright exploitative acts. The financial burden does not end with the dowry that the family of a daughter gives at her wedding. Each time the daughter has a child, jewelry, gifts, clothes, fruit, dried fruit and cash have to be given to the son-in-law and his family. In fact, the financial burden for a daughter continues for all ritual celebrations until the day she dies and even extends beyond, as the community meal after the death of a daughter is also the responsibility of her family.

Indeed, rituals are very important to all of us everywhere. Though they are enacted for a short time, the ideology behind them drafts us into the roles we live throughout our life. Consciously and unconsciously, ritual performances perpetuate the dominant societal values. The fact that most rituals in any religious tradition are officiated by men sends internal messages of inferiority to their women, and keeps them locked into a secondary position. Across religions, we need to be self-critical. As we shall discuss in more detail in Chapter VI, Sikhism has no priesthood, and yet even here the public functions are discharged by men. The equal role of women in private worship must play out in the performance of Sikh public rites and ceremonies as well.

Sikh men worked hard to get the Anand Marriage Act of 1909 passed, which changed the ancient marriage rite to its present-day form. But we can make further progressive changes in the twenty-first century. Currently, the groom leads the four circles. The ritual would be more balanced and even if both bride and groom took turns leading, or both walked together side by side. Such a performance would be a fulfillment of the intrinsic circularity of Lavan – without beginning or end, and without any linear hierarchies.

Some of the pan-Indian cultural rituals are clearly gender-biased. The winter ritual of Lohri is chiefly celebrated in homes where a boy is born. While parents and grandparents of a boy dole out money and gifts around crackling bonfires, those of a girl remain sad during the cold, dark nights of Lohri. Likewise, the pan-Indian rite of Rakhri takes place in homes where there are brothers. Sadness and tears, blame and abuse is the lot of mothers without sons, or sisters without brothers.

Even some of the Sikh ceremonies show favoritism to boys. Affluent Sikh families have begun to celebrate the *dastar bandhan* (turban-tying) for their sons as a rite of passage with great pomp and show. This is upsetting for families with only daughters. Theoretically, Sikh rites are the same for both girls and boys, but there are double standards.[6] The elaborate name-giving ceremonies of the sons are never quite the same for the daughters!

The impulse to bring the infinite Divine into the daily rhythms is definitely alive in the Sikh community, and it serves as a motivating factor for change and growth. Their simple greetings welcome the Divine, for whenever Sikhs say hello or goodbye, they join their hands and say *Sat Sri Akal* (truth is timeless). Their frequent exclamation *Waheguru* (before a meal, after a sneeze, etc.) surges with a sense of wonder and echoes Guru Nanak's awe (*wah!*) as he experienced the transcendent One. The Sikh Gurus wanted to bring about a genuine transformation in society by breaking open the inner fount of joy suppressed by religious officials and power-wielders. Practitioners today must free their rites and ceremonies from stifling economic and social pressures, and invest them with the spiritual energy derived directly from their Gurus.

Chapter VI

Feminist Text in a Patriarchal Context

Though the voice is that of male Gurus, Sikh scripture is a remarkably 'feminist' text. Living in a 'doubly' patriarchal medieval Indian society, the Sikh Gurus witnessed the subordinate role of women. From time immemorial, the patriarchal society of northern India has been obsessed with sons: the region resounds with the blessing 'may you be the mother of a hundred sons!'[1] The great Rig Veda, one of the earliest textual pieces produced in India, begins with a prayer to Agni (Fire) to grant many 'heroic sons' to his worshipers. Later, the Brahmin elites, in their popular Code of Manu, restricted women's legal independence, and made them subservient to their fathers, husbands and sons.[2] Total devotion to the husband (*pativrata*) was the sanctioned norm. With the socio-political rule of the Mughal Empire, another patriarchal layer with West Asian values such as *purdah* and multiple wives, relegated Indian women even further. The Gurus empathized with their situation, and tried to create a window of opportunity through which women could achieve liberty, equality and sorority.

But the followers have been unable to grasp the broadmindedness of their Gurus. Instead of the liberating message of the Gurus, ancient oppressive feudal values have dominated Sikh society. Ironically, just a few decades after Guru Gobind Singh created the democratic and inclusive family of the Khalsa through his *amrit* initiation in 1699, women were barred from joining it! We hear Chaupa Singh, a tutor and aide of the Tenth Guru, overturn the radical implications of Guru Gobind Singh's Baisakhi and revert to the norms of *stridharma*, spelled out in the traditional *Dharmashastras*. His ethical manual (*The Chaupa Singh Rahit-Nama*) dictates a Sikh woman's primary mode of religiosity as the worship of her husband: she is to 'know her husband as god' (*apne bharte nu karta janai*; 556); she is to 'keep fasts for the sake of her husband' (*patibratu rakhe*; 567).[3]

The ideals and practices of the first Sikh community established by Guru Nanak in Kartarpur, where men and women recited sacred verse, cooked and ate together, are reversed by Chaupa Singh. Instead, he stipulates segregation and discrimination: women may listen to but are prohibited from reading the Guru Granth in public (CS: 538). And among many other *dos* and *don'ts*, Chaupa Singh categorically outlaws men from administering *amrit* to women: '*sikhani nu khande di pahul deve so tankhaia* – he is an offender who gives Sikhni *amrit* prepared by the sword' (506)![4] The waves of wonder, joy and equality generated by the Gurus quickly found their way back to a stagnant pond of discrimination and androcentric norms that were definitely outside of the Sikh practices instituted by Guru Nanak and his successor Gurus. The voices and views of early patriarchs such as Chaupa Singh have been very harmful to the community as a whole.

The glamorous regime of Maharaja Ranjit Singh (1799–1839) brought great splendor to the Sikh religion in many ways; but unfortunately, the situation for women deteriorated even more. With the elaboration of pomp and ceremony at his royal court, formal rituals and ceremonies discarded by the Gurus entered into the Sikh way of life. The customs of *purdah* and *sati* undergone by women from elite Muslim and Hindu families, respectively, began to be emulated by the upper echelons of Sikh society. At Maharaja Ranjit Singh's death, several queens underwent *sati*.[5]

British colonialism made matters worse. The Punjab was annexed by the British in 1849, and the imperial masters, who greatly admired the 'martial' character and strong physique of Sikh men, produced a 'hyper-masculine' culture. That drive continues. With the Green Revolution and the enterprising spirit of its people, post-colonial Punjab became the breadbasket of India. Today, it is in the ferment of globalization. Contemporary economic and technological priorities have made the patriarchal imperative for sons even stronger. Parents regard sons as their social security, financial insurance, and as religious functionaries who will eventually perform their funeral rites. Sons are deemed to be essential to carry on the family name, property and land. When a son marries, he brings his wife into the family home, and she takes care of her in-laws into their old age. With *his* wife comes *her* dowry which adds to the economic resources of his family. Simple marriage ceremonies have become extremely opulent, dowries extravagant, and gifts to the daughter and her in-laws for every rite, ritual and festival, exorbitant. Both in India and in Sikh diasporas, marriages are transformed into elaborate affairs, and the quantity and quality of what is hosted for or given to the daughter reinforces the power and prestige of her father. Daughters have no rights over their natal homes; they are viewed as beautiful commodities and investments in their father's status and honor. The not-so-wealthy feel extreme pressure to squeeze out their hard-earned money to keep up with the cultural norms. While a son is desired for the accretion of his father's assets, a daughter is rejected because she represents its depletion. The economic and social demands of contemporary Sikh culture are extremely challenging.

With the combination of ancient patriarchal values and new globalization, gender disparity is deteriorating at an alarming rate. The proportion of baby girls is beginning to decline rapidly. In India's population of 1.027 billion, the last census showed only 927 girls for every 1,000 boys – down from 945 ten years earlier. Prenatal sex identification using ultrasound have made gender-selective abortions increasingly easy. Female fetuses are being aborted to preserve the legacy, business, property and status of fathers and sons. With technological and economic advances, Punjab, the home of the Sikhs, is ironically facing a terrible situation. Newspaper articles have focused on the tragedy of female feticide in the affluent agrarian area of the Punjab. A 'diabolic link' exists between sex-selection technologies and the abortion of female fetuses, with the result that there is an increasing imbalance in the ratio of males to females in the population of the Punjab. The selective abortion of females reinforces this devaluation of girls and further entrenches gender prejudices. Since immigrant Sikhs maintain transnational ties with their families and friends in the Punjab, the customs and values from home are quickly exported to diasporic communities across the globe.[6]

The government of India even banned the use of sex determination techniques two decades ago. But people have found ways to evade the law. The SGPC, the Sikh governing body, is trying to support the ban. In the city of Fatehgarh Sahib in the Punjab – where the ratio of females is 750 per 1,000 males – some 250 Sikh religious leaders discussed ways to prevent female feticide. The general population has not confronted this situation seriously, and the laws are obviously not working. In this context, the feminist message of Sikh scripture acquires all the more relevance. The text does not give any direct injunctions. Neither is it prescriptive, nor proscriptive. The Gurus offered only sublime poetry with intimations, which, more than rules, has the capacity to reach the inner recesses of the mind and bring about social change. This chapter explores the feminist import of Sikh scripture from a theological, psychological and social perspective, and concludes with some thoughts on how to access its vast potential so that gender-justice can be practiced.

Theological

By designating the Divine as the numeral 'One' at the very outset, Sikh scripture breaks centuries-old images of male dominance, and opens the way to experiencing the One in a female modality. The unique configuration of *Ikk Oan Kar* has the potential of the radical 'meta-patriarchal journey' proposed by the feminist philosopher Mary Daly – to exorcise an internalized father-God in his various manifestations and incarnations.[7] As the powerful Nanakian numeral shatters the dominance of male imagery, it creates a space for the Divine to be experienced in other new and important ways. Logically, it does not matter how the Divine is understood in human terms; the One is totally transcendent and beyond all categories. But in the poetry of the Gurus, both female and male dimensions run in parallel. The Divine is identified as *both* male and female: '*ape purakh ape hi nar* – itself male, itself is female' (GG: 1020). Thus we receive a balanced perspective, which is crucial for mental and spiritual health.

Scriptural verses unleash multiple relationships with the Infinite. Guru Arjan says ecstatically: 'You are my father, you are my mother; you are my brother, you are my friend…' (GG: 103). Thus the One is passionately embraced in numerous relationships. This sense of plenitude strips off patriarchal stratifications and blots out masculine identity as the norm for imaging the Divine. It stretches the imagination. We feel new emotions. We see new vistas. We experience joy in so many different ways.

Rather than orient us to a distant 'heavenly' future, the Guru Granth regularly turns attention to our primal home – the mother's body, the ontological base of every person. It offers multivalent womb imagery. Conceived by different poets with different emphases and in different contexts, we find here an extremely fertile ground inspiring a wide range of responses. The womb is celebrated as the matrix for all life and living. However, it also serves as an eschatological expression for the return of the self into this world. According to Sikh scripture, birth is rare and precious, like a diamond, but it can be frittered away for naught. An immoral life generates a negative rebirth, and the mother's womb in that instance is pictured as a scorching and painful mode of being – empty of the Divine. Under positive circumstances, however, the womb is a vital space permeated with the Divine, and the fetus functions as a symbol for cultivating Sikh morality, spirituality and esthetics.

The womb (*garbh* or *udar*) is affirmed as the source of life: 'in the first stage of life, O friend, you by the Divine will, lodged in the womb … says Nanak, in the first stage of life, the creature by the Divine is lodged in the womb' (GG: 74). The reader is directed away from death and the otherworld to the very source of life. In contrast with the 'necrophilic imagery' of patriarchal theology, the pervasive womb imagery in Sikh scripture affirms life and living in diverse forms. The womb is the space (*thanu*) where we become the self, both body and spirit. Even the pervasive usage of *rahim* ('compassionate' – an expression for the Divine) draws attention to her maternal space. In the speculations of the Muslim philosopher, Ibn Arabi, the root of the word '*rahimat*' is womb, and the meaning of compassion or mercy is derived from it.[8] Similarly, feminist scholars relate the Hebrew word *rachum* ('compassion') with *racham*, the word for womb.[9] Sikh scripture continues to resonate with many positive memories of our lodging in the womb, the mother's creative organ: 'in the mother's womb are we taken care of' (GG: 1086); 'in the womb you worked to preserve us' (GG: 177); and 'in the mother's womb you nurture us' (GG: 132).

We hear the Guru Granth honoring the maternal space as a social utopia in which the fetus is free from patriarchal designations of class, caste and name: 'in the dwelling of the womb, there is neither name nor caste' (GG: 324). The scriptural verses transparently reveal that the placental waters of the mother – primal and nourishing – are free of distinctions and hierarchies. The Sikh Gurus were acutely aware of their oppressive patrilineal and patricentered north Indian society in which the family name, caste and profession came down through birth. So the mother's pregnant body is envisioned as free from all sorts of 'ism's' and social hegemonies. Her fetus is nurtured by *her* life-giving uterus; it is not suffocated by the father's name, class or professional ties.

The Tenth Guru absorbed these ideals and brought about a change in the patriarchal framework. In the Khalsa family he created, people from different castes, classes and regions sipped *amrit* from the same bowl and received a new identity. As noted earlier, in parallel with the surname 'Singh', for men, Sikh women have the surname 'Kaur' (meaning princess). Women are thus free from the lineage of fathers and husbands. As 'Kaur', a woman retains her own identity for her whole life. She does not have to adopt the name of her father at birth nor that of her husband at marriage. Sons and daughters, husbands and wives retain their selfhood equally throughout their lives. This transformation in the patrilineal structure, traced to the Gurus, has radical implications for the identity and autonomy of women.

The Guru Granth takes women's genealogy seriously and acknowledges Mother's milk full of biological and spiritual nutrients. Even the recitation of the Divine name is succulently experienced as milk in the mouth. The language of the Gurus is echoed by the words of contemporary French feminist scholar, Hélenè Cixous: 'Voice: milk that could go on forever. Found again. The lost mother/bitter-lost. Eternity: its voice mixed with milk.'[10] Her milk is a biological necessity, keeping us from dying. So is *bani*, the Divine Word. By pouring the two together, the Sikh Gurus make knowledge essential for everybody. The textuality of the Guru Granth lies in its physical sensuality – drinking the words as though they were the mother's life-giving milk.

The Gurus compare the intensity of saintly devotion to that of an infant's love for the mother's milk (GG: 613). In an unforgettable juxtaposition of analogies, the Divine is like a 'cane for the blind' and 'like mother's milk for the child' (GG: 679). In a tender passage: 'says Nanak, the child, you are my father and my mother, and your name is like milk in my mouth' (GG: 713). Throughout the Guru Granth, the Sikh Gurus unabashedly express their attachment to the Divine through an infant's attachment to the mother's breast: 'my mind loves the Divine, O my life, like a child loves suckling milk' (GG: 538).

However, the maternal imaginary in the Guru Granth is not a matter of religious deification, because 'she' is not idolized into some distant goddess – an object of worship. It is when the Divine is genuinely imagined as Mother that her positive characteristics begin to filter into our mind, and ignite respect for our mothers, sisters, daughters and wives. We regard them as life-and-blood individuals who take on the qualities and powers of the Divine One. We thank them for creating and nurturing us. We remember real women, and our lips utter the Granthian exaltation '*dhan janedi mau* – blessed are the mothers!' Our respect goes to all the mothers from all the species, and so the scriptural imaginary fills us with pride in our own bodies, and charges us all, men and women, to relish our Divine in the daily rhythms of life.

As Jewish and Christian thinkers have observed, *Hers* is a different model of creation from that of an omnipotent Creator who simply makes his Creation out of nothing, or even of an artist who admittedly 'creates' but does not embody his/her creation.[11] In the Mother model of theology, a future 'kingdom' of God is not awaited nor is its justice concerned with condemning in the future.[12] Such theories are articulated in the love that extends from the pervasive Granthian maternal symbol into our immediate families, into our primary communities, and into other species. Since the whole community – of human beings and nature alike – constitutes *her* family, she does not favor humankind over nature nor does she favor the immediate advantage of the dominant class, race and sex. A profound sensitivity to the environment, and new ethical paradigms of justice and equality, will emerge if we truly imagine the Divine as the Mother. Half a millennium ago the Sikh Gurus might not have known the empowering potential of their maternal symbol. But it is there. We in the twenty-first century can actualize it and bring about gender justice.

There is yet another strong feminist current in their poetry: a vocative for the Mother – '*meri mai*' – flows vibrantly in the Sikh textual body. For example, the daily hymn Anand begins with '*anand bhaia meri mai* – Oh mother of mine, I am in bliss!' The Third Guru experiences unicity, and in his ecstasy, he lyrically and polymorphously addresses his Mother, '*meri mai* – my Mother!' Coming from the lips of male poets, it is a verbal embrace gushing from the point closest to their unconscious. *She* is the bedrock of their identity, and so they ask of her passionate questions: 'How can I live without the Name, O my Mother?' (GG: 226); 'How could I forget That, O my Mother?' (GG: 349); 'How do I unite with truth,

O my Mother?' (GG: 661); and 'What virtues will unite me with my life, O my Mother?' (GG: 204). While they seek her knowledge, they also share passionate moments with her: 'I am in love O my Mother!' Each time, the Mother carries their language forward, making their experience come alive. This is not a dualistic opposition between *the male Gurus* versus *her*, but a healthy 'dialogic' relationship, which is rooted in openness and leads to a deeper self-awareness, a deeper communion.

Clearly, it is not in opposition to, but rather pulling towards, the Mother that the Sikh Gurus establish their identity. The oceanic experience in her body and of her wisdom, strength and physical closeness melt away any splintered or patriarchal individuality. The verses of the male Gurus resonate with the views of feminist theologians and object-relations psychoanalysts who posit the maternal–infant relationship at the heart of an individual's psychological and social development. Instead of the Freudian Oedipal conflict, castration complex and individuality, feminist theologians (Naomi Goldenberg, for example) and object-relations psychoanalysts (Melanie Klein and D. W. Winnicott, for example) shift the focus to the maternal–infant relationship. Both theology and object-relations theory 'derive their insights into the matrices that support human life from an image of a woman-in-the-past'.[13] Sikh scriptural language displaces the father from his dominating symbolic position and cherishes the love of the mother, the care of the mother, the caresses of the mother, the transverbal communion with the mother. The male Gurus remember her prebirth and postbirth creativity, and our reading of their verses in turn can help us to improve the individual and social fabric of our lives: 'Just as the mother takes care of her children, so the Divine sustains us' (GG: 680). The abundant joy of envisioning the Ultimate is 'like the look between a child and its mother' (GG: 452). When we feel the Divine arms around us – 'like a mother tightly hugs her child' (GG: 629) – we cannot but recharge our innermost selves, and renew our relationships with our family, friends and community.

Psychological

Psychologically, the Gurus connect with the female at a very deep level. Throughout the Guru Granth, they identify themselves with *her* in their search for the Divine. Woman is regarded as physically and spiritually refined, so it is in her tone, her mood, her image and her mode of dress that the Gurus express their yearning. They envision The One as a handsome Groom, and take on the personality of a bride, totally merging with her feminine feelings and thoughts in their desire for spiritual union. The male–female duality which violates the wholeness of human nature and deprives each person of the other half is overcome, establishing, in turn, the significance of being human. Men and women are united, and share their human angst and human hopes.

The pervasive bridal symbol establishes a sensuous and palpable union with the Infinite One. The Groom (*sahu*) is known as *agam* (infinite), *agocaru* (unfathomable) and *ajoni* (unborn); He is utterly metaphysical and beyond all perception through the senses. It is 'the Wholly Other', as Rudoph Otto, the eminent German theologian, said.[14] The bride perceives and proclaims the infiniteness of her Groom: 'O my Beloved, your limits I cannot fathom.' She is perplexed and wonders how she is going to 'see' her True Groom when 'He has no color, no garb, no form' (GG: 945). How is she going to know the unknowable? She imagines Him to be 'a deep and unfathomable ocean full of precious jewels' and 'she dedicates herself entirely to Him – *avar nahi an puja*' (GG: 1233). The bride understands the Singularity of her Groom and declares fervently that she would attach herself to none other: 'Without the One, I know no other.'

Ultimately, it is the bride who succeeds in creating proximity to this distant Groom. She is the one to chart the way that will make the Transcendent accessible to human experience. She addresses the 'Wholly Other' in most personal terms: '*mere sundar gahir gambhir lal* – O my handsome, unfathomable Beloved'; 'my Beloved is the most delicious inebriation'. The Wholly Other is perceived so intimately that the bride announces: 'My loved Groom isn't far at all' (GG: 1197). She praises him lavishly:

> My Beloved is utterly glorious, brilliantly crimson,
> Compassionate, beneficent, beloved, enticer of the hearts,
> overflowing with *rasa*, like the *lala* flower. (GG: 1331)

The backdrop to this scenario is nuptial union. The red color, the *lala* flower, the enticing of hearts, the latent joy – all point to this consummation. The bride in this phenomenal world sees her transcendental Groom directly and physically. In her eyes, He is like the *lala* flower. He is dyed deep in glorious beauty; He is mind-bedazzling. He is overflowing with *rasa*. The senses of sight (crimson, brilliant), smell (like the fragrance of the flower) and taste (*rasa* – the juice, the essence) all unite to convey to the reader the bride's complete and thoroughly sensuous unity with her divine Lover. The female is the model to be emulated for spiritual union.

The Guru's expression of unity points in the direction of a more egalitarian and open-ended social structure than the 'Lord' and 'Father'[15] symbolism dominant in many religions. As Jewish and Christian feminist scholars have analyzed, the Lord–Father symbol basically upholds a hierarchical, patriarchal frame of reference from which the female experience is excluded. In contrast, the bride symbol in Sikh scripture exalts feminine love. Here, equality is the basis of the relationship. The bride, simply by loving, not by fearing or remaining in awe, or being totally dependent, senses the proximity of her Infinite Groom and is then able to share that feeling with her sisters and friends. Through her intense love, she is able to establish a free and non-authoritarian relationship with the Divine. Her experience has much to offer women who are struggling to free themselves from a Father–Lord symbol that they find oppressive.[16] Moreover, she does not need any mediators such as priests or theologians. The Sikh bridal symbol suggests a freedom from patriarchal media; with no one standing in between, the bride directly and passionately seeks to embrace the Wholly Other.

But the bridal symbol has to be fully understood and not read simplistically as though women must be dependent on their husbands. Not at all. The Granthian bride is dependent only on the Divine One, and men, women and the entire cosmos share this dependence. The Sikh scriptural message is not the subjugation of the female to the male, for her Groom is beyond gender; rather, it is the rising of the individual spirit towards the Absolute. The rich variety of Granthian images reveals the complexity and dignity of the female experience, and loosens the grip of masculine symbols on the contemporary imagination. She is spiritually refined. Her emotions are strong. Her body is regarded positively. She is the model to be emulated. The lingering effect of such passages produces an emotional strength that helps to confront sexist attitudes and practices.

Social

Devotees and scholars cite the Guru Granth widely for its rejection of caste and class; however, its bold rejection of sexism is barely noted. The Sikh text dramatically affirms women's creative and natural processes in the social fabric. Not only are there images celebrating *her* gestation, birthing and lactation processes, but also a condemnation of taboos surrounding menstruation and post-partum pollution. The Gurus also criticize the institutions of *purdah* (confinement of women) and *sati* (the self-immolation of women on the funeral pyres of their husbands). Their passionate poetry relays their empathy, and discloses their intention that society should discard oppressive androcentric codes.

Even now, society in general is horrified at the sight of women's blood – whether it is her monthly period or the blood that accompanies every birth. Considered a private, shameful process, menstruation is equated with being ill or weak. Because of their menstrual periods, women are barred from religious services. As feminist scholars have been reminding us, disdain for this natural feminine phenomenon has contributed to the low status of women. The Sikh Gurus were aware of the sexism prevalent in their society and denounced taboos against women. The fear of the gaze, touch and speech of a menstruating woman had been internalized by Indian society for centuries. These deeply-rooted negative attitudes to women have seeped into all of India's religious traditions. The Guru Granth dramatically dispels conventional taboos against female pollution, menstruation and sexuality. Menstrual bleeding is regarded as an essential, natural process. Life itself begins with it. The first Guru reprimands those who stigmatize the garment stained with menstrual blood as polluted (GG: 140). Many scriptural verses celebrate the female body, and affirm the centrality of menstrual blood in the creative process: 'from mother's blood and father's semen' is created the human form (GG: 1022). Here, priority is given to *ma ki raktu* (mother's blood). Another scriptural passage confirms it: 'from blood and semen is one created' (GG: 706).

Like menstrual blood, blood of parturition is also stereotyped by society as impure and dangerous, and is ritually avoided. The mother giving birth is a biologically natural and organic mode of creation. Yet birth, *every* mother's most fantastic miracle, is deemed to be dirty, with all sorts of lingering fears of pollution attached to it. In medieval India, any home with a new birth was considered to be toxic for 40 days, and only the performance of elaborate rituals could bring it back to normality. It is quite remarkable how publicly the Sikh Gurus condemned such notions of pollution:

> If pollution attaches to birth, then pollution is everywhere (for birth is universal).
> Cow-dung [used as fuel] and firewood breed maggots;
> Not one grain of corn is without life;
> Water itself is a living substance, imparting life to all vegetation.
> How can we then believe in pollution, when pollution inheres within staples?
> Says Nanak, pollution is not washed away by purification rituals;
> Pollution is removed by true knowledge alone. (GG: 472)

From the Sikh scriptural perspective, pollution is an inner reality, a state of mind, and not the product of any natural birth. Female inferiority is dismissed: 'How can we call her inferior from whom kings are born?' asks Guru Nanak poignantly (GG: 473). The Sikh Guru strongly questioned the legitimacy and purpose of devaluing women on the basis of their reproductive energy. Set upon Guru Nanak's egalitarian vision, Sikh scripture continually erases negative connotations associated with women's bodies.

It also draws attention to the exploitive customs of *purdah* and *sati*. Guru Nanak's passages depicting Babur's invasion carry profound empathy for Indian women. Muslim and Hindu women from different sectors of society are graphically depicted as victims of patriarchal institutions:

> Hindu, Turk, Bhatt and Thakur women –
> Some have their veils sundered from head to toe,
> Others make the crematorium their abode. (GG: 418)

The Sikh Guru's compassion extends to both Hindu and Muslim women – equally for those who practice *purdah* (Muslim) and for those who practice *sati* (Hindu). The straight horizontal sequence of his verse bridges any chasms that may segregate women – 'Turks,

Figure 14: Female worshiper at the Golden Temple

Hindus, Bhatts or Thakurs'. They are all victims, irrespective of religious or societal hierarchies. With a radically feminist sensibility, Guru Nanak tells us how the veils of Muslim women are ripped from head to toe by the invaders.

Purdah, as we all know, is not just a piece of material with which the Muslim women cover their hair, their faces and their bodies, but also a bundle of complex norms involving patriarchal control of female sexuality. Initially observed by Muslim elites, the custom soon penetrated the Indian masses. The Guru Granth urges the excision of such artificial social confinements. In an entirely different image, the Guru says:

> When she dances in ecstasy,
> How could she be veiled?
> So break the vessel and be utterly free! (GG: 1112)

Here is an autonomous subject in joyous movement – without any *ghungat* (north Indian term for veil). In her ecstasy for the Divine, she has discarded the shackles of immobility and invisibility. Considering its heavily controlled patriarchal social context, the freely dancing unveiled scriptural figure is quite a revolutionary model for spiritual liberation.

Along with *purdah*, the custom of *sati* is denounced. Literally meaning pure or good wife, *sati* in social history is understood as a widow's sacrifice of her life on her husband's funeral pyre. Her characteristic markers are purity and devotion to her husband – alive or dead. *Sati* was a common practice in Guru Nanak's milieu. Battling against Babur's invasion, many Hindu men lost their lives. Their widows performed their duty (*stridharma*; *pativrata*). Guru Nanak's haunting words cited earlier '*ikkna vasu masani*' ('others make the crematorium their abode'), vividly evoke robust women being lapped by cruel fires. They also raise questions: Was this really *her* duty? Who made it normative? How could society have clung to such horrific customs? Displacing ancient norms, the Guru Granth offers a new form of '*sati*' that is performed not for the sake of the husband who died but for the infinite, eternal, universal Husband:

> These are not called *satis* who burn themselves in crematory
> pyres

Says Nanak, know them as *satis* who die in the shock of
separation.
They are *satis* who live in harmony and contentment
Serving their Husband by daily remembering him. (GG: 787)

Thus the conventional rite of *sati* is no longer a woman's consignment of her body to the flames of her dead husband. From an external ritual, *sati* is transformed into an inner experience of love for the Divine, our universal Husband; from a cruel death, *sati* is transformed into a peaceful and harmonious mode of life; from sleep eternal to constant service and remembrance of the singular One. In the Guru Granth, the final test of a woman's sexual and emotional purity is changed into a life-long devotion by both men *and* women, at every stage of their life.

Such scriptural verses raise questions not only about the past but also about present-day assumptions. What are our values and attitudes towards women? The practice of *sati* has been illegal since the early nineteenth century, yet tragically, its lethal flames continue to char the psyche of Indian women. Yes, the widow lives, but can we call her dreary, dead existence *living*? Indian culture continues to stereotype widows as inauspicious figures who bring death to the husband and bad luck to his family by their own bad karma. However young she may be, a widow must not wear bright colors, jewelry or makeup.[17] Ostracized by their society, they are liminal figures who learn to shun entertainment or sexual experience, and are forced to swallow all sorts of emotional and physical abuse. Do the daughters, sisters, nieces and wives live as fully or freely as their male counterparts – at *any* stage of their life?

Purdah also continues to be widely practiced. Bangladeshi feminist, Taslima Nasrin, has made 'Let's Burn the Burqa' a global slogan. Even if it is not a literal veil for Sikh women, their life is restricted: marriage and care of children, husband and in-laws takes priority over anything personal. Globalism has only amplified androcentrism. The Sikh community retains patriarchal feudal values. In the contemporary reality, daughters are bound to 'honor codes', huge dowries are doled out for their marriages, and female fetuses are being aborted, making alarming statistics. The enlightening lyrics of the Guru poets raise our consciousness and make us self-critical. Their poetic intimations force us to examine:

Figure 15: Upper-class Punjabi woman with companions, Punjab, 1867

do sons, *purdah* and female purity fulfill *religious* and ethical obligations, or are they merely veils and coverings for individual obsessions and greed?

Activating the Text

Indeed, the verses of the Gurus uttered some five centuries ago, during an exceptionally trying religio-political situation, are replete with phrases and imagery that could give a new meaning, a new direction and a new authenticity to the cause of equality chartered only in recent decades in the West. So what are the ways to appropriate them?

Engage Directly with the Text

Everybody needs to read and understand the text from their individual perspective. There has been no disclosure of feminist possibilities because it has only been the male elites who have served as intermediaries. Their one-sided, androcentric approach has dominated interpretations and commentaries. In Gurdwaras, congregations hear interpretations of the Guru Granth from *gyanijis* (Sikh intellectuals), who speak in a male voice and from a male point of view. It is their voice that is broadcast around the world through radio and television. Similarly, Sikh scholarship has been dominated by males, with the result that female images are neglected, sometimes even misinterpreted, and their feminist import is invariably lost. The Book was hailed as the Guru (by the Tenth Guru in 1708) precisely to promote a personal relationship. It is imperative that men and women access their scriptural Guru on their own, without relying on male theologians, exegetes and scholars.

Create New Translations

Likewise, there must be new translations of the sacred verse. The existing adaptations in English are marred by aberrations and distortions. Whereas the Divine is the transcendent, metaphysical One, the term is invariably translated into God and given a male identity. Profoundly simple in its beauty, the original verse celebrates the Divine intimately present in and with everybody. But translators over and over insert archaic phrases that exalt and extol, and lend mystique and authority to that One, making 'Him' wholly distant and other. 'Hallowed be thy name', which is still used in English, is adapted in Sikh scriptural translations. Perhaps 'God' is wondering why people are talking to him in this archaic language that he has not heard for 500 years! Religious Jacobean English is distanced from everyday English, and when it is used in the Sikh context, it becomes doubly foreign, alienating and misleading.

Another tendency of the translators is to reduce the robust and authentic presence of female scriptural models into a mere figure of speech.[18] In some way or other, 'soul' gets latched on to the powerful females, killing their vibrant bodies. A simple *suhagan*, for example, in translation becomes 'bride-soul'. The term 'soul', sturdily appropriated by translators (and exegetes), is utterly inappropriate in the Sikh context. Laden with Jewish–Christian connotations, the soul imposes the mind–body dualism, shifting attention from the present situation to an afterlife and heaven out there. Feminist scholars have warned us about the terrible consequences of the bipartite 'body–soul' framework on the devaluing of bodies, of life on earth and of female gender and sexuality.[19] In spite of the fact that the original verse does not contain any reference to the soul, it is lavishly present in English translations. Its usage dichotomizes the fullness of the Gurus' experience and vision, and sends misogynistic and geophobic messages to readers. New gender-inclusive, female-sensitive translations are urgently needed.

Women Must Have an Equal Role in Public Worship

In Sikh places of worship, male *granthis* (readers) or *bhaijis* (custodians of Gurdwaras) are the ones in closest touch with the Guru Granth. Their hands dress the venerated book, their hands open the holy book, and their voices read out the sacred verses from the book. They lead the liturgical prayers. Even the sweet sacrament (*karah-prashad*) is distributed by men and boys. Sikhism has no priesthood, and nowhere in the Scripture are men delegated to be the sole custodians of their sacred text and leaders in worship, and yet women are tacitly discouraged from conducting public ceremonies. Women are in the vicinity – praying, cleaning the sacred precincts, cooking, doing the dishes – but they rarely lead services. There are many Gurdwaras, but are there any female Granthis? The Sikh egalitarian practices in private worship must be extended outside the home. Otherwise, Sikh men and women will continue to internalize the predominant role played by men in public, which has only legitimized women's deference and subordination to their fathers, brothers, uncles and husbands.

Follow the Sikh Ethical Code

In its attempt to formalize the message of the scripture, the SGPC developed several rules in the *Sikh Rahit Maryada* (the Sikh Ethical Code, published in 1950; see Chapter 4) that would combat female oppression. This standard authoritative statement of Sikh conduct categorically states that neither a girl nor a boy should be married for money. The giving of a dowry is specifically forbidden. Twice the Code makes the point that Sikh women should not veil their faces (12, 18). It prohibits infanticide, especially female infanticide, and even prohibits association with people who would practice it. The *Sikh Rahit Maryada* allows for the remarriage of widows, and it underscores that such a ceremony must be the same as that for the first marriage – a marked difference from the old Punjabi custom, when a widow was shamefully wrapped in a sheet and carried away to a brother of her dead husband. The *Sikh Rahit Maryada* denounces this custom, which treats a daughter like an object or a piece of property passed to her husband and his family. In traditional Indian families, there is also a superstitious custom that people should not eat at the home of their married daughter – forgetting that Nanak himself lived with his married sister, Nanaki, and her husband!

The community needs to propagate and follow such clearly articulated rules. Sikh families should feel empowered by their Ethical Code and not be put under social pressure to provide a dowry for their daughter and gifts for her and her in-laws throughout their lives – or aborting her even before she enters this world.

Existential Correlation

Whereas Sikh scripture is radically open, the community has been slow to acknowledge and implement its innovative ideas. Instead of discovering the new and unique contribution of their Gurus, Sikhs perpetuate the centuries-old values that surround their religion, historically and geographically. Sikhs represent less than 2 per cent of the Indian population, and the customs and veils of the ancient feudal system have slipped easily into Sikh ideas and practices. Sikh

Scripture validates women's natural processes, and yet menstruating women are tacitly forbidden to perform *prakash* or *sukhasan*. So ingrained are the false memories that Sikh women see themselves as polluted and perpetuate these fallacies through their own daughters and granddaughters. When the sacred Book exalts women, how could the ardent devotees of that very Book consider them otherwise? But instead of blaming external contingencies, the community needs to be self-critical. What was the innovative message of the Gurus? Why is it not being followed through? What steps need to be taken to match the existential reality with the vision of the Gurus?

There is optimism on the horizon, though, because Sikh men and women are beginning to take steps toward gender justice. Dr Upinderjit Kaur, Education and Languages Minister of the Punjab, is implementing new plans to expand and improve the standards of secondary education. This far-sighted political leader (author of *Sikh Religion and Economic Development*) is committed to eradicating gender, socio-economic and disability barriers throughout the Punjab. Campaigns geared specifically to counter female feticide are being initiated by the Shiromani Gurdwara Parbandhak Committee (SGPC), in collaboration with the Punjab government and the Ranbaxy Corporation. Political leaders and non-governmental organizations (NGOs) are forging important infrastructures for the protection, welfare, education and employment of girls and women. Preneet Kaur, India's Minister of State for External Affairs, is raising mass awareness in both rural and urban areas that daughters can support their families – *just like sons*. In its two-pronged objective, the Nanhi Chaan Foundation is actively working towards the protection of baby girls and the environment. Harsimrat Kaur, Member of the Indian Parliament from the Bathinda Lok Sabha Constituency, is urging the Punjab State government to provide incentives of fixed deposits for financially weak parents of newborn girls. With Sikh women such as Dr Upinderjit Kaur, Preneet Kaur and Harsimarat Kaur in the political arena, gender equality becomes more of a reality.[20] The courageous Mai Bhago, who fought valiantly alongside Guru Gobind Singh against oppressive forces, can serve as a historical role model for contemporary Sikh men and women to collaborate together in their fight against gender injustice. Together they can bring about a change, and live the egalitarian and liberating life intended by their Gurus.

Poets, novelists, artists and filmmakers are also engaged in raising societal consciousness. In subsequent chapters, we shall sample the works of poet Amrita Pritam, writer Shauna Singh Baldwin, filmmaker Gurinder Chadha, and the artists Arpana Caur, Amrit and Rabindra Kaur. The meeting between the Sikh Prime Minister Manmohan Singh and President Barack Obama in November 2009 brings new hope for women internationally. The leaders of the world's two largest democracies jointly declared that women's participation and equality in all spheres of life is an essential goal of the US–India Strategic Dialog initiatives. To respond to the pain and victimization of any woman in any part of the world is now a moral obligation for every citizen in this global village.

Chapter VII
Colonial Encounters

The Punjab, the home of the Sikhs, is the strategic, north-western gateway to the Indian subcontinent. This fertile region was the cradle of the ancient Indus valley civilization (2500–1700 BCE). Later the Punjab was the birthplace of the Rig Veda (1500–1200 BCE) with its Sanskrit hymns and its horse-riding warriors. The Sikhs are believed to have descended from them. In 326 BCE, Alexander the Great conquered the Punjab, and he and his successors left some Greek cultural and linguistic influences on the region. The discovery of ancient coins provides evidence for the Hellenic impact on the Punjab. Over the centuries, the lure of the land of the five rivers also brought in waves of other foreigners – Scythians, Sassanids, Huns, Afghans, Persians, Turks, Mughals and, closer to our own times, the British.

Like their European counterparts – the Portuguese, the Dutch and the French – the British came by sea to trade with India. The first ships of the East India Company (chartered in 1600 by some English merchants) arrived at the port of Surat in 1608. Sir Thomas Roe, the ambassador for King James I, negotiated with the Mughal Emperor Jahangir, and acquired the right to establish a factory at Surat. Soon, the East India Company began to expand its commercial ventures. Trading posts were set up all along the eastern and western coasts, and British communities developed around Bombay, Madras and Calcutta. With its commercial success, the Company started to make territorial conquests and made its way steadily toward the Punjab, annexing it in 1849. After the Indian Mutiny against the Company in 1857, the East India Company was dissolved, and India was ruled directly by the Crown. Indian independence came on 15 August 1947, and with it the tragic split of the Punjab between India and the newly created country of Pakistan. Over the years, Sikh–British encounters have been very complex.

In this chapter we shall explore a few of them from precolonial and colonial times. Basically, they correspond to the periods: (i) before the establishment of the Sikh Empire by Maharaja Ranjit Singh in 1799; (ii) at the zenith of his Empire (1799–1839); and (iii) after the fall of the Sikh Empire – from the annexation of the Punjab in 1849 to the Radcliffe Line dividing it in 1947. As we shall examine in this chapter, during the century of colonial rule there were points of convergence and divergence between the imperial masters and their Sikh subjects. Their postcolonial encounters will be taken up in the final chapter on diaspora, but an overlap between the two chapters is inevitable. As the 'favored sons', Sikhs traveled along vast networks to fight, patrol, administer and build railways for the British Empire. From Shanghai to Vancouver, the turbaned Sikh soldier was a conspicuous imperial symbol. Soon after independence, Sikhs flocked to Britain to meet the labor shortage in its post-war industrial towns. Just as in the past, the mobile Sikhs continue to remain in close touch with their roots in the Punjab. Indeed, the precolonial, colonial and postcolonial relationship with Britain is profoundly significant to the dynamic Sikh faith.

Before the Sikh Empire

Charles Wilkins at the 'College of the Seeks'

The first Anglo-Sikh encounter was recorded by Charles Wilkins (1749–1836). Wilkins also happens to be the first English translator of the Bhagvad Gita, he created the first Devnagari typeface, and he was the first director of the India Office Library in London. He was a close colleague of Sir William Jones, the founder of the Asiatic Society of Bengal. Wilkins went to India as a typographer and writer for the East India Company. On his way to Benares in 1781, he stopped off at Gurdwara Sahib in Patna for a few hours. Wilkins refers to this Sikh site, commemorating the birth of Guru Gobind Singh, as the 'College of the Seeks'. He wrote his narrative for the Asiatic Society, which was published in 1788.[1]

When Wilkins asked his Sikh hosts if he 'might ascend into the hall', he was told that it was a place of worship 'open to all men'. The visitor was perceptive on reading their intimation 'that I must take off my shoes'. Rather than get annoyed, Wilkins considered 'this ceremony in the same light as uncovering my head upon entering any of our temples dedicated to the Deity'. Mutual respect and understanding marks their meeting.

Wilkins went on to describe the Sikh shrine as an expansive and joyous space, permeated with sacred music and the reading of scripture, a space in which meals and sweetmeats are enjoyed. He tried to explain the philosophical principles of the 'great book of folio size' from which the hymns that he heard were read: 'there is but One God, Omnipotent and Omnipresent, filling all space and pervading all matter ... commands universal toleration ... and inculcates the practice of all the virtues, but particularly universal philanthropy'. Being familiar with Sanskrit and Persian, he was able to follow much of the original. The Englishman – much taken by the old man reading from the text – remarked: 'I never saw a countenance so expressible of infelt joy, whilst he turned about from one to another, as if it were, bespeaking their assents to those truths which his very soul seemed to be engaged in chanting forth.' Wilkins' account ends with the 'ceremonies used in admitting a proselyte'. This would be a description of Guru Gobind Singh's Khalsa initiation, which, he went on to explain, can be 'in any place, as well on the highway as in a house of worship'. With sugar puffs diluted in pure water they 'sprinkle some of it on the body, and into the eyes of the convert … They offered to admit me in their Society'.[2]

This is a remarkably significant interfaith encounter. More than two centuries ago, an eminent British scholar personally visited the birthplace of the Tenth Guru in the heart of Patna and listened avidly to Sikh Scripture, ate their sacred food, reflected on their ethical values, and recognized their universal values. In turn, the community warmly welcomed his participation, and even invited him to join the Sikh initiation ceremony! At the Gurdwara, Wilkins expressed the hope that he would one day translate Sikh sacred verse, but this unfortunately did not happen.

Such encounters are rare in the history of religion. Just a few years earlier, a Swiss Frenchman had called the Sikh initiation 'a filthy, beastly ceremony'.[3] Normally, the British too looked at the Sikhs from a political and colonial angle, and often through secondary sources, which resulted in misinformation. Wilkins' example demonstrates how meaningful it is to actually visit the sacred place of another faith.

The History of the Origin and Progress of the Sikhs, by James Browne

With their growing political power in the last quarter of the eighteenth century, Sikhs became a matter of curiosity – and even concern – for the East India Company. Major James Browne, an envoy of the East India Company at the Mughal Court of Shah Alam in Delhi, produced the earliest historical European work on the Sikhs in 1788 (the same year as Wilkins' discourse).[4] Entitled *The History of the Origin and Progress of the Sikhs*, it includes Browne's English translation of a Persian text he came across at the Delhi Court. He acknowledged that the original text in Devnagari was in the possession of 'two Hindoos of considerable knowledge', and they reproduced this for him in an abridged Persian version. But he also gathered his own data and made personal observations during the two and a half years he was employed in Delhi, and 'accompanied the whole with a map, specifying the extent of their territories, the names of their chiefs, together with the places of their respective residence, and the number of their forces'. Primarily written for the political benefit of the East India Company, Browne's document forms an interesting Western 'discovery' of the 'tribe of people called Sicks'.[5]

Trying to make sense of the unknown faith, Browne uses Protestant terminology and an interpretive framework with which the Company men would have been familiar: '[it] appears to bear that kind of relation to the Hindoo religion, which the Protestant does to the Romish'. He is quite taken by the way 'religion and politics unite in its aggrandizement', citing a host of examples: 'their confederacy is Khalsa Gee'; Sikh coins display 'the name of the Guru'; it is by the holy Tank of Amritsar that 'the commander for the campaign is chosen and their expeditions for the season planned'. Like Wilkins, he too describes the Sikh initiation ceremony, the symbols worn by the Sikhs, and importantly captures their egalitarian spirit: 'designed to signify that every distinction is abolished except that of being a Sick'. Browne mentions the fraternity of the Khalsa, with unshorn hair and beard.

Equally observant of the commercial and agricultural success of the Sikhs, he comments on their 'state of high cultivation' and 'the very fine cloth, which they make at Lahore, and also the best arms in Hindostan'. Having met several Sikhs, he describes their physical characteristics: 'I perceived a manly boldness in their manner and conversation, very unlike other inhabitants of Hindostan.'

By suggesting that Sikhism in Hindustan could be seen as similar to Protestantism in Britain, Browne intended to familiarize his British peers with these very different 'inhabitants of Hindostan'; and through his investigations and personal observations, he intended to warn them about emerging Sikh power. In effect, this pioneering 'Western' sketch created mental patterns that were only reinforced over time. While his Protestant/Catholic parallel stereotyped Sikhism as a 'reform movement out of Hinduism', Browne's appreciation for Sikh 'manly boldness' championed a hyper-masculine Sikh identity that prevails even today.

The Sikh Empire

Maharaja Ranjit Singh and the Establishment of the Sikh Empire

Between the death of their Tenth Guru in 1708 and the victory of their first monarch in 1799, the Sikhs went through a very difficult period. The Guru had initiated Banda (who had been a Hindu ascetic) into the order of the Khalsa just before he passed away in Nander. Armed with Guru Gobind Singh's blessing, Banda Singh Bahadur (1670–1716) came to the Punjab as a zealous commander of the Khalsa force. He captured the town of Sirhind in 1710, and thus created the foundation for Sikh sovereignty. But the immediate result of his victory was the severe persecution of the Sikhs by the Mughal authorities. The ruler Farrukh-Siyar passed an edict to exterminate Sikhs. Banda was finally captured in December 1715 and subsequently executed in Delhi, along with many other Sikhs. Some of these horrific massacres were recorded by the ambassadors of the East India Company.

While being fraught with internal battles, eighteenth-century Punjab was also invaded by the Persian Nadir Shah and the Afghani Ahmad Shah Durrani. The oppressive regime of the Emperor Aurangzeb had demoralized the people. After the death of Aurangzeb in 1707, the Mughal Empire was shrinking, and the commercial East India Company was expanding its military dominance. The Punjab became a battleground for the Persians, Afghanis, British and Sikhs – each group fighting to establish its own empire. In this volatile period, 19-year-old Ranjit Singh, with the help of his mother-in-law, Sada Kaur, peacefully captured the capital city of Lahore on 7 July 1799. He integrated 12 warring Sikh bands into one sovereign State.

Crowned Emperor of the Sikhs on the Baisakhi day of 1801, he ruled in the name of the Khalsa, and introduced coins with Gurmukhi script. Lahore was his administrative capital; and Amritsar, his religious centre. For 40 years, the Maharaja ruled with pomp and glory a kingdom that even the powerful British Empire was afraid to challenge. Comparisons between Ranjit Singh and his near contemporary Napoleon abound in the Sikh imagination.

British–Sikh 'Perpetual Friendship'

A 'political' encounter between the Sikhs and the British took place on 12 September 1808, when 22-year-old Charles Metcalfe arrived at Maharaja Ranjit Singh's court with an offer of friendship from the British government. Metcalfe met the Maharaja in his camp near Kasur, bringing with him numerous gifts sent by the Governor-General of India. A few months later, they signed the Amritsar Treaty of 1809. In this historic treaty, the British and the Sikh governments pledged 'perpetual friendship' and exchanged ambassadors. The first article of the treaty specified: 'The British Government will have no concern with the territories and subjects of the Rajah to the northward of the Sutlej.' Though it prevented Ranjit Singh from extending his kingdom beyond the River Sutlej in the south, the treaty allowed him in theory to expand in all other directions.

Provided with a sense of security by the British, Ranjit Singh was able to consolidate his power in the Punjab, build up a powerful army, and pursue his territorial aspirations. Called 'the Lion of the Punjab', Ranjit Singh took over Multan in 1818, Kashmir in 1819, Dera Ghazi Khan in 1820, Dera Ishmail Khan in 1821 and Peshawar in 1834. By the time of his death, his formidable Empire stretched from the Sutlej in the south to the Khyber Pass in the north, and Kashmir and Ladakh in the east to Sindh in the west. Queen Victoria called it an 'enormous and splendid kingdom'.

Looking At All Religions 'With One Eye'

The Sikh Emperor usually dressed quite simply. But he did wear the celebrated Koh-i-noor diamond, 'the mountain of light', on his arm. As a child he was scarred by smallpox, which left him blind in one eye. With his usual wit, he would explain: 'god wanted me to look upon all religions with one eye, that is why I was deprived of the other'.

In the religious demography of his empire, Sikhs were a minority and Muslims constituted the bulk of the population. Ranjit Singh was respectful of all religious communities, and extended his patronage equally to his Muslim, Hindu and Sikh subjects. The day he was crowned by the revered Baba Sahib Singh Bedi (1756–1834), a descendant of Guru Nanak, prayers were said in Islamic mosques and Hindu temples for his long life. Sikhs, Muslims and Hindus alike held important positions in all areas of Maharaja Ranjit Singh's kingdom. The language of his court was Persian, which had been the official language of the Mughal emperors since the time of Akbar. Even the first coins struck by the Sikh King were in the Persian script. He fostered the celebration of Muslim festivals and, respectful of Hindu sentiments, prohibited the slaughter of cows. A devoted Sikh, he celebrated his victories with thanksgiving prayers at the Harmandar. During his reign, the Harmandar was lavishly plated with gold set with semi-precious jewels, and came to be known as the Golden Temple. New Gurdwaras were built, and many old ones were renovated and given grants of land. Mosques and Hindu temples were also constructed, and Muslim, Hindu and Sikh artists were commissioned extensively.

The Maharaja loved meeting new people of different nationalities and faiths. Many foreigners found employment at his court. Martin Honiberger, a native of Hungary, was the personal physician of the Maharaja, and enjoyed his trust. He also took care of Ranjit Singh's favorite horse, which was one of the five presented to the Maharaja by the King of England. After Waterloo, soldiers who lost their employment with Napoleon – including the Frenchman Jean-François Allard and the Italian-born Jean-Baptiste Ventura – came to work for Ranjit Singh. But they had to sign an agreement that, in the event of a clash between the Maharaja and a European power, they would remain loyal to their master and fight for him. They were also to wear their beards long, refrain from eating beef and smoking tobacco in public, and were to take care not to offend against the Sikh religion. The surgeon-general of the Khalsa army was French, one of the battalion commanders was German, and one of the engineers was a Spaniard. The Maharaja appointed an Italian and an American as governors of some of his provinces. Several Englishmen were employed on various civil and military duties. With men of such diverse races, nationalities and faiths to

Figure 16: General Jean-François Allard and his family, Lahore, 1838

serve him, Ranjit Singh maintained a cosmopolitan court. Writers and painters were very taken with its colorful diversity. On a monumental canvas that was displayed at an exibition in Vienna in 1855, the Hungarian artist August Shoefft depicted approximately a hundred people in the Sikh Court. Along with the Maharaja's family, numerous employees from multiple religions and ethnicities can be identified.[6]

Other Europeans and Americans produced their own commentaries. Baron Charles Hugel, a German scientist, wrote that the Punjab under Ranjit Singh was safer than territories ruled by the British. When the English missionary, Dr Joseph Wolff, arrived at the palace, he was greatly surprised to hear someone singing 'Yankee Doodle' with a typical American accent. It happened to be one of the Maharaja's governors – Dr Joshian Harlan, a native of Philadelphia. Reverend John C. Lowrie, the first American missionary to India, arrived in Ranjit Singh's Punjab in 1834. On visiting Amritsar he made a telling remark: 'Amritsar is the Sikh Athens and Jerusalem.' For Lowrie, Amritsar combined the beauty, light and reason represented by Athens, and the strength, faith and morality represented by Jerusalem – a combination that was to represent modern civilization for author Matthew Arnold some years later.

Alexander Burnes in Lahore and Amritsar

The Maharaja was a fine diplomat and was often successful in interceding between other Indian princes and the British-run East India Company. After the Amritsar Treaty of 1809, he maintained cordial relations with the British, and there was a regular exchange of embassies and gifts. In 1830, Alexander Burnes made a long journey via the River Indus to present the Maharaja with five horses (as noted earlier) 'of gigantic breed that is peculiar to England', a gift from King William IV, along with a letter addressed to 'His highness Maharaja Runjeet Sing, chief of the Seik nation, and Lord of Cashmere'.[7] Sikh historians, however, read his motive quite differently, in that Burnes came to survey the River Indus so that the British could expand their influence in the region of Sindh, and prevent the Sikhs from advancing southwards.

In his memoir, *Travels into Bokhara*, Burnes provides interesting glimpses of his month in Lahore, during which he experienced the hospitality and grandeur of the Sikh Empire. He depicts the layout of the city, its architecture and its cosmopolitan atmosphere. His breakfast at Mr. Allard's home and the Maharaja's display of the Koh-i-noor diamond, form the two bookends of his trip to Lahore, and with his keen sensibility, Burnes graphically reproduces the sights, sounds and tastes that he witnessed. On arrival, he visited Allard's home and was struck by Mughal art and décor, French champagnes and British trumpets. Burnes writes: 'the walls and roof of the apartment were entirely inlaid with small pieces of mirror. Champagne usurped the place of tea and coffee. M. Allard is the Maharaja's general of cavalry; and we had the trumpets of his division in attendance during breakfast.'[8] Before Burnes departed, the Maharaja acquiesced to his request and showed him the Koh-i-noor, and according to the spectator:

> Nothing can be imagined more superb than this stone: it is of the finest water, and about half the size of an egg? … the Kohinoor is set as an armlet, with a diamond on each side about the size of a

> sparrow's egg. And with the diamond was brought a large ruby ... with names of several kings engraved on it, including Aurganzebe and Ahmed Shah....[9]

Whatever his political motives may have been, Burnes portrays Ranjit Singh with much empathy and admiration. He felt bad about Singh's physical disabilities, and thought that he would not last much longer. He admires him for his warm and generous personality. His anecdotes give us a deep understanding of Ranjit Singh's personality. The first time Burnes went to the palace to meet him: 'just as I was stooping down to remove my shoes at the threshold, I suddenly found myself in the arms and tight embrace of a diminutive old-looking man – the great Maharaja Runjeet Singh'. Another day, the Maharaja suddenly invited the Englishman and his companion to join him for a simple breakfast, and 'Runjeet selected the choicest parts [of the mango] and handed them to us himself'.[10] The Maharaja's sharp wit comes across as he introduces Burnes to a group of nautch girls: 'this is one of my regiments (*pultuns*) but they tell me it is one I cannot discipline'.[11] After their dance performance, the Maharaja made sure they were escorted back to their homes on elephants, and paid handsomely. For Burnes: 'The most creditable trait in Runjeet's character is his humanity.'[12] Again:

> Ranjeet Singh is, in every respect, an extraordinary character. I have heard his French officers observe that he has no equal from Constantinople to India; and all of them have seen the intermediate powers.[13]

On his way back to Simla to report his impressions of the Lahore Court to the Governor General, Burnes stopped off in Amritsar 'to view the rites of Siek holiness'. He recounts visiting the Golden Temple and attending the evening ceremonies. Referring to it as the 'national temple', he describes: 'it stands in the centre of a lake, and is a handsome building covered with burnished gold. After making the circuit of it, we entered, and made an offering to the "Grinth Sahib", or holy book, which lay open before a priest....' Indeed, Burnes followed the Sikh form of worship and made a generous offering of 250 rupees. Before departing: 'I begged the orator to declare our desire for a continuance of friendship.'[14] Thus, in the precincts of the sacred space, the British ambassador solicits divine support for the perpetual friendship with the Sikh State. His visit was a prelude to the meeting between the Governor General Bentinck and the Sikh Maharaja – remembered as the 'most spectacular occasion in the history of Anglo-Indian relations'. It took place a few months later on the River Sutlej.

Superpowers Meet by the Sutlej

Since the signing of the Treaty of Amritsar in 1809, much had accrued on both sides. The Sikh Empire was now at its zenith. The grandeur of the Maharaja had become a legend. The Governor General wished to meet him. Through his emissaries, he proposed a summit, which was welcomed by the Maharaja. The venue chosen was Ropar, on the River Sutlej, which marked the boundary between the British and the Sikh Maharaja's kingdom. Elaborate camps were prepared on either side of the river for the respective rulers. The date of the meeting between the two 'superpowers' of the subcontinent was fixed for 26 October 1831.

A party of Englishmen came to escort Ranjit Singh to the Governor General's camp. The Maharaja had already dispatched 3,000 horsemen dressed in resplendent yellow silk. They crossed the Sutlej and waited in rows to greet him. Decked in pearls and jewels, the Maharaja arrived with a train of a hundred gorgeously decorated elephants. A large number of nobles and courtiers, in their glittering brocades and diamonds, arrived in a stately manner. The gifts to Ranjit Singh from Bentinck included British canons, jewels, two horses with saddles of gold, and an elephant trimmed with red velvet.[15] Two hundred trays were needed to carry the presents!

The following day, Ranjit Singh played host to the Governor General. The ground was spread with intricate silk carpets. In the center was placed a pair of royal thrones, with the canopy above inlaid with gems. The Koh-i-noor sparkled on Ranjit Singh's upper arm, adding luster to the scene. The gifts presented to Bentinck included two bejeweled Afghan swords, Persian guns with golden carving, a large number of pashmina shawls, and an elephant with a silver howdah. The Maharaja personally put a pearl necklace around the Governor General's neck.

Such lavish Anglo-Sikh encounters carried on for five days. There were parades and gun salutes, sumptuous dishes and choicest wines, bands and displays of horsemanship. At that critical geographic marker, two heads of state exchanged gifts, sat together, ate together and conversed together. But what actually transpired, neither the Sikhs nor the British recorded. The surface of the Sutlej does not betray its inner currents. The ornate spectacle echoed the 'Amritsar Treaty of 1809'. By the end of the nineteenth century, the British had recognized that

> the result of Lord William Bentinck's diplomacy with the Lion of the Punjab was a great increase in Ranjit's friendliness to us, and the establishment of that understanding which resulted in the alliance a few years later against Afghanistan, and which held good through all the troubles at Kabul ten years afterwards ... It is enough to record Lord William Bentinck's marked success in coming to a satisfactory understanding with Ranjit Singh, who at an earlier period of his career had been hostile and even defiant.[16]

Emily Eden Sketches 'Brothers and Friends'

The writer and artist Emily Eden traveled to India to visit her brother Lord George Auckland during his tenure as governor-general (1836-42). She recorded her tour of the sub-continent in her sketches, watercolors, and letters to her sister back in England (*Up the Country*). In 1838 she went to the Punjab to visit the Kingdom of Lahore and voluminously captured the splendor of the Sikh court. Eden's female perspective, her Victorian sensibility, and her refined artistic lens offer important visual and literary insights.

There are extremely rare references to meetings between English and Sikh women, so her encounter with Prince Sher Singh's wife carries much historical significance. While Eden was being escorted to her residence by the Prince, she observed a Sikh tent 'fitted up very much like an English drawing-room, full of plate, and musical-boxes, and china'. On meeting Mrs Sher Singh, Eden was taken by her delicate beauty – 'the longest almond eyes in the world, and with hands like a little child's'. Eden was equally taken by her emotional strength – 'she did not seem at all afraid of Shere Singh, which is very unusual...'. The English visitor does express her regret, though, about not having been able to meet upper-class women: 'so as to hear their story, and their way of life, and their thoughts'.[17] Patriarchal barriers and protocols did not promote cross-cultural female communication.

Eden's work captures the splendor of the Sikh court, the debonair quality of Sikh princes and nobles, their dazzling clothes and their ornamented horses. She describes the Sikhs eclipsing European pageantry:

> fifty horses were led past us. The first had on it emerald trappings, necklaces arranged on its neck and between its ears, and in front of the saddle two enormous emeralds, nearly two inches square, carved all over, and set in gold frames, like little looking-glasses … The next horse was simply attired in diamonds and turquoises, another in pearls, and there was one with trappings of coral and pearl that was very pretty. Their saddle-cloths have stones woven into them. It reduces European magnificent to a very low pitch.[18]

With both pen and brush, Eden evocatively depicts Ranjit Singh sitting in his typical comfortable pose with one foot in his hand, speaking animatedly and sipping his 'fiery spirit' – a drink which seemed to have upset her Victorian principles. She captures his childlike excitement for horses, as 'he ran out in the sun to feel the legs and examine [the horse]'. Personally, she is amazed by the Sikh Maharaja's interest in Christianity: 'Runjeet has got a fit of curiosity about our religion … he wants to have translations … asked a great many questions about our prayers etc….'[19] Again: 'Runjeet has been extremely curious about our Sundays and Christmas-days.'[20] Eden also communicates his enthusiastic response to the painting Queen Victoria had done as a gift for him. As the painting was being carried:

> all the English stood up, and a salute of twenty-one guns was fired. Runjeet took it up in his hands, though it was a great weight, and examined it for at least five minutes with his one piercing eye, and asked for an explanation of the orb and sceptre, and whether the dress were correct, and if it were really like; and then said it was the most gratifying present he could have received, and that on his return to his camp, the picture would be hung in front of his tent, and a royal salute fired.[21]

That was not all. Queen Victoria must have made an indelible impression on the Sikh Maharaja, as the next day he had more questions about her for Eden's English coachman. This poor chap, who had lost his mother-tongue by serving in India, came to Eden displaying extravagant gifts that the Maharaja had given him, along with the complaint: 'He talked about it for an hour and a half, and I telled him I never seed the Queen.'[22]

Like Alexander Burnes, Emily Eden underscores the Maharaja's penetrating intelligence and admires him for his boundless generosity: 'Runjeet feeds the whole camp while we are in his country, men and beasts – the men 15,000….' That there was no capital punishment in his kingdom is noted by both. In Eden's words: 'He has made himself a great king; he has conquered a great many powerful enemies; he is remarkably just in his government; he has disciplined a large army; he hardly ever takes away life … and he is excessively beloved by his people.'[23]

During their trip, the Maharaja escorted the Governor General to the Golden Temple. Eden's sketch of their visit to the Sikh sacred spot captures an important moment in British–Sikh relations: 'you never saw two gentlemen on better terms with themselves and each other', she concludes. Eden begins with a description of the holy book at the center under a canopy of gold cloth: 'quite stiff with pearls and small emeralds'. The British Governor General and his sister sat in front of the holy book: 'Runjeet made us sit down with him on a common velvet carpet.' She then gives the sequence of three speeches, each proclaiming the intimate British–Sikh bond. The first was made by an official from the Golden Temple: 'to the effect that the two great potentates were now brothers and friends, and never could be otherwise'. The second was made by the Governor General: 'that the two armies had joined, and they could now conquer the whole world'. Finally, the Sikh Maharaja 'carried on the compliment, and said that here the oracle had prompted him to make his treaty, and now they saw that he and the English were all one family'.[24]

The Waning Sikh Raj

Only a few months later, the Maharaja died (27 June 1839), and along with him vanished those claims of power and friendship. Chaos ensued in that splendid Empire. It became a bloodbath of warring factions. After a series of brutal murders, the Sikh Raj passed to Ranjit Singh's youngest son, Dalip Singh. The five-year-old Dalip ascended the throne in 1843, with his mother Jindan (1817–63) appointed as the regent. Maharani Jindan, the robust queen of Ranjit Singh, was famous for her sharp intelligence, and the British were in awe of her, calling her the only courageous 'man' in the area. Maharani Jindan came out of Purdah, she held court and conducted the State in public with enormous strength and wisdom. She reviewed the troops and restored a working balance between the army and the civil administration. The young Maharaja's first few years were spent in the luxury of the palaces in Lahore. Surrounded by attendants, he rode elephants and horses, went on hunting and shooting sprees, he was taught Persian and Gurmukhi, he received the love of his mother and maternal uncle. But soon everything toppled. The British, who had coveted Ranjit Singh's splendid empire, took advantage of its weakened situation. They broke their pledge of perpetual friendship and, after the Anglo-Sikh wars, conquered the Punjab. On 24 March 1849, the Sikh soldiers surrendered in Ferozepur. The 'absolute subjugation and humiliation of so powerful an enemy' witnessed by the Governor General Dalhousie was proudly reported to Queen Victoria: 'the remains of the Sikh army, 16,000 strong were marched into camp, by 1,000 at a time, and laid down their arms as they passed between the lines of the British troops … Many of [the Sikhs] … exclaimed as they threw their arms down upon the heap: "This day Runjeet Singh has died!"'[25]

Sikhs Under Colonial Rule

The Sikh Maharaja and Queen Victoria

Dalip Singh was quickly dethroned. The East India Company seized his property, along with the famous Koh-i-noor. The little boy was separated from his mother and exiled from the Punjab to Fatehgarh in Uttar Pradesh, to live with a devout Christian couple, Dr and Lady Login, who served as his guardians. Maharani Jindan was treated with unnecessary hostility. Colonial administrators like Henry Lawrence and Henry Hardinge had been accusing her of fomenting intrigue in the Court at Lahore. Jindan was expelled from the Punjab, interned at Benaras under strict surveillance, and while she was held hostage at the Fort of Chunar in Uttar Pradesh she made a dramatic escape to Nepal disguised as a maid. In Kathmandu, she was given political asylum by Prime Minister Jung Bahadur. The British Government confiscated her precious jewels and rescinded her pension. Fearful of the fact that she had the power to restore the Sikh kingdom in the Punjab, the British Residency in Kathmandu

Figure 17: Maharaja Dalip Singh

continued to keep a vigilant eye on Jindan. Meanwhile, in his new environment, Dalip converted to Christianity. In 1854 he sailed to London, where he was to settle on a pension provided by the British.

Queen Victoria hosted him in London, and soon became very fond of him. She was charmed with the dignified manner of the 15-year-old deposed Indian Maharaja, and equally so with his 'Sikh costume' and his 'extremely handsome' appearance. It is as though the Queen, in her enthusiasm, was echoing his father's excitement about her when he received the young Queen's portrait! Victoria commissioned painters and sculptors to depict the young Dalip. During the week that he was modeling for the German painter Franz Winterhalter (10–17 July 1854), the Queen sat across from him, with Prince Albert, and composed her own sketches of her exotic subject. Her ink drawings happened to focus on two items: his turban – ironically, the young fellow had neither *kesha* (for his long hair had been shorn) nor the *kangha* underneath – and the Queen's own miniature portrait studded in pearls around his neck. Governor General Dalhousie had expressed interest in Dalip's turban as well: '[the] night-cappy appearance of his turban is his strongest national feature'.[26] During this Winterhalter week, the young Dalip placed in the Queen's hand the Koh-i-noor, the quintessential symbol of her conquest. In order to refine its shape and luster, the diamond had been sharply reduced from its original size by a Dutch diamond cutter. The Queen later wore it as a brooch. After her death, the Koh-i-noor was used in the coronation crowns of the King's consorts – Queen Alexandra, Queen Mary and Queen Elizabeth (later, the Queen Mother), and is now on display among the Crown Jewels in the Tower of London.

In 1859 Dalip Singh went to India to bring back his aging mother from her political exile in Nepal. In her fragile condition, attendants, including her maid Soortoo, accompanied the Maharani to England. Dalip arranged for his mother to live in Abingdon House, in Kensington. The Maharani died in 1863. Dalip Singh followed her wishes and took her remains back to India for cremation, but was not allowed to perform the last rites in the Punjab. The dethroned heir of Maharaja Ranjit Singh was viewed as too powerful a threat to the Empire. Dalip eventually performed the final ceremony for his mother by the banks of the River Godavari, near Nasik in Maharashtra.

Queen Victoria and the Logins tried to arrange a marriage for him with Princess Gouramma, the daughter of an ex-Rajah of

Coorg. She had also converted to Christianity. In fact, the Queen was her godmother, and was keen to see her married to Dalip. But in the end he married Bamba Muller, the daughter of a German father and an Ethiopian mother. Bamba spoke Arabic and was educated at the American Presbyterian Mission School in Cairo. Dalip and Bamba started their married life at his newly acquired estate at Elveden. The Sikh Maharaja restored the country house with an eclectic mix of Italian and Mughal decor. Its sparkling glass mosaics recreated the magnificence of his lost palaces, and the paintings on the walls replayed the glorious reign of his father. He also built an aviary, where he kept exotic birds. Exiled from the Punjab, the Maharaja lived the extravagant life of a British aristocrat, hosting a wide range of sporting activities. He even acquired the nickname of the 'Black Prince of Perthshire' when he was in Scotland.

Nevertheless, his Sikh heritage, that essential part of his being, came back to life with a renewed vigor. His mother had all along been a strong reminder of his faith. His relatives and the general Sikh community began to campaign for his return to the Punjab as the ruler of the Sikh nation. Dalip Singh began to negotiate with Punjabi revolutionaries to overthrow the colonial state with the help of Russia and return to the Punjab. In 1886 he left for India, where the Sikhs were preparing for his glorious return. But he was arrested in Aden by the British police. He was not allowed to sail onward to Bombay. At this juncture, Dalip Singh took the Amrit initiation and reconverted to Sikhism. He then went to Paris, and slipped into Russia, where he became entangled in an anti-British party, which included Sikh, Irish republican, Russian, Afghan and Egyptian agents. Unfortunately, he subsequently had a massive stroke and died in Paris in 1893 – without any financial or political support. His wish for his body to be returned to India was rejected. He was buried in Elveden Church, beside the grave of his wife Bamba, and his son Prince Edward Albert Duleep Singh. Both Queen Victoria and the Prince of Wales sent wreaths. To pay off his debts, Elveden was sold off to the Guinness family. The Maharaja had several children but they left no heirs. The Sikh Raj, built by his father, completely crumbled away.

The large painting of Dalip Singh by Winterhalter continues to hang in Osborne House on the Isle of Wight, where the 15-year-old had been entertained by Queen Victoria and Prince Albert in 1854. Three small paintings on porcelain of the Maharaja, his wife Maharani

Bamba, and their son Victor Albert, are also displayed. The elaborate carvings in the Durbar Room at Osborne House were crafted by Bhai Ram Singh, a Sikh artist especially invited to England from Amritsar. Bhai Ram Singh's architectural designs are a perfect setting for the display of the exquisite collection of gifts given to Queen Victoria by Indian Maharajas and nobles.

Though the Sikh kingdom above the Sutlej had been annexed, the Sikh states in the Cis-Sutlej region signed treaties with the British. Under British protection, they were allowed to keep their own courts and armies until India's independence in 1947. For their territorial integrity and 'autonomy', the princely rulers of Patiala, Nabha, Jind, Faridkot and Malerkotla maintained a friendship with the British. A few of them opened schools modeled on elite British public schools, and the lessons were taught in English. The rulers and their families traveled to England, and in turn entertained British visitors in palaces specially built for them. The Maharaja of Patiala hosted them at the Baradari Palace, which had a skating rink, swimming pool and cricket club. Its guesthouse had drawing rooms furnished with elaborate Victorian furniture, mahogany card tables, Russian teasets and German porcelain. Its bathrooms were ultra modern – there was even a bathtub encased in glass, where water sprayed from all sides. The building overlooked beautifully manicured gardens, interspersed with ponds full of blooming lilies and statues of frolicking cupids. An enormous sculpture of Queen Victoria dominated the scene. In post-independent India, this guesthouse became the headquarters of the Punjabi University, with Queen Victoria still holding her scepter. Over the decades the Queen's statue has disappeared, but the friendship between the royal families continues. The Maharaja of Patiala and his wife, Preneet Kaur, attended Prince Charles' and Lady Diana's wedding. In 2006, Prince Charles, with his second wife Camilla Parker Bowles, visited the ancient fort of the Maharaja of Patiala, located in the heart of the sprawling bazaars.[27]

'Favored Sons of the Empire'

From being arch enemies of the British during the Anglo-Sikh wars, the Sikhs became their loyal supporters. During the Indian rebellion of 1857 (which began with the mutiny of Sepoys at Meerut and soon erupted into rebellions against the East India Company across the whole of the upper Gangetic plain and central India), the Sikhs, along with other conquered Punjabis, followed the British authorities. The Punjab was relatively stable at this time. Since Sikh soldiers were allowed to wear turbans and beards, and to observe their religious practices, they did not share the grievances of other Indian Sepoys. Moreover, the harvest had been good, and since the revenue demanded by the Government was modest enough, there was general contentment among the Punjabis.[28] The Phulkian rulers, who had been bolstered by the British, reciprocated by backing the Company at this critical time, providing them with both soldiers and support. Sikh troops defended English establishments and families, they escorted convoys of the sick and wounded, and played a pivotal role in ending the Mutiny.

Within a week of the Mutiny, the British began to claim: 'If we survive this, never will a Hindustani be enlisted again. Our army should be entirely European, Afghan, Gurkha and Sikh.'[29] A year later, *The Lahore Chronicle* duly acknowledged Sikh loyalty and military prowess: 'English skill and English valor succumbed, and but for the fidelity of the Sikhs every vestige of European civilization would in all probability have been eradicated.'[30] The British General, Henry Havelock, witnessed the gallantry of the Ferozepur Regiment during the early days of the Mutiny and declared: 'Soldiers! Your labours, your privations, your sufferings and your valour will not be forgotten by a grateful country.' His words are inscribed on his statue in Trafalgar Square in London. The Ferozepur Regiment was known as 'Brasyer's Sikhs' after Colonel C. B. Brasyer, the first Englishman to recruit Sikhs into the British Army. They had the right to wear red turbans as part of their uniform.

After the Mutiny, the rule of the East India Company came to an end and the British government began to administer India directly. In 1877, Queen Victoria was declared the Empress of India. The army, the financial system and the administration underwent a major transformation and Sikhs, as the ideal subaltern community, took on an intrinsic role in the Raj's new infrastructure. The Sikhs, with their 'manly boldness' that James Browne had first recognized, began to enter imperial institutions, military service and labor networks all over the British Empire. They received enormous professional and material advantages. The incomes, pensions, grants, land preference policies and colonial patronage created a special Anglo-Sikh relationship. After the Indian Councils Act of 1861, the

Maharaja of Patiala was nominated to the Governor General's Council.

Sikhs were recruited in disproportionately large numbers to serve in the British Army. The lucrative employment attracted Sikh agriculturalists, thus temporarily alleviating the pressure on land from population growth. The caste names that Sikhs had learned to discard were reintroduced, as many of them were registered in the army under the old system of family name, and the occupational boundaries they had rejected also came into play, as the colonialists created 'traditional agriculturists', 'martial races' and 'trading castes'.[31] Sikh regiments were separated from the other 'martial races' of Pathans, Gorkhas and Rajputs, and were also separated from the more peaceful Bengalis, who were denounced as 'effeminate' by the British. Sikh troops were required to go through the Amrit initiation and wear the five symbols of their Khalsa identity. Both military discipline and religious discipline were instilled among the Sikh regiments and monitored by their commanding officers. Exploiting the rhetoric of Sikh loyalty and manliness, a vigorous new patriarchal discourse with its patriotism and paternalism became attached to the 'brotherhood of the Khalsa'.

Fiery speeches were made by influential Sikhs on behalf of the British Army, stressing, as did the Maharaja of Patiala, 'loyalty to the King-Emperor, and Sikh readiness to fight and die as good warriors'.[32] Sikhs formed about one-fifth of the imperial army in the First World War, with numbers reaching 100,000 by the end of the war. They fought bravely for the Empire in Europe, Africa, West Asia, Burma, Malaya and China. The Sikhs won 14 of the 22 military crosses awarded to Indians for conspicuous gallantry. From Shanghai to Mesopotamia, Sikhs heroically guarded the outposts of the Empire. In return, they received grand honors and handsome grants of land in the new canal colonies in the Punjab (which the muscular lads whom the British admired so much had helped to build), and became the richest agriculturists in Asia.[33]

The Singh Sabha Response to Colonialism

With the British occupation of the Punjab, missionary activity was extended to cover the newly acquired territory. An American Presbyterian Mission, established in Ludhiana in 1835, set up a printing press, which produced translations into Punjabi from the Bible and from English literature. The first book to be printed in the Gurmukhi script was the Bible itself. The Evangelists read in the Sikhs' rejection of caste and idolatry their openness to scriptural truth. Their optimism regarding the potential of finding converts from the Sikh faith is apparent in the valedictory instructions given to T. H. Fitzpatrick and Robert Clark, the first missionaries of the Church of England, appointed to the Punjab in 1852:

> Though the Brahman religion still sways the minds of a large proportion of the population of the Punjab, and the Mohammedan of another, the dominant religion and power for the last century has been the Sikh religion, a species of pure theism, formed in the first instance by a dissenting sect from Hinduism. A few hopeful instances lead us to believe that the Sikhs may prove more accessible to scriptural truth than the Hindus and Mohammedans.[34]

Catholics, Methodists, Episcopalians, Moravians and other Orders competed with each other to convert this 'species of pure theism'. The missionary activity received government patronage. With the loss of their Raj, the Sikhs were in a low psychological state. The conversion of Maharaja Dalip Singh was a shock too. The faith of the new rulers appeared attractive to Sikhs and they started giving up their own heritage. From their high point under Maharaja Ranjit Singh, the Sikhs after 20 years of British rule had dwindled to a little over one million by 1868.

The Christian enterprise spread into spheres of social welfare such as education and medical care. After the famous 1854 dispatch of Sir Charles Wood, the Government's policy was directed toward opening schools and colleges, and made it a 'sacred duty' to promote education in both English and the vernacular languages. Such activities initiated a new process of literary, social and cultural resurgence among the Indians. Powerful movements of reform and renewal arose in the three major traditions of India – Brahmo Samaj in Hinduism; Aligarh in Islam; and Singh Sabha in Sikhism. The Brahmo Samaj, founded by Raja Rammohun Roy in Bengal in 1828, comprised Western-educated intellectuals who wished to create a synthesis of enlightened Hinduism and European liberalism. Aligarh, founded by Sir Sayyid Ahmad Khan, initially began as a secondary school patterned after European models in 1875 in India and soon established itself as an influential modernizing movement in Islam. The Singh Sabha issued from the deliberations of leading Sikhs of the time, such as Thakur Singh Sandhanwalia, Baba Sir Khem Singh Bedi and Kanwar Bikrama Singh of Kapurthala, who met in Amritsar in 1873.

The Singh Sabha aimed at recapturing the original message of the Gurus and recovering and re-establishing Sikh identity. There was a deep concern for the decline of ethical standards. As well as the problem of Sikhs converting to Christianity, many Sikhs were adopting practices discarded by the Gurus. During the pomp and ceremony of the Sikh Empire, social customs such as *sati* and *purdah*, and elaborate Brahmanical rituals, re-entered Sikh life. The Singh Sabha activists wanted to purge Sikhism of such extraneous influences. There was also the challenge from the Arya Samaj (a Hindu reform movement established in the Punjab in 1875), as many of its leaders with an anti-Sikh bias began to suggest that Sikhism was a branch of Hinduism. Furthermore, with the British occupation of the Punjab, Urdu (the Persianized form of the language spoken around Delhi), along with English, became the official medium of provincial administration. The Singh Sabha therefore aimed to address issues of personal identity, formulate theological concepts, reform social customs and give prominence to Punjabi, the language of their Gurus, with its Gurmukhi script. Soon after the Singh Sabha in Amritsar, another was set up in Lahore, with the patronage of Sir Robert Egerton, the governor of the Punjab.[35] Within a decade, some 121 Singh Sabhas had sprung up. Committed to mass education and print culture, they tried to reach illiterate villagers, create liaisons with Sikh regiments, as well as beginning a flurry of literary activity, including the publication of numerous journals and newspapers in the Punjabi language.

The Lyall Khalsa College in Amritsar

To meet its goals, the Singh Sabha ideology tried to combine modern-style education with Sikh religious education. This led to the creation of the Khalsa College at Amritsar in 1892 – the premier Sikh educational institution. It received enthusiastic support from the British government, so, in honor and gratitude, it was renamed the Lyall Khalsa College, after Sir Charles James Lyall (1845–1920), the Lieutenant Governor of the Punjab. Soon Khalsa colleges and Khalsa schools were being established all over the Punjab. At primary, secondary and advanced levels, these institutions promoted the study of science, literature, English and Gurmukhi, and Sikh scripture. With such an Anglo-vernacular curriculum, the Punjab entered the orbit of a new consciousness.

Pioneers of Sikh Women's Education

Bhai Takht Singh (1870–1937) was a graduate of the Oriental College in Lahore. Influenced by his teachers, who were prominent Singh Sabha leaders, Bhai Tahkt Singh became a strong advocate of women's education. He started a modest open-air Gurmukhi school at Ferozepur in 1892. With the help of his wife, Harnam Kaur, and their tireless efforts, a boarding house was added in 1904. This launched the Sikh Kanya Mahavidyala, a vital institution in the promotion of Sikh women's education. Takht Singh did not accept government support; instead he traveled to migrant Sikh communities in Rangoon, Malaya and Singapore to raise funds. In 1907, the Sikh Kanya Mahavidyalaya started *Punjabi Bhain* ('Punjabi Sister'), a literary and social magazine, which transmitted the ideologies of the Singh Sabha. The school became a center of cultural and literary activity. Following its example, schools exclusively for the education of girls were opened at Lahore, Amritsar, Rawalpindi and Ropar. The aristocrat Baba Khem Singh Bedi (1832–1905), an influential ally of the British, also made important contributions toward the education of Sikh girls and women. He donated large sums toward the establishment of schools and colleges for females.

M. A. Macauliffe: A Devout Scholar of Sikhism

The German philologist, Ernest Trumpp (1828–85), made the first attempt to translate Sikh Scripture into English. Trumpp had studied several Indian languages and prepared their grammars and glossaries for the use of Christian missionaries. The India Office commissioned him to produce the translation of Sikh Scripture, but because of his blatant orientalism, Trumpp's work, published in 1877, had an extremely negative reception. The damage to Sikh sentiment was reversed by Max Arthur Macauliffe (1841–1913), a senior administrator for the British government. He gave up his job, and with great devotion, sensitivity and accuracy, produced a translation of Sikh Scripture along with a study of the Gurus and saints (published by Oxford University Press in 1909). The Sikhs were jubilant. Macauliffe was invited by the custodians of the Golden Temple to lecture on his work, and three complete readings (*akhand paths*) of the Guru Granth were held for his scholarly success. Though Macauliffe regretted his work had not received the British government's patronage, *The Sikh Religion: Its Gurus, Sacred Writings and Authors*, is regarded as 'a beacon in the Sikh literary world'. Sikhs frequently quote the observation of his assistant Muhammad that Macauliffe was reciting the Jap (Sikh morning prayer) ten minutes before his death.

Bhai Kahn Singh Nabha: Ham Hindu Nahin

In response to the prevailing Arya Samaj rhetoric that the Sikh religion was a branch of Hinduism, Singh Sabha writers articulated their distinct identity. In 1898, Bhai Kahn Singh (1861–1938), the chief minister of Nabha and a leading scholar, published *Ham Hindu Nahin* ('We are not Hindus'). Through a dialog between a Hindu and a Sikh, the author explains the differences between their scripture, society, rituals and belief systems. Citing important references, he proves that Sikhism is a separate and autonomous socio-religious entity. Initially in Hindi, Bhai Kahn Singh's text was later translated into Punjabi. He also produced the *Gur Shabad Ratnakar Mahan Kosh* ('Encyclopedia of Sikh Literature'), which is regarded as the most reliable reference material on matters Sikh. His books *Gurmat Prabhakar* and *Gurmat Sudhakar* are the standard texts for understanding Sikh faith and belief. Macauliffe went to Nabha in 1885 to study Sikh history and literature with this revered scholar.

Sikh Anand Act 1909

As the Sikhs became more conscious of their identity, they wanted to practice their rites of passage and their ceremonies in their own distinctive way. The Sikh rite of marriage was legalized by the Anand Marriage Bill passed in 1909, after which Sikh weddings were no longer patterned on Hindu ritual.

Bhai Vir Singh: The Poetic Voice

Less than a year old at the time of the birth of the Singh Sabha, Bhai Vir Singh (1872–1957) eventually became its most ardent exponent and eloquent spokesman. He attended the Church Mission School, read English writers and philosophers, absorbed Western ideas, and thus broke away from the constricting classical structures and tropes. At the same time, he learnt Persian, Urdu and Sanskrit; then went back to his Sikh heritage, and to his mother tongue, Punjabi. He recognized the essential bond between culture and language, and seizing the new energy around him, transformed the Punjabi language into a powerful medium to express new literary, artistic and social ideas. He adopted many different genres to awaken his community to their own past, using fresh and innovative insights.

Bhai Vir Singh was a voluminous writer. He published eight collections of poetry, four novels, a play, five biographies and nine major texts, that he annotated and commented upon meticulously – while still keeping up with journalism. He began to work on a formal commentary on the Guru Granth late in his career, and devoted several years to the project. Unfortunately, it was not completed during his lifetime and was published posthumously, in seven large volumes. His exegesis of the Jap in 178 pages (*Japuji Sahib Santhya*) is a telling illustration of his erudite scholarship. The verses are analyzed at great length and in depth; allusions, symbols and a glossary of terms are provided; individual words are traced etymologically; and extensive references to preceding commentators are made.

Like other Singh Sabha thinkers, Bhai Vir Singh realized the important role of women. In order to reform his society and restore the ethical values of the Gurus, he wrote fiction and poetry with strong female role-models such as Sundari, Rani Raj Kaur, Satvant Kaur, Subhagji and Sushil Kaur. These women are paradigms of moral strength, spiritual sensitivity and physical courage. They are not fairyland characters, but human beings of flesh and blood. Through them Bhai Vir Singh wanted to remind his people of the revelation of the One mediated through Guru Nanak, and of its implication for society.

Sundari is the first novel in the Punjabi language. The story was conceived when Bhai Vir Singh was still in high school, and a part of it was written then. Fed on stories of Sikh heroism and sacrifice dating back to the eighteenth century, he chose that historical period as a backdrop for his narrative. His protagonist Sundari is born into a Hindu family, but converts to Sikhism, and subsequently abandons the traditional texts and mores. Sundari embodies total faith in the infinite One, she wears the five Sikh symbols, she rejects superfluous rituals, she cheerfully prepares *langar*, she fights courageously, and she even bandages and gives water to an injured soldier from the enemy camp. The author's objective, in his own voice:

> In writing this book our purpose is that by reading these accounts of bygone days the Sikhs should recover their faith. They should be prepared actively to pursue their worldly duty as well as their spiritual ideal … They should learn to own their high principles … and adhere to the Guru's teaching: 'Recognize all humankind as one.'[36]

Bhai Vir Singh's novel is a call to action, demanding a shift in consciousness and a transformation of society.

Similarly, his epic *Rana Surat Singh*, modeled on Edmund Spenser's *Faerie Queene*, presents the quintessence of Sikh mysticism through its female protagonist Rani Raj Kaur. The final stanzas of Guru Nanak's Jap come to life artistically and comprehensively as Rani Raj Kaur journeys through the five spheres with her divine companion. Like the Gurus who wrote in the poetic mode, Bhai Vir Singh made poetry an integral part of his hermeneutic technique. *Rana Surat Singh* (12,000 lines of verse) was published in 1905. Several collections of shorter poems appeared subsequently. The form of these poems was an innovation in Punjabi literature and they became instantly popular. Romantic poets such as William Wordsworth and John Keats had their impact, and the new form brought about a revolutionary transformation in Punjabi poetry. Bhai Vir Singh's sole objective was to evoke, elucidate and expand the Sikh scriptural message. Poetically he grasped the Guru Granth, and poetically he made it transparent and alive for his readers.

The poet often probes into the many complexities of the human psyche. The glimpses he offers into the innocence and pristine joy of childhood are delightful. For example, in his poem 'Wild Berries', the almighty Lover is compared with a naughty child who not only snatches fig-candy from his mother's hand, but also takes enormous pleasure in eating each and every bite. By gathering the transcendent Infinite in the lap of a mother, Bhai Vir Singh unfolds images of the Divine that are generally neglected by society.

Throughout his works, he championed a distinct Sikh identity, but he did so in the pluralistic model of the Sikh Gurus. His works evoke the singular reality shared by humanity. Sikhism, like Islam, is an aniconic tradition, but Bhai Vir Singh condemns religious fanatics who fear images and become victims of their phobias. In his work entitled *Avantipur de Khandar*, he laments the destruction of Hindu idols at Avantipur in Kashmir. The Punjabi poem serves as a poignant reminder of the recent attacks on the giant Buddhist statues in the Bamiyan Caves in northern Afghanistan by the Taliban. How could hatchets and explosives be employed to destroy art that embodied such peace and serenity? What did the eyes see in these ancient images that they had to be destroyed with acts of sheer brutality? According to the poet, idols can be put back together from rubble, but the critical problem is the distorted vision: how do we begin *to see* reality? In keeping with the message of the Gurus, his works reveal the urgency for 'eyes' that see through external differences into the intrinsic beauty of art belonging to humanity. Through his wide-ranging texts, the Singh Sabha poet inspired his Sikh community; and his works have relevance for global readership too.

Anti-Colonial wave

After the First World War, the amicable Anglo-Sikh relationship underwent a major change, which is apparent in the events detailed below. These took place in colonial India, but they were compounded by forces ignited oversees. The shabby treatment and the racist policies inflicted on Sikh immigrants to Canada in the early twentieth century disillusioned the loyal sons of the Empire. Simultaneously, there was a revolutionary awakening against British colonialism brought about by the Ghadar movement that had its genesis on the West coast of the New World (see also Chapter IX on the Sikh diaspora). The revolutionary ideas, shared via communication networks over the continents, fueled the sentiments of the Sikhs in colonial Punjab.

Ram Singh Namdhari

Even prior to the First World War, Ram Singh Namdhari (1816–85) had launched a non-violent and civil disobedience movement in the Punjab. He was the religious leader of the Namdharis. (Meaning literally the adopters of *nam*, this sect of Sikhs revere their leader as the living Guru, whereas for mainstream Sikhs the Scripture is the only living Guru. Namdharis are easily recognized by their white homespun clothing and horizontally-styled turbans. Some expert classical musicians have emerged from this group.) Ram Singh championed the self-rule movement in the Punjab against British imperialism. He is probably the first Indian to use non-cooperation and boycotting of British goods, educational services and law courts as a political weapon.

Rakab Ganj Gurdwara Wall

In 1912, the British Raj moved its capital from Calcutta to Delhi. During the construction of the road to the new viceregal lodge (modern Rashtrapati Bhavan), the outer wall of the Rakab Ganj Gurdwara was dismantled. This Gurdwara is venerated as the cremation site of Guru Tegh Bahadur: on his execution in 1675, his disciple Lakhi Shah escaped with the Guru's body, and since open cremation would not have been allowed, Lakhi Shah set fire to his house, burning with it the body of the martyred Guru. The demolition of its wall by the Raj evoked deep hurt and anger in the community. Telegrams and petitions were sent to the Viceroy of India, the lieutenant Governor of the Punjab, and the commissioner of Delhi. The wall was eventually rebuilt in 1921.

Jallian Wallah Bagh Massacre

A critical date in the transformation of the Sikh attitude towards the Raj was 13 April 1919. For their Baisakhi celebrations, Sikhs, as usual, had come to their sacred Golden Temple. Adjoining the shrine is an enclosed garden with high brick walls, called the Jallian Wallah Bagh. Here, a large crowd had assembled for a peaceful public gathering, despite the ban on such meetings by the British authorities. When Brigadier-General Reginald Dyer found out about it, he brought in his army. Standing at the narrow entrance of the compound, he ordered his men to fire at the large gathering of unarmed and innocent men, women and children. According to official estimates, nearly 400 civilians were killed, and another 1,200 were left wounded with no medical attention. Dyer, who claimed his action was necessary to produce a 'moral and widespread effect', apparently felt no remorse. Baisakhi 1919 intensified the urgency for India's independence, and Sikhs changed from being loyalists to ardent nationalists. They wanted the British to quit India. Twenty-one years later, a young survivor of the massacre, named Udham Singh, went to London and assassinated Michael O'Dywer at Caxton Hall. O'Dywer had been the governor of the Punjab at the time of the Jallian Wallah Bagh tragedy.

Claiming their Sacred Spaces

Under the British, the overall governance of Gurdwaras passed into the hands of the Mahants (clergy-cum-managers). The Mahants owned the land attached to the Gurdwaras and they were in charge of performing rites of passage. Since they had the support of the British, the Mahants did not care much for Sikh sentiment. Misappropriation of funds and deviation from Sikh norms became common practice. The Sikhs wanted to free their Gurdwaras from the recalcitrant Mahants so they could manage them collectively and utilize their incomes for the education and well-being of the community. On 12 October 1920, students and faculty members of the Khalsa College called a meeting to take immediate action to free the Gurdwaras from the control of the Mahants.

Shromani Gurdwara Prabhandak Committee and the Shromani Akali Dal

The Sikh Shromani Gurdwara Prabhandak Committee (SGPC) was constituted on 15 November 1920 with 175 members, to manage and reform Sikh shrines. The removal of Hindu images, icons, practices and ideologies was crucial for its members. They fought tragic battles against the Mahants and the British administrators to take control of Sikh shrines, and re-establish the Sikh essentials in their sacred spaces.

With many Gurdwaras shifting into their orbit, Sikh leaders found there was a need to organize a political party, and so the Shromani Akali Dal came into being in January 1921. As the political arm of the SGPC, the members of the Akali Dal promoted the ideas of the SGPC among the Sikh public, and the Gurdwara reform movement itself came to be known as the Akali movement. In many cases, the Akalis had it easy: the transition was smooth; however, there were many others in which the Akalis met severe challenges in their attempt to bring Gurdwaras under the management of the SGPC. In a sequence of tragedies – the Nankana Holocaust (1921), Guru ka Bagh (1922) and Jaito (1924) – hundreds of Akalis lost their lives. But each incident made them stronger and more fervent. According to Khushwant Singh:

> The Akali movement was the first example of passive resistance organized on a mass scale which proved wholly successful; the largest civil disobedience movements launched by Mahatma Gandhi and organized by the Indian National Congress were but pale imitations of the Akali achievement.[37]

When the Punjab government tried to divest the Sikhs of the symbol of the sword by restricting its size, the Sikhs boldly denounced their repressive measures. The Secretary of the Sikh Young Men's Association declared: 'the sword is to the Sikh what the sacred thread is to the Brahmin'. (It was a reminder that the Ninth Guru had sacrificed his life for the upkeep of religious freedom of the Hindus.)

Keys to the Golden Temple Treasury

On 7 November 1921, the keys of the Golden Temple treasury were forcibly taken by the British, which deeply offended the Sikhs. The SGPC protested strongly, and asked the Sikhs to hold assemblies to condemn the action of the Government. Sikhs did not participate in any function connected with the forthcoming visit of the Prince of Wales, and instead went on strike on the day of his arrival. Sikh leaders were arrested by the Deputy Commissioner, and so were many more. Dressed in black and singing hymns, the Sikhs gladly filled British jails. Under pressure of the growing agitation, the Government gave in. On 19 January 1922, at a huge gathering at the Golden Temple, Sardar Kharak Singh, President of the SGPC, received the bunch of keys wrapped in red cloth – symbolic of an auspicious transition. Mahatma Gandhi sent him a telegram message: 'First decisive battle for India's freedom won. Congratulations.'[38]

The Radcliffe Line

Sikhs who were gaining so much lost it all when their homeland was partitioned. Hindus, Muslims and Sikhs together had fought for their country's independence from British rule. To break their cross ethnic solidarity, the British promoted communalism. They prompted the elite land-holding Muslims of the United Provinces to establish the Muslim League in 1906 to represent Muslim interests. In 1909 they instituted separate electorates for the Indian population. As the movement for independence gathered momentum, the political leaders could not agree on how their new power was to be shared. The Muslims, who had ruled India until the British took over, demanded their own state of Pakistan. The Sikhs were for a united India. But if Pakistan were to be conceded, Sikh leaders expressed their demand for a separate Sikh state with the right to federate with either India or Pakistan. From the time of Guru Gobind Singh, the concept of a sovereign Sikh state has been imprinted on the Sikh psyche: '*raj karega khalsa* – the Khalsa will rule' is remembered in the daily liturgical prayer. Maharaja Ranjit Singh had crystallized their aspiration. Now that the British were leaving, they felt the Punjab should belong to the Sikhs again. If there was going to be a 'Pakistan' and a 'Hindustan', there also had to be a 'Sikhistan' (at times called 'Azad Punjab' or 'Khalistan'). On the eve of the British departure, Muslim–Hindu–Sikh divisions gained enormous force, and the colonial policy of 'divide and rule' reached a horrific finale.

It was poets such as Amrita Pritam, Mohan Singh, Prabhjot Kaur, Amarjit Chandan, Surjit Patar, Gopal Singh Dardi, Dhani Ram Chatrik, Firozdin Sharaf and Dr Fakir Muhammad Fakir, who have been bringing in the message of hope. Their works reminded Punjabis of their common literary inheritance. These poets frequently returned to the waters they drank from together, the fields they harvested together, the land they danced in together. The most famous among them are Mohan Singh (1905–78) and Amrita Pritam (1919–2005). They championed the ideals of liberty and togetherness, often synthesizing their ambitious new forms with the traditional folk rhythms of the Punjab. Aligned with the progressive movement, both were prolific poets and won many distinguished awards.

Mohan Singh called to Indians to come out of their compartmentalized mode of existence. His poem, *Come Let's Dance*, seethes with patriotic sentiments. The dynamic dance is the gesture of stepping forward into the realm of new possibilities and intimate relationships. The dreams and ideals of his contemporaries would crystallize only if they came out of their 'curtains and veils' – their hegemonies of caste and class, their segregation of gender and religion, their divisions of *we* and *they*. The love of their motherland had the force of flushing out their communal phobias so that they could embrace one another intimately. To cite just the opening segment of his poem *Come Let's Dance*:

Come people of India
  Let's get together
Let's create a strong
  Rhythm of love

Open up the curtains
  Lift up the veils
Let's dance
  Closely together

Let's drink
  The wine of patriotism
Let's get inebriated and
  Lose ourselves
In sinuous steps
  Our arms wide open
Let's join in and
  Tightly hug one another…

In Mohan Singh's vibrant choreography, rich and poor, Muslim and Hindu, men and women, should dance together. His sonorous melodies incite people to open up their arms. The poet called for a celebration of inclusivity, freedom and ecstasy.

Instead, there were internecine massacres. India gained independence on 15 August 1947, but the subcontinent was divided along religious lines. Sir Cyril Radcliffe, who had never been to India, was put in charge of drawing the boundaries. Working with outdated maps and census figures, he drew the line that split the Punjab between the nations of India and Pakistan. His haphazard 'Radcliffe Line' cut through even tiny villages (such as Wagah), where Sikhs, Muslims and Hindus had been living together for centuries. The Muslim population began to migrate to West Punjab, which now belonged to the new nation of Pakistan, with its distinct Muslim identity. Likewise, Sikhs and Hindus from the western part were forced to cross over to East Punjab, which now formed a part of free and secular India. In her famous *Ode to Waris Shah*, Amrita Pritam depicted the brutal destruction of joy and togetherness that she witnessed during those riot-torn days. The land of the *punj* (five) *ab* (rivers) is sheeted with corpses; its waters are full of blood:

Today I ask Waris Shah to speak from his grave!
And turn to the next page of his book of love.
You saw one Punjabi daughter weep, you wrote page after page,
Today countless daughters weep, they cry out to you Waris Shah:

Rise! O sympathizer of the afflicted! Rise! Look at your Punjab!
The land is sheeted with corpses, the Chenab is full of blood.
Somebody has poured poison into its five rivers –
And their waters are irrigating our farms and fields.
Each pore of this lush land is bursting with venom:
Redness flares up inch by inch, wrath flies high.
The poisonous breeze wafts across forests –
Turning each bamboo flute into a snake.
The snakes cast a spell, and bite again and again,
The limbs of the Punjab suddenly become blue.
Songs are broken into silence, weaving strings have snapped;
Friends are torn asunder, their spinning-wheels lie hushed.
Aloft with nuptial beds the rafts are floating away –
Branches along with swings are breaking apart.
Lost is the flute that once played on the breath of love,
All of Ranjha's brothers have forgotten its art.
The blood spilt on the ground is seeping into the graves,
The princesses of love are weeping in their sacred spots.
Today everyone has become a villain, a thief of beauty and love,
From where can we bring today another Waris Shah?
Today I ask Waris Shah to speak from his grave!
And turn to the next page of his book of love!

Amrita exhorts the Sufi poet – loved by the Muslims, Sikhs and Hindus alike – to come out of his grave and grapple with the unimaginable atrocities being afflicted on millions of Punjabis.

During that mass migration of over 12 million people,[39] Sikhs lost their historical Gurdwaras, including Nankana Sahib, the birthplace of their founder Guru. They lost their rich lands in the canal-irrigated zones of West Punjab that they had cultivated with their own efforts. They lost Lahore, the magnificent capital of their Empire under Maharaja Ranjit Singh. They lost their homes. They were not given a separate Sikh state as the Muslims were. They were left with the horrific memories of Punjabis – Sikh, Muslim and Hindu – being seized by a mad communal frenzy. In that blind rage, countless innocent men, women and children were murdered; their bodies, their psyches, their families, their homes and their shrines were all brutally destroyed. To recover their wholeness has been difficult.

Chapter VIII
Sikh Art

Sikh art is aniconic. The most ubiquitous visual Sikh symbol is shown here; it expresses Guru Nanak's theological construct of the One transcendent Reality. *Ikk Oan Kar* is used extensively as a form of ornamentation in arts, crafts and architecture. It can be seen on gateways, walls and windows of homes, shrines and shops. The image is elaborately inscribed in silk, marble, steel and gold. It is embroidered on oxen covers and precious canopies; it is embossed on books, and on earrings and pendants. Without confining the Divine in any way, the rhythmic unity sustained by the numeral 1, the syllabic *oan*, and the unending geometric arc, launches the spectator toward an all-encompassing infinity. Its inherent openness permeates Sikh art and forges innovative patterns.

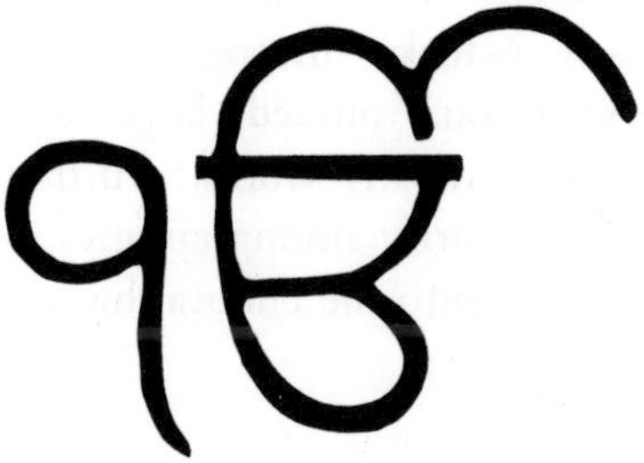

The category 'Sikh Art' goes beyond ritual and religious objects commissioned by the community. It includes sacred and secular items that were produced by Sikhs, those that were made under Sikh patronage or in territories dominated by Sikhs, and those items that depict Sikh themes. Geographically, its span is from Central Asia and Afghanistan in the west to Patna in the east. But much of these rich visual materials remain unexplored. Whereas the art of the Buddhists, Jains, Hindus, Muslims and Christians from the Indian subcontinent has been an important academic subject, Sikh art has only recently begun to gain attention. The tercentenary celebrations in 1999 of the Founding of the Khalsa generated a number of exhibitions and conferences. Among them was 'Arts of the Sikh Kingdoms' curated by Susan Stronge for the Victoria and Albert

Museum in London. The exhibition was subsequently taken to the Asian Arts Museum of San Francisco and the Royal Ontario Museum in Toronto.[1] In India, B. N. Goswamy put together a comprehensive exhibition, entitled 'Piety and Splendour', for the National Museum of India in New Delhi.[2] In 2003, the Satinder Kaur Kapany, the first permanent gallery displaying Sikh art in the West, was inaugurated at the Asian Arts Museum in San Francisco. In July 2004, through the efforts of Paul Taylor, the Smithsonian's National Museum of Natural History opened 'Sikhs: Legacy of the Punjab'. In 2006, B. N. Goswamy and Caron Smith brought together materials on Sikh art and devotion for the Rubin Museum of Art in New York. The title of their exhibition, 'I See No Stranger', appropriately carries Guru Nanak's message of the common human bond. These exhibitions offered large and spectacular displays and generated major scholarly works.[3] Further research into Sikh art is sure to foster familiarity among cultures in contemporary times and provide a window into the cultural history of India.

Janamsakhi Illustrations

The pictorial representations of Janamsakhis constitute one of the earliest expressions of Sikh art. The narratives about the life of the founder Guru (discussed in Chapter I) attracted the popular imagination and invited their visual rendering. Wherever sizable and influential communities developed, the familiar stories were put in easily identifiable forms for them. These happened to be not only in the religious centers in the Punjab such as Amritsar, Anandpur and Damdama, but also in Patna in Bihar, where the Tenth Guru was born, and in Nander in Maharashtra, where he passed away. Patrons from these centers commissioned local artists, and consequently, numerous Janamsakhi renderings have come down from different regions and different periods.

This wide dispersion, of course, makes the dating and exact place of production difficult for many of the items. Nevertheless, it lends a fascinating variation. The First Guru is depicted in the Guler and Kangra styles of Northern India, just as he is in the Eastern Murshidabadi or Southern Deccani styles. The artists who painted him were also Hindu, Muslim, Buddhist or Jain and they presented the Sikh Guru through the lens of their respective religious beliefs. The stories they chose to paint depended on their personal interest and much was contingent on their individual talent. The quantity of illustrations varies in the extant manuscripts: the Bala Janamsakhi (dated 1658) has 29 illustrations; the Bagarian manuscript (dated 1724) has 42; while the B-40 Janamsakhi (dated 1733) has 57.[4] Some of the later versions have over a hundred illustrations. The quality varies too: some artists are preoccupied with the contents and hastily move the narrative forward, while others linger on subtle details to evoke esthetic sentiments. The paintings from the Nainsukh family of artists are especially lauded for their refined work.

Yet there is a remarkable similarity among the illustrations, and scholars have wondered for some time about the possibility of templates being in circulation. The recent discovery of a creased sheet, filled with thumbnail depictions of 74 events in Guru Nanak's life, has proved their speculation. Though the drawings are extremely sketchy, each episode is numbered and identified, with a brief inscription in Persian and Gurmukhi characters.[5] Such templates would have been used by different groups of painters and scribes to retell Guru Nanak's life story.

And so, in bright colors and dramatic sequences, they paint the parables, allegories and miraculous happenings associated with the founder Guru of Sikhism. We see a little boy going to school, with a wooden board in his hand for writing. This board, with a tiny handle, serves as a poignant symbol that its holder would write up a new morality. We find a teenager asleep in the fields, while a cobra – a familiar Pan-Indian artistic motif – protects him from the harsh sun. The artists tell stories in easily identifiable forms to intimate Nanak's divinity. The moment of his revelation is profoundly captured in the B-40 Janamsakhi (#28). According to its written text, '*baba nanak*' is endowed with Guruship in this 'divine palace of the formless One – *baba nanak nrinakar de mahal vic*'. Visually, Guru Nanak is positioned standing in the middle of the frame. His hands joined in reverence reach above him and his tilted face extends both below and above, producing an intriguing multidimensional perspective. The panoramic view with trees and shrubs on the far horizon, bunches of colorful little flowers popping up all over the green grass, and Bhai Mardana playing his *rabab*, constitutes the Divine palace of the formless One. Situated in its tangible latitudes and longitudes, Guru Nanak appears to be in total ecstasy. With his eyes half closed, his lips smiling, he stands (*stasis*) outside of himself (*ec*), a perfect intersection of the physical and the spiritual spheres (for image, see p. 3).

The manuscripts illustrate his marriage festivities: Nanak the groom is on horseback, while his bride Sulakhni is in a palanquin with a group of women. They show his sons, Siri Chand and Lakhmi Chand. But it is his relationship with his sister that is captured most tenderly. In a meeting between the siblings (from the Kapany collection), affection pours out as their arms reach out to greet each other.[6] In this triangular scene, the spectator moves briskly from the wide floral designs among the rhythmic designs of the 60-degree interior angled walls to the ever-narrowing distance between brother and sister. The two stand facing each other: Guru Nanak is with his companions, Bala and Mardana; Nanaki is with a female relative. The architectural backdrop and the physical setting of the protagonists visually reinforce the emotional union between the siblings. With his intrinsic divine nature, the Sikh Guru is presented as a person belonging very much to this world.

The various Janamsakhi illustrations portray the Guru carrying his progressive message to people from different religious and social backgrounds. In various scenarios, he delivers his message about the importance of truth, the futility of empty rituals, the value of honest work and the submission to the singular Divine over any other agent. The artists triumph in relaying the impact of his lessons. A glance at Guru Nanak with, in his left hand, crimson blood dripping from the bread offered by a wealthy man and, in his right hand, nurturing milk dripping from the bread offered by a humble carpenter, leaves a lifelong imprint of the value of honest labor.

In a painting from the family workshop of Nainsukh of Guler (1710–78), we see Guru Nanak and his companions looking at an ash-besmeared, meagerly clad renunciate asleep on the ground.[7] Through this double gaze at a sleeping figure lying on an ochre-colored cloth spread on a tiger skin, the utter futility of renunciation is brought home. The artist displays an ironic contrast, not only between the oblivious sleeper and his wide-eyed audience, but also between his inert body and the dead tiger's lively tail that seems to curl up from behind. The scene resounds with the question: why would anybody alive give up this precious human life? '*Hire jaisa janam hai kaudi badle jae* – this life worth a diamond goes for naught' said the Guru (GG: 156).

Another work, 'Guru Nanak and the Priests of Kurukshetra', shows Guru Nanak challenging the rigidity with which vegetarianism was upheld by the orthodox.[8] The Guru is in the historic field (*kshetra*) where the Mahabharata was fought between the Kurus and Pandavas. The sun above, set in a dark blue horizon at the center of the painting, indicates a solar eclipse. From a conventional perspective, the landscape is intensely sacred, both spatially and temporally. In the foreground of the painting pilgrims are seen bathing in the waters. However, in the middle, Guru Nanak sits under a tree and behind him deer meat is being cooked in a pot over a fire. A host of perturbed ascetics approach the Guru, pointing their fingers at him for his sacrilegious act of cooking meat in such a holy coordinate of place and hour. But the Guru remains calmly positioned with his legs tucked under him. His hands rest on his lap. His robe is unruffled. A pink shawl remains gently draped over his right shoulder and a golden halo surrounds his serene face. The painting elucidates his message that 'meat is neither prohibited in the Puranas, nor in Western scriptures'; 'it is used in ritual feasts and wedding festivities' (GG: 1290).

When Guru Nanak engages with Muslims, Islamic esthetics come to the fore. The popular narrative of the Ka'ba turning around along with the movement of Guru Nanak's feet captured the fancy of the painters too.[9] But the Indian artists may not have known exactly what the Ka'ba in Arabia looked like. Therefore, relying on their imaginations, they drew up a mosque-like domed construct with minarets that move the eyes vertically beyond the painting, and design a ground filled with endless arabesques. In this essential Islamic setting, we find Guru Nanak and Mardana peacefully asleep while an angry Mullah, pointing his finger at them, leans on an intimidating staff. It is a compelling venue for the Guru to instruct the Mullah that there is no place devoid of the Divine. Similarly, Guru Nanak's conversation with the Muslim holy men, Pir Sayyad Ahmad Hassan and Pir Jalal-ud-din, takes place in a typical Mughal courtyard: the back wall has latticed windows and the floor has diamond-shaped yellow tiles, each decorated with an abstract orange flower.[10] During the meeting between Guru Nanak and Emperor Babur, the two are seated face to face, each on his own square carpet with intricate geometric designs.[11] The floor too is elaborately tiled in geometric patterns flowing out in orange, yellow and white, echoing the colors of the robes and shawls of the Sikh Guru and the Mughal monarch.

Over the course of his biographical descriptions, the garments change and so do the facial features as the Guru matures from a baby to a young boy to a dark-bearded youth, into gray-bearded middle age and subsequently to a full-white-bearded and dignified old man (*Baba*). The artists concentrate most often on his sage-like reservoir of spiritual wisdom and personal peace. Later painters began to depict him with a halo. A pan-religious figure, he wears a patchwork cloak with an ascetic's cord (*seli*) on his shoulder and a roundish turban on his head. He has a book with him – either in his hand or placed in front of him. Some iconographic cliches that developed over time include a water-pot (*kamandalu*) by his side, an arm-rest (*bairangan*) under his left arm, a necklace of beads around his neck, a rosary in his right hand, a pair of wooden sandals and a staff. He is portrayed as a central figure sitting cross-legged, along with his inseparable Muslim companion, the musician Mardana, and his Hindu devotee, Bhai Bala. While Bhai Bala sits in his mendicant's robes wrapped in devotion (though sometimes he stands behind the Guru, reverently waving a flywhisk – a symbol of Guru Nanak's sovereignty), Bhai Mardana appears to move his fingers along his *rabab*, the stringed instrument he invariably carries.

Wherever he goes and with whichever group he interacts, Guru Nanak triumphs. His spiritual power is visually translated by the gentle expression on his face, the profound look in his eyes and the calm authority he exudes by being positioned as a central figure. His openness is apparent from the inclusive style of his dress and the diverse setting in which he appears. The visual iconography vibrates with Guru Nanak's Word as it merges into Mardana's *rabab* and flows along landscapes teeming with monkeys, birds, trees and streams. The effect of the Janamsakhi paintings is enchanting.

Guru Angad

Since the Second Guru was a critical person in Guru Nanak's biography, the illustrators depict him with enormous interest and reverence. In the B-40 Janamsakhi, he is pictured at least five times. We first see Lahina before he comes into the Sikh fold and is renamed Angad. He is going to the shrine of goddess Durga with three other men (#21). The bounce in their gait, their flexed knees and raised heels, and the animated birds and trees in the background, impart a briskness to the scene. All four carry banners in their hands. Lahina also has a tiny white flower in his right hand and appears to be enjoying its fragrance as he walks along. The image makes the ideological point that Lahina was the rightful heir to Guru Nanak, for whom sensuous experience was the criterion for Divine knowledge: 'Only the relisher of fragrance can recognize the flower' (GG: 725).

The next painting in the B-40 Janamsakhi (#22) marks a nuanced reverse: the group is now entering the frame from the left. The men are paying homage to Guru Nanak, who is seated under a tree on the far right with Mardana striking the strings of his *rabab*. Lahina, identified in the text as wearing 'pure white', is bowing to the Guru, who reciprocates by showering blessings with his extended right hand. The narrative reads: 'You will not be parted from my body' (*tun mere ang thi juda na hohiga*); 'You are born from my body' (*meriah angahu tun paida hoia hai*); 'Light merged with light' (*joti mahi joti samai*). The painting depicts the quintessential phenomenon of Guru Nanak transforming his disciple Lahina into Angad, literally making him his *Anga* (*limb*).

In illustration #54, they are facing each other symmetrically. Guru Nanak is on the left, Guru Angad is on the right. Guru Nanak's beard is white, Guru Angad's is dark. Guru Nanak has a rosary in one hand and looks into the far distance, Guru Angad has his eyes lowered and his hands are joined in veneration to Guru Nanak. The scene poignantly captures the moment of succession from the venerable Nanak to the middle-aged Angad. While Guru Nanak looks into his timeless and spaceless future, his younger successor, with his folded hands, accepts the responsibility to replace him as the Guru. The sounds of Mardana's *rabab* merge with the spiritual flow from Nanak's lips, creating a cosmic symphony, which chimes with the music of the blooming flowers and the chirping birds. The red bird above is witnessing the scene. According to the Janamsakhi text, Guru Nanak says: '*mai tudh upar hath rakhia hai / Jio e tio aakh* – I have put my hand on you; recite what comes to you'. The founder Guru of Sikhism is clearly bestowing his divine heritage to the Second Guru in the form of the formless Word. The next painting shows Guru Angad resuming his spiritual legacy: his chin is higher, his eyes are wider, and to the figure whose human contours appear to be merging with infinite space, he says: '*guru bhi tu hai gobind bhi tu hai duja koi najari nahin avda* – You are the Guru, you are Gobind; I see no other' (B-40 Janamsakhi, #55). The visual translation of the text reinforces its literary impact.

The Portraits of the Gurus

The early portraits of the Sikh Gurus were painted in the courtly Mughal style, which was developed by Emperor Akbar, and refined by his son Jahangir and grandson Shah Jahan. Its foundations were established by Hamayun (the second Mughal Emperor) who, from his exile in Iran, brought back two artists, Sayyid Ali and Abdus Samad. These accomplished Persian painters integrated the Hindu, Jain and Buddhist local styles, and over the succeeding decades gave shape to the distinct style of 'Mughal' art. With the cultural expansion under Mughal rulers, artists from the Punjab plains and the Pahari areas were trained in the Mughal style of painting and portraiture. Consequently, when they painted the Sikh Gurus, the physical features of the Gurus, as well as their outfits, turbans and poses, looked very much like Mughal princes and nobles. Some works have the intricate patterns and technical finesse that were characteristic of Mughal miniatures. Refined portraits of the Gurus were produced at flourishing centers of art, such as Guler, Kangra, Bilaspur, Nurpur and Mandi.

For the growing Sikh community, the 'image' of their historical Gurus must have been extremely crucial. It is likely, then, that they were portrayed during their lifetime and there is some mention of portraits made of Guru Hargobind, Guru Tegh Bahadur and Guru Gobind Singh – but to date no authentic works have come to light.[12] The disapproval of idolatry among the Sikhs was a factor in the lack of their visual representations. The Ram Rai collection in Dehra Dun is known to be the earliest example of the genre of portraiture in Sikh art.[13] This set of paintings was commissioned by Ram Rai (b. 1646), the elder son of Guru Har Rai (Nanak 7). According to Sikh tradition, Ram Rai was disowned by his father for misquoting scripture to win the favor of Emperor Aurangzeb, so his younger brother, Har Kishen, was nominated as the Eighth Guru. Ram Rai therefore established his own rival following and proclaimed himself Guru.[14] The precious 'earliest' set of paintings of the Gurus has been in the custody of his descendants at the Gurdwara Ram Rai in Dehra Dun. A painter from the Mughal School produced the series as early as 1685, and it subsequently served as a model for the murals extant on the walls of the southern gate of the Gurdwara complex.[15]

Guru Nanak's spiritual line must have been very important for Ram Rai because, in spite of a 100-year gap between them, he is seen seated with the founder Guru. In a portrait of the First Guru, dressed in white and holding a book in his hand, Ram Rai is pictured sitting behind him on the same carpet in a bright red outfit, with his left hand stretched out animatedly. There is a tree above them. Both are listening to Mardana and Bala playing the *rabab* and *sarangi* respectively. The portraits of Guru Angad, Guru Amar Das, Guru Ram Das and Guru Ajran (Nanak 2–5) follow a conventionalized scheme worked out by the artist. These four Gurus are seated respectively on a low platform-like throne, with an attendant standing behind holding a *chauri* flywhisk. There is an air of formality about these images, as they stress the sovereignty of the Gurus.

The exception is Guru Hargobind, Ram Rai's great-grandfather (the Sixth Sikh Guru). He appears with extra verve. There are five portraits of him in this collection and each is uniquely appealing. In one of them, he is seated on a chair with his sons, which reflects the Guru's tender affection for his family. In another, he is standing under a willow tree, and his right hand is raised to touch its leaves. In the third, the Guru has a bird on his hand that he appears to be caressing. In the fourth, he is holding a long sword with a swirling design in his right hand; and in the fifth he is riding a horse. The Guru we encounter in these images is delicate in his manner, but large and muscular in his physique. In fact, the horse that he rides or people standing beside him, appear relatively very small. The portrait of the Seventh Guru (Ram Rai's father) is in all too familiar a pose stereotypical of Mughal Emperors: he stands bedecked in precious jewels, in a regal robe and tight trousers – looking sideways to the right with a flower in his hand. In his own portraits, a broad-shouldered Ram Rai is profiled with a falcon in his hand, an emblem of power. Gurus Har Kishen, Tegh Bahadur and Guru Gobind Singh do not feature in this collection.

The mainstream portraits of the Ten Gurus appear in the first half of the eighteenth century. The Gurus are identified on the borders with brief labels in Persian, Gurmukhi or Devnagri scripts. Like the portraits commissioned by Ram Rai, these are composed in a provincial Mughal style. A set of symbols associated with the particular Gurus is firmly established. Guru Nanak is the most conspicuous figure, of course, and his four successor Gurus from Angad through Arjan are modeled on his image. Their simple garments are those of a religious person, and the rosaries in their hands symbolize their contemplative nature. The transformation comes with the Sixth Guru, who is portrayed in royal regalia, wearing an aigrette on his turban, carrying weapons, riding horses and almost always sporting a falcon on a gloved hand. His broad shoulders and heaviness of girth celebrate his muscular physique. As we noted in Chapter III, Guru Hargobind ascended to the Guruship after the martyrdom of his father (Guru Arjan) in 1606. In those tragic historical circumstances, he resolved to instill a spirit of freedom in his people so that they could resist the oppressive political officials. For the Sikhs he was their *sacha* (true) *padhsah* (emperor), their spiritual and political leader, with a rosary in one hand and sporting a falcon on the other. With the Sixth Guru, an iconography of political resistance and power came into play.

The next three Gurus (Har Rai, Har Kishen and Tegh Bahadur) replicate the style of the first five. Even when they are depicted with parasols and attendants – signs (*lakshanas*) of royal grandeur – a quiet spirituality resonates in their portraits. For example, in the early nineteenth-century Pahari painting of Guru Har Rai (from the family workshop of Nainsukh of Guler), the Guru is on a walk with an attendant carrying a majestic umbrella at a 45-degree angle.[16] Ornamented with a brilliant peacock feather, the parasol seeks to protect the Guru from the dazzling sun. Yet somehow, it is the Guru's plain halo, the symbol of his inner radiance, that takes over from the huge parasol and even the brightness of the sun. Unlike his portrait from the Dehra Dun collection (commissioned by his son), Guru Har Rai here wears very little jewelry. He is dressed in a white muslin knee-length cloak – so fine that it reveals the rich material of his pajama trousers and matches the transparent white skies above, as well as the delicate white blossoms on the tree across from him. Instead of hunting dogs, a cute little dog walks ahead of him, but the artist catches him turning back as though to have a peek at the Guru. The scene vividly captures the spirituality of the Seventh Guru engaged in his normal routine.

The Eighth Guru, Guru Har Kishen, is easily recognizable because of his boyish looks. He is the only Guru without a beard. He was five years old when he succeeded his father in 1661 and died three years later from smallpox. Artists portray him with a soft smile. The Ninth Guru, Tegh Bahadur, is again depicted in a contemplative mode. An eighteenth-century painting from the Punjab plains shows him standing in a long, yellow cloak on an elegant marble terrace with lace-like balustrades.[17] Behind him is his attendant carrying a flywhisk in his honor. But the dull green, rather empty, backdrop and the simple hand-spun striped rug on the ground, take away the opulence of the setting. The dignified Guru, who has no weapons, only a simple staff in his hand, remains the sole focus. And his eyes looking afar carry the spectator to distant horizons.

The pageantry returns with Guru Gobind Singh and does so with phenomenal grandeur and vigor. The Tenth Guru, popularly called '*Shah-i-Shahan*' (King of Kings, a title used in the Persian tradition for the Emperors of Iran), is depicted with all the icons of sovereignty. He rides spirited stallions dappled with ornate decorations and jeweled harnesses. The Guru himself is invariably decked out in royal outfits, precious jewels, elegant shoes and with a towering aigrette in his turban. The supreme warrior carries a host of weapons: a bow is slung across his shoulder, a quiver of arrows appears on one side, a sword on the other, and a dagger is tucked into his waistband. He can carry a long, rather frightening javelin in one hand and an arrow in the other, and give the sense of galloping faster than wind. Hunting dogs cavort alongside his stallion. A majestic parasol carried by his attendant augments his imperial glory. We see the hero depicted, who is extolled in folk songs – holding a white falcon (*chitteh baaja wala*), riding a blue horse (*neele ghore wala*) and wearing a royal aigrette (*kalghi*). Guru Gobind Singh was a great poet, a great patron of the arts, but it is his royal persona and martial finesse that artists have illustrated most lavishly. Such portraits subsequently became popular in bazaar art.

A memorable image is a watercolor of Guru Nanak from the late nineteenth century (now at the Government Museum and Art Gallery in Chandigarh).[18] The Guru has a full beard, a halo, a turban with a high flap and a domed top, and he wears a full-sleeved robe that is mesmerizing. One of the Janamsakhis recount Guru Nanak receiving a cloak of honor during his visit to Baghdad, with verses from the holy Qu'ran embroidered on it.[19] In the watercolor, tinted in a golden hue, the Guru's robe is inscribed all over with calligraphy in Arabic characters, in the *naksh* script. The Guru, deep in thought, with a rosary in his hands, is seated on a terrace. Some branches in brush strokes on the right echo his profile. In the far background is an impressionist rendering of massed foliage. Closer, we get a glimpse of the Mughal-style latticework balcony balustrade. Closer still is a large, round, pillow-cushion associated with emperors, and the Guru – with his left leg tucked under and the right one placed over the left knee – sits perfectly aligned with his royal backdrop. The rich, horizontal folds of his pillow-cushion intersect dynamically with the vertical stripes of his pajama trousers; the circular designs on his turban rhythmically repeat the circles on the pillow, the necklace around his neck and the rosary in his right hand; the triangles decorated with yet more triangular florets on his draping shawl join the rectangular border of the carpet on which he is seated.

In this scene of perpetual motion, the Guru is wrapped in a robe woven with verses from the holy Qu'ran and the sublime Jap that cover the entire front and sleeves. The Islamic invocation *bismillah al rahman al rahim* and the Sikh *adi sacu jugadi sacu hai bhi sacu nanak hosi bhi sacu* appear together.[20] The diverse threads of Guru Nanak's dress powerfully weave that One who is beyond all external designs and forms. In its visual hermeneutics, the work unravels not only the meaning of the term 'text' (derived from *texere*, to weave), but also the singular transcendent matrix from which all the materials derive. The call for *rahimat* or *rahim* is the perennial womb of Truth (*sacu*), which always was (*jugadi sacu*), is (*hai bhi sacu*) and will be evermore (*hosi bhi sacu*). Without halting the mind anywhere, the painting gives a visual and sonorous push to imagine and intuit that Infinite One, *Ikk Oan Kar*.

Scriptural Manuscripts

Very important expressions of Sikh devotion are the illuminated and illustrated manuscripts of the Guru Granth. At this stage of research, not much is known about their artists, scribes or patrons. Jeevan

Singh Deol, a pioneer in this field, distinguishes three types: early manuscripts with *nisans* (from the Persian 'sign' or 'emblem'); those with illumination or floral adornment (*minakari* or *bel buta*); and illustrated manuscripts.[21] The first type are relatively simple, with their artistic grandeur coming from the autograph of one of the Gurus on their opening folios. These *nisans* generally consist of the prelude to the Guru Granth (Mul Mantar),[22] written in the Guru's own hand on a fragment of unadorned paper. The devotees placed these in their sacred volume as a token of the Guru's blessing.

The second genre of manuscripts consists of elaborate decorations and illuminations reminiscent of Persian work. Instead of the simple cursive lettering (*naqqashi*), a highly ornamental script (*tazheeb*) begins to appear.[23] The Persian sunburst (*shamsa*), the divine light (*nur* of the holy Qu'ran) and the highly ornate Islamicate blue and gold lettering (*unvan*), filter through Sikh sacred volumes from the seventeenth century to the mid-nineteenth. These artistic patterns indicate that the Sikh volumes were a product of professional book illuminators (*muzahhibs*), who were trained in illustrating Arabic and Persian manuscripts. During the regime of Maharaja Ranjit Singh, extensive use of gold was made in the writing and illumination of texts – literally called '*sunehri beeds*' or 'golden volumes'. It is believed that the most lavish Sikh sacred volume was created for the Maharaja by a scribe using an ink mixed with gold, diamonds and emeralds.[24]

The addition of figural adornment constitutes the third category. Around the middle of the eighteenth century, the style of adorning manuscripts of the Guru Granth changed, largely as a result of the introduction of large numbers of Kashmiri painters and scribes into the Punjab. Some of the artists were itinerants from the Pahari schools or the Mughal ateliers, having lost their employment with the collapse of the Mughal Empire. Some of these would offer their talents to clients in the plains during the winter months, while others were often engaged for years at a time by a single patron. In their decorative style and their choice of colors, the illuminations produced by the Kashmiri artists differ from the earlier Islamicate ones. The Kashmiri painters and scribes also began to illustrate manuscripts of the Guru Granth, with portraits of the Ten Gurus on the opening folio of the main text. Sometimes the Gurus are shown with their families and at other times with Indic gods and goddesses, usually with Devi, Sarasvati or Ganesha. In a folio from the extravagantly illustrated manuscript at the National Museum in New Delhi, the configuration *Ikk Oan Kar* includes the traditional figures of Devi, Brahma, Shiva, Vishnu and Laxmi, at the same time reaching out to the formless One. Since Sikhism is an aniconic tradition, such figural images in copies of its sacred text have been controversial, and have raised questions about the authenticity of the works.

The practice of illuminating or illustrating the scriptural manuscripts disappeared abruptly at the close of the nineteenth century. The printing press took over the production of scriptural copies. The vines, flowers and geometric borders in modern volumes are faint memories of a lost beauty.

Arts in the Sikh Kingdoms

During the reign of Maharaja Ranjit Singh (1799–1839), Sikh art received unprecedented royal patronage and the Gurus and their message found expression in many different media. The Maharaja's tolerance promoted harmonious coexistence among Muslims, Hindus and Sikhs, and his patronage extended to artists of all religious denominations, which resulted in many spectacular creations. Thus, while building a strong army, collecting revenue and expanding his Sikh empire, Maharaja Ranjit Singh also invigorated the artistic talents of people practicing different faiths across his vast domains. He provided countless opportunities for folk vitality to develop into refined art. During his prosperous reign, there was the construction of magnificent forts, palaces, gurdwaras, mosques and temples; an enormous production of gold and silver objects; the designing of precious jewelry; crafting of exquisite arms; and the creation of luxurious tents, canopies, caparisons and large woolen shawls that could be slipped through a tiny ring! Centers such as Lahore, Amritsar, Srinagar, Multan and Sialkot produced artifacts for the Maharaja and his court. The highlights include the embellishment of the Golden Temple, the bejeweled canopy for the Guru Granth, the golden volume (*sunehri beed*) presented to the Gurdwara at Nander in Maharashtra, the gold throne made by Hafez Muhammad Multani, and exquisite jewelry for both men and women, including the legendary Koh-i-noor diamond that the

Maharaja very reluctantly received from the Afghani royal family in exchange for rescuing their ruler, Shah Shuja (in 1813).

Coinage

Maharaja Ranjit Singh displayed his independence by issuing coins, but he did so in the name of the Ten Sikh Gurus. He recognized their supreme authority, and, paradoxically, through his submission to the Ten, the Maharaja justified his own supremacy and legitimized his divine right to rule his vast empire. His model was Banda Bahadur (1708–16), who was the first to create Sikh state political power in the early seventeenth century. The coins concretized an important ideal of Sikh life – the victory of *degh* (cooking pot) and *tegh* (sword). While *degh* represents food from the common kitchen so that nobody would go hungry, *tegh* denotes security: the sword being an instrument of resistance to political, religious and racial oppression. The first Sikh coin celebrates in Persian the spiritual transmission from Guru Nanak to Guru Gobind Singh: 'Guru Nanak received without delay from Nanak/The pot and the sword, conquest and victory.'[25] The early coins were inscribed in Persian, though later on Gurmukhi and Devanagari characters begin to appear, often with the words *Guru Nanakji* and *Akal Sahai* (Timeless One is the Protector). On the coins issued under Maharaja Ranjit Singh, the ubiquitous *pipal* leaf appears with images of a sword, dagger, lion, trident, fish and banner.[26] A striking gold coin from Amritsar, minted in 1806, bears the name *Guru Gobind Singh* in Persian and has a flower with eight petals on the reverse.[27] Maharaja Ranjit Singh also produced Sikh tokens in the shape of coins in different metals. Most of them depict the first Sikh Guru with his companions Mardana and Bala on one side and the Tenth Guru with his royal falcon on the other. Many are engraved with the words *Sat Kartar* (True Creator). A gold token has Guru Nanak seated under a tree, with his Mul Mantra in Gurmukhi characters on the reverse.[28]

In the same vein, later Sikh rulers continued to promote the Gurus and their words as markers of their political power. During the reign of Maharaja Bhupindra Singh of Patiala (1891–1938), the civilian medals were imprinted with the royal image of Guru Gobind Singh, as well as with the *Degh Tegh Fateh* configuration.[29] The medals looked very European in their floral decorations and the ribbons around them, but essentially conveyed Sikh religious images and ideals.

Weapons

The weapons wielded by Guru Gobind Singh became powerful symbols of the Sikh Empire. Maharaja Ranjit Singh's passion for fine arms shows up in the spears, swords, daggers, bows, arrows, shields and armor crafted during his reign. A dramatic pommel of a sword known to have belonged to him is designed in the shape of a horse's head: its mouth is slightly open, its nostrils flare, its eyes shine with rubies and the gold quillon has the Maharaja's portrait on ivory, set in a circle of precious stones.[30] What is interesting is the imagery of the Gurus and Sikh sacred verses displayed on some of his weapons. For example, a sword from the Arms Gallery in the Old Fort in Patiala shows Guru Nanak seated with Bhai Mardana and Bhai Bala close to its hilt, while along the blade are depicted his successor Gurus, seated in the company of their devotees.[31] Also from the Arms Gallery in Patiala is a dagger inscribed with Gurmukhi characters, deciphered as 'words of prayer'.[32] Some quoits worn on the tall conical turbans of Maharaja Ranjit Singh's soldiers (to be deployed as weapons) are embellished with verses from the Guru Granth in gold.[33] The Tenth Guru had composed poetry on the feats of the invincible Durga, and she too appears on an exquisite brass shield covered with scenes of combat, hunting and equestrian skills.[34] A synthesis of Mughal and Pahari craftsmanship, this shield from Maharaja Ranjit Singh's reign vibrantly shows camels in combat, a lion and a dragon battling, a warrior taking on two ferocious lions, two men wrestling and the many-armed Goddess Durga attacking the buffalo demon. The weapons from this Maharaja's reign display a keen artistic sensibility.

Shawls

Like the Mughal Emperor Akbar, Maharaja Ranjit Singh was very fond of shawls. When he annexed Kashmir in 1819, a portion of the annual tribute sent to his court at Lahore was paid in shawls. Lahore had been a major center of the shawl trade and its luxurious items were greatly admired by Europeans. As early as 1784, the Governor General, Warren Hastings, was commissioning shawls for his wife, describing them in a letter to her as 'beautiful beyond imagination'.[35] Napoleon Bonaparte's Empress Josephine, known to have had a huge collection of Kashmiri shawls, was painted on several occasions draped in their elegance.[36] Migrants to Ranjit Singh's army, Napoleon's Generals Allard and Ventura exported shawls to Paris with designs specially produced for the French market. The material of the delicate wool from the pashmina goat had great appeal for Europeans. The designs varied from the simple floral motifs of the Mughal court in the seventeenth century to overblown European motifs. Some even had maps woven into them. A shawl belonging to Gulab Singh (a successor of Ranjit Singh) shows elaborate episodes from *Sikander Nama*, the Book of Alexander the Great.[37] Unfortunately, with the famine of 1877 in colonial Punjab, the shawl weaving trade collapsed.

A long tradition of other arts, such as silk weaving, also received immense impetus during the prosperous times of the Sikh Maharaja. Since there was negligible production of silkworms in the area, the yarn was imported from Bokhara via Peshawar, and later from China via Bombay. Silk yarn was spun, dyed and woven at several centers in the Punjab, such as Amritsar, Lahore, Patiala, Multan and Jallundhar.

The most popular of all embroidery types in the Punjab is Phulkari (*phul*/flower + *kari*/work). Made by rural Muslim, Hindu and Sikh women, the colorful Phulkaris are worn at weddings and on festive occasions. The cloth is usually the locally made khaddar cotton, dyed a rusty brown, which is then embroidered with geometric folk patterns in a darning stitch in floss silk. Its more refined version is the *bagh*, which is so sumptuously embroidered that the cloth becomes a garden (*bagh*), with the background material disappearing entirely. The intricate stylized designs of Phulkaris resonate with the spirit of joy and togetherness.

With his pluralistic vision, the Maharaja built gurdwaras, mosques and mandirs (Hindu temples) for his people. He is remembered for contributing the expensive silver doors at the Temple of Goddess Kali, and for paying an inordinately high price for a manuscript copy of the holy Qu'ran.[38] His staunch faith in Sikhism did not deter him from promoting the religious sentiments of all his subjects. The themes and styles in painting and architecture from his era disclose a rich religious diversity. The refurbishing of the Harmandar was, of course, his major accomplishment. He made a huge monetary grant towards it and invited skilled Muslim architects, masons, wood carvers and other craftsmen to Amritsar. In the vicinity of the Harmandar, a residence for the artists was built along with a mosque. Yar Mohommad Khan Mistri was the technical expert responsible for the gold plating.

The Maharaja's service is commemorated in an inscription in Gurmukhi over the entrance of the Harmandar: 'The Great Guru in his wisdom looked upon Maharaja Ranjit Singh as the chief servitor and Sikh, and in his benevolence, bestowed on him the privilege of serving the Temple.'[39] The Golden Temple of today rises from the center of the sacred pool, approached by a causeway bordered with marble balustrades. Its exterior marble walls on the lower side are embellished in lapis lazuli, onyx and other semi-precious stones, set using the *pietre dure* technique. Its upper parts are covered with plates of gilded copper, the reflections of which shimmer in the surrounding water. The interior of its second storey, with walls and ceiling sparkling with mirrors and colored glass in kaleidoscopic motifs, is open in the center to reveal the Guru Ganth enshrined on the ground floor below. A gorgeous canopy studded with pearls and jewels was offered by the Maharaja to place above the Scriptural Guru. Arabesque designs flow vibrantly on the walls of the Harmandar, creating rich borders to the deer, lions, cobras and elephants, as they hold flower vases, fruit and fairies.

Painting

The Sikh devotee also embellished hundreds of other Gurdwaras as well, with artists from different religious backgrounds being employed to paint their walls. Likewise, beautiful illustrations of the Guru Granth, portraits of the Gurus, and Janamsakhi depictions were taken up in different parts of his vast empire. The miniature portraits of the Sikh Gurus regarded as the finest set of paintings in the Pahari style were created under his patronage.[40] In addition to the ruler, there were his sons, other aristocratic families such as the Sandhawalias and Majithias, and the Europeans at his Court who enthusiastically commissioned artists. Themes from other religious traditions and mythologies were also produced, as was erotic art on the walls of his forts and palaces, and in the homes and estates of his nobles. Artists from Guler, Kangra, Kotla and Nurpur moved to the Sikh Court at Lahore and Amritsar for patronage, transforming their techniques to suit the esthetics of their new clients. The Sikh School of Painting flourished in the Sikh Kingdom.

Because of his smallpox and physical disabilities, it is said that Ranjit Singh was averse to portraiture. Nevertheless, artists were wildly enthusiastic about him and his glamorous Court. The

Hungarian, August Schoefft (1809–88), was one of them. As well as *The Court of Lahore*, which won him great acclaim when he exhibited it in Vienna in 1855 (also noted in Chapter VII), Schoefft painted the Maharaja in the presence of the Guru Granth at the Golden Temple. With the houses and minarets of the city of Amritsar in the background, the Golden Temple rises from the shimmering water, and in the foreground of the painting we see the Maharaja listening respectfully to the Scripture in the open air. Shoefft's oil painting proves the literary testimony of an English visitor that 'the Granth was constantly read to him'.[41] Many other artists portrayed him sitting grandly in his court, or riding horses in all his strength and glory. Emily Eden sketched Ranjit Singh sitting in his typical pose with his leg folded under, and she also sketched his horses decorated with precious emeralds.

His son and successor, Maharaja Sher Singh, also patronized Shoefft and his famous glittering portrait shows him draped in jewels, seated on Maharaja Ranjit Singh's golden throne, holding an upright sword.[42] Enamored by Western perfumes and other exotic items, Sher Singh is believed to be the first Sikh pictured with his beard tied. In another work, Shoefft painted Sher Singh surrounded by his Council in an elegantly latticed hall in the Lahore Fort. He also painted the young prince Dalip Singh, dressed in ornate red outfit with Punjabi gold-embroidered shoes and a jeweled sword in his hand, sitting, rather out of place, on a branch of a tree.[43] He is too much lost in his own child's world to notice the blatant contrast between the rustic landscape and his opulent outfit. Shoefft also did sketches of Maharani Jindan sitting confidently on a cushion, resting against a pillow with her head held high.[44] The European artists were inspirational for Sikh painters. After Shoefft's huge canvases, their miniature painting style was transformed. A three-dimensional perspective was introduced and painting in oils became common practice. The earlier Mughal naturalism and Pahari lyricism, combined with Western realism, added a whole new dimension to the Sikh School of Painting.

With the exception of Rani Jindan, depictions of women have generally been neglected, but the extant few have a special appeal as they offer glimpses into life beyond the opulence of the Maharaja's Court. In a scene from General Allard's household, we find Mrs Allard in a combined Indian-European outfit.[45] Her head is covered

Figure 18: Maharani Jindan

and she is seated coyly against a pillow with a rosary in her hand. While her children are in front of her playing with their toys, her husband is grandly seated on a chair behind her. On either side of the frame are two Punjabi maids in service: the one on the left is pouring tea from a dainty European teapot, while the one on the right is holding an Allard child in her arms. Both have their heads covered, but their faces are not veiled. Dressed in typical Punjabi outfits (salwars, shirts and dupattas), these tall Punjabi women standing upright indicate enormous strength. The painting replays the cultural stereotypical binary in which the 'lower class' women enjoy a freedom that the 'upper class' lady, in her heavy gowns and oppressive paraphernalia, does not.

During Maharaja Ranjit Singh's period, Punjabi folk heroines Sassi and Heer, cherished by Muslims, Sikhs and Hindus alike, appear frequently in the language of colors. As a helpless Punnu is taken away on the camel, an anguished Sassi runs towards her treacherously drunk lover, while her friends try to hold her back.[46] Under Sikh patronage, paintings began to display a shift from a mythological naturalism to a new realism. Whether seated in the harem, stepping up to dance, or standing in attendance, the characters are animated. The interior settings also become less imposing. On the canvas of a Punjabi artist, we see a lady comfortably sitting on a bed with one leg up and her elbow resting on it.[47] A close dynamic is created as she leans forward to converse with her attendant, who is standing at the foot of the bed. In another painting, two couples are framed along a vertical plane, saying goodbye.[48] Perhaps the men are going to battle. In this scene of departure, the women hold their husbands in a tight embrace. Clearly, these women are not some idealized romantic figures, but strong, hearty, three-dimensional subjects.

In contrast, however, a heart-wrenching scene of the Maharaja's funeral (in the British Museum in London)[49] discloses the prevalence of patriarchal codes: four queens and seven slave girls are heroically prepared to commit *sati*. W. G. Archer's comment, 'The picture lacks the majesty of a great painting', trivializes the colossal sacrifice and bravery of these women.[50] The Maharaja lies in his shroud, but his face, with the full beard, is recognizable; behind him is an attendant with a flywhisk, exalting the person who is no more. The Gaddan Rani, commemorated for honoring her Rajput heritage and breeding, leads the other queens and maids as she ascends the lethal ladder up to the sandalwood pyre. The women are seen seated around the royal corpse according to their rank: the queens at the head of their husband and the maids at his feet. All are strangely serene and respectful of their royal master. While the flames below are beginning to ignite the thick mats of reed doused with oil that will soon reduce their living bodies to ash, the dark, threatening clouds above choreograph the gruesome reality of their so-called 'honor'. Painted by a local Kangra artist, the picture poignantly shows how the practice of *sati*, discarded by the Gurus, had been incorporated into the pageantry of the great Sikh Maharaja.

With his death (on 27 June 1839) and without a strong ruler to succeed him, Maharaja Ranjit Singh's powerful kingdom was soon lost to the British (1849). The ensuing nostalgia gave rise to the large-scale production of sets of paintings on ivory. These portrayed the Maharaja, his family members, ministers, warriors, advisors and other talented men. The clusters of figures in a small, oval format evoked the presence of the Sikh glory of the past. With their industry-like production, the workmanship of the ivory paintings declined and other art forms began to emerge in the Punjab, among them lithographs, woodcuts and photography.

The fall of the Lahore Kingdom brought to light the splendor of other Sikh Kingdoms. The chiefs of the Phulkian States of Patiala, Nabha, Jind, Faridkot and Kapurthala had their ruling powers confirmed by the British. After Lahore, Patiala emerged as the most important Sikh Kingdom of the Panjab. If Maharaja Ranjit Singh is famous for his Koh-i-noor, the Maharaja of Patiala is famous for his 'Patiala necklace'. Maharaja Bhupinder Singh (1891–1938), who inherited the De Beers diamond 'nearly as big as a golf ball' had Cartier mount it in a necklace, along with his two Burmese rubies. The Maharaja was often photographed wearing this Art Deco parade necklace with its half a pound of diamonds. It was last seen intact being worn by his son, Maharaja Yadavindra Singh, in 1941.[51]

His ancestor, Maharaja Narinder Singh (1845–62), widely regarded as the 'most enlightened' ruler of Patiala, was a great patron of the arts. With him, Patiala became a cultural hub for painters, poets, musicians, builders, craftsmen and gardeners from different religious backgrounds and different parts of North India. Eminent classical singers were invited to the court and the Patiala *gharana* of Hindustani music acquired much fame. Eminent artists from Jaipur, from the Pahari regions and from the Mughal court migrated to Patiala to work on the extensive murals for his forts, palaces and shrines. The varied artists, working simultaneously, created eclectic works. On the walls in the old fort, located in the heart of the Patiala bazaar, or in the hall of mirrors in the Motibagh Palace a few miles away, we see not only the Sikh Gurus but also Vaishnava, Shaiva, Shakta, Buddhist and Jain deities.[52] But the Maharaja's supreme devotion to the Word of the Gurus is perfectly captured on canvas. In a scene of a huge procession, the haloed and dignified Maharaja Narinder Singh is seated on an elephant, with his entourage of princes, courtiers and uniformed soldiers in serried ranks. As our eyes move with the movement of the colorful convoy, we recognize that it is the Guru Granth, under a domed howdah with an attendant, that leads the procession. As the distinguished art historian Goswamy notes, the Maharaja is merely a humble follower, a devotee in service to his Scriptural Guru.[53]

The way Maharaja Narinder Singh promoted the arts served as a model for his successors at Patiala and for the rulers of Nabha, Kapurthala, Faridkot and Jind. Paintings of the Sikh Gurus, illustrated manuscripts, rich murals, series of royal portraits and works capturing the unsung 'lower' segment of society, were produced all over the Sikh Kingdoms. Sikh painters such as Kishen Singh, Bishan Singh and Kapur Singh gained much popularity. The lost glory of the Sikh Raj was reproduced and the realism of their situation recorded in gouache, watercolor and oils. Along with the arts, the Maharajas promoted Sikh scholarship. The celebrated writer Bhai Kahn Singh was appointed tutor to the heir apparent of Nabha State. The first complete exegesis of Sikh Scripture was prepared under the patronage of the princely rulers of the state of Faridkot. In 1897, the Maharaja of Faridkot donated a large sum of money for electric power to be installed at the Golden Temple, as well as for a new building for its community kitchen.

The city of Patiala continues to be famous for the crafts that once supplied the Court of the Maharaja: jewelry, *zari* work (gold embroidery), *juttis* (gold-embroidered footwear), and *parandis* (silk braids with fancy tassels) and *nalas* (drawstrings). It is also known for its tailors, who make the loose Punjabi salwars worn by Sikh women, and for its dyers. With his special knowledge of colors inherited from his ancestors, the Muslim 'Masterji' is the beloved dyer of the Punjab – even washing machines cannot wash out the color of his turbans (worn by men) or dupattas (worn by women). For weddings and special occasions, shopping sprees in the narrow, bustling bazaars of Patiala are a must for Sikhs from near and far.

Twentieth-century Painters

The cultural and political shifts of the twentieth century generated a new momentum, with many men and women creating exciting works. We shall explore below just a few of them and try to gain a sense of their esthetic vision.

Amrita Sher-Gil

Daughter of a Sikh father and a Hungarian mother, Amrita Sher-Gil in her short life (1913–41) transformed the course of Indian art. In her oft-quoted words: 'Europe belongs to Picasso, Matisse and Braque and many others. India belongs only to me.' The prodigious young female artist took up the challenge to bring to Indian painting a bold new esthetic with an existentialist realism. Fiercely outspoken, she publicly denounced the work of the prominent Bengal School of her times: 'entirely illustrative in quality, and depends for its popularity not on pictorial merit, but on romantic appeal'.[54] She rejected the orientalized romanticism dominating the Indian art scene and heralded a modern movement where the individual artist had the freedom to depict reality from his or her own perspective. In her paintings and her letters, she raised questions of identity, autonomy and authenticity. Sher-Gil is the most celebrated icon of modern Indian painting. Her works constitute the core collection of the National Gallery of Modern Art in New Delhi. She is the first Indian artist to have a solo exhibition at the Tate Modern in London. Her ability to combine the classical artistic traditions of India with her Parisian training led to several inventive works, which showed the way for many succeeding generations of Indian artists. Indeed, her unique style has a place in both Western and Indian art history.

Sher-Gil was born in Budapest in 1913. Her aristocratic Sikh father had fallen in love with the flaming red-haired, vivacious Hungarian opera singer, who accompanied Princess Bamba Jindan (Maharaja Dalip Singh's daughter) during her visit to the Punjab. During the First World War, the family stayed in Hungary and returned to India in 1921, two years after the Jallian Wallah Bagh tragedy. They settled in Simla, the summer capital of the British Raj. Recognizing her precocious talents, the family subsequently moved to Paris and Amrita, at the age of 16, was enrolled at the École Nationale des Beaux Arts where she studied under the postimpressionist painter,

Lucien Simon. She spent her summers in Hungary. During these formative years, Sher-Gil took time to explore her hybrid Punjabi and Hungarian identity. Catholic and Jewish on her mother's side, she inherited the Sikh tradition from her father. The spheres of music and art from her mother's side were complemented by language and photography from her 'star-gazing' father.

Paris was the perfect place for the free-spirited teenager. With her exotic looks, her large searching eyes, full-lipped mouth and flamboyant manner, Sher-Gil befriended painters, musicians, dancers, exiles and adventurers from all over the world who came to Paris. The city offered her a Bohemian lifestyle very different from the stifling aristocratic atmosphere of her home. She became aware of her sensuality and with her artistic genius was able to bring that private energy into the public sphere. Her paintings show her working in vivid colors. She found her subject in the female form and began to paint a series of sensuous, highly-charged nudes. In *Sleep* (1932), she painted her younger sister, Indira, from a traditional Western perspective, recalling Manet's provocative 'Olympia'. Indira lies in natural repose, her left arm resting on a pink shawl with an embroidered design of a scaly dragon, which not only echoes Indira's hair, but also follows the sinuous fluctuations of her flesh. Two years later, inspired by Paul Gauguin, Sher-Gil painted 'Self-Portrait as Tahitian' (1934). She painted her body in its exotic, non-Western form, while retaining the basics of the European male painters. Her facial features make her easily recognizable, for she imbues her portrait with much more personality than Gauguin did with his figures.

Being away from India helped her to mature and realize its artistic wealth. In a letter to her parents, she admits:

> Modern art has led me to the comprehension and apprehension of Indian painting and sculpture … It seems paradoxical, but I know for certain, that had we not come away to Europe, I should perhaps never have realized that a fresco from Ajanta or a small piece of sculpture in the Musée Guimet is worth more than the whole Renaissance.[55]

On returning to India, she traveled extensively through the subcontinent, visiting museums, temples and caves. With her keen eyes, she took in the many different artistic genres of her fatherland. She was rapt by the frescoes in the Buddhist and Hindu caves at Ajanta: 'vital,

Figure 19: Amrita Sher-Gil and her father, Sardar Umrao Singh

vibrant, subtle and unutterably lovely' was how she described them in a letter.[56] In Bombay, she met Karl Khandalavala, who exposed her to the seductive appeal of the Rajput, Mughal, Basholi and Pahari schools of miniatures. An avid collector of miniature paintings and a leading art critic, Khandalavala subsequently became Sher-Gil's most ardent champion. With her discovery of Indian art, Sher-Gil's

Western art training went through a major change. Her fascination for Indian painting and sculpture was superimposed on the techniques she had absorbed from artists such as Paul Gauguin, Cezanne, Manet and Modigliani. She developed a unique signature style that demonstrated her multicultural vision. Her paintings became more and more modernist, simple and stylized in form. The vibrant colors and textures were given foremost importance.

On her return to India, Sher-Gil witnessed the rise of the nationalist movement. Many Indian artists began to paint strong mythological figures in golden hues. India's indigenous name 'Bharat' identified as the body of the goddess – with rivers, mountains, forests and deserts as her organic whole – acquired a new fervor. A powerful 'Bharat Mata' (Mother India) became the symbol of the independent movement against the British Raj. In contrast to grand visualizations, Amrita started to explore the vacant lives of the ordinary people living on feudal estates in colonial India. In *Mother India* (1935), she depicts a pathetic peasant woman, her head lowered in despair, sitting huddled with her sickly son and daughter, whose large eyes brim with fear. Sher-Gil's *Mother India* is a poignant antithesis to the image of the overarching and controlling female figure, created by the sons of 'Mother India' in their nationalist ideology.

The bleakness of India enchanted Sher-Gil in an utterly unexpected way. In her own words:

> It was the vision of a winter in India – desolate, yet strangely beautiful – of endless tracks of luminous yellow-grey land, of dark-bodied, sad-faced, incredibly thin men and women who move silently looking almost like silhouettes and over which an indefinable melancholy reigns. It was different from the India, voluptuous, colorful, sunny and superficial, the India so false to the tempting travel posters that I had expected to see.[57]

At a rapid rate she began to paint 'Hill Men', 'Hill Women', 'The Beggars', 'Coolie Boy' and 'Women With Sunflower'. Her subjects were the emaciated men pulling rich Sahibs in their rickshaws, vendors and beggars on the glamorous streets of Simla, and male and female servants in the mansions of her wealthy family and friends. Sher-Gil's paintings capture the depleted spirit of these men and women in servitude to the upper echelons of society. In this phase she moves away from the style of realism in which she was trained.

Her figures become elongated, flatter and more inspired by color. As she acknowledges: 'I am personally trying to be, through the medium of line, colour and design, an interpreter of the life of the people, particularly the life of the poor and the sad....'[58]

Her female subjects are vitally complex. They appear to come from different classes, castes and regions, but an existential vacuity overflows in each case. In her later works, Punjabi subjects became prominent. Though they are dressed in typical Punjabi salwar-kameez and dupatta, it is difficult to identify their particular Sikh, Hindu or Muslim affiliation. In a subtle way the artist conveys their common predicament: these Punjabi women are equally victims of patriarchy. Without being sensational, her works elicit enormous empathy. On Sher-Gil's canvas, ordinary subjects, in ordinary situations, articulate the extraordinary harshness of reality that words simply fail to express. Even so-called happy moments, such as being with friends or marriage rites display a deep emotional dislocation. We shall examine two illustrations: 'The Bride' and 'Woman on the Charpoi'.

Both were painted toward the end of Sher-Gil's life. Her Bride is dressed in flamboyant red, against a pale green wall. The roundness of her upper arms and breasts, lyrically replayed in her voluptuous hips, echoes the domed gold *chok* ornamenting her dark hair. The tight-fitting shirt at the bodice, hips and arms are seen through the gauzy scarf swirling around the bride. Ironically, the vibrant circles of the Bride's sensual body are slashed with the downward slant of her face, a laceration duplicated by the sequined scarf as it cuts sharply across diagonally from the top of the domed hairpiece to the ground below. With a resigned look in her eyes, she gazes into an empty future. Her bright crimson outfit, the sequined scarf and the jewel on her head augment her dark psyche. Her tight outfit controls her overflowing sensuality, just as the cruel societal codes control her subjectivity. She is withdrawn, both from herself and from the world around her. She is leaving her natal home to go and serve her husband and his family for the rest of her life, and her own parents will have to bear the unceasing burden of dowry and gifts.

This painted Bride takes on the form of the 'helpless toy', depicted by the artist as a 12-year-old. The young Sher-Gil had just seen a bride, barely a year older than herself, being married off to a 50-year-old man who already had three wives. Empathetically, she wrote in her diary about the forlorn child bride with her 'lovely liquid eyes', silently accepting the oppression enforced on her by her family.[59] From the lips of Amrita Sher-Gil's mute Bride, we can hear the poem 'Kanya Dan', composed by Amrita Pritam:

> Blotched in auspicious henna
> Shrouded in shimmering crimson,
> Bound in chains of yellow gold,
> Part of his flesh, daughter of her womb.
> O great father, O great mother,
> How many blessings you gather!
> ....
> A diamond never cries,
> A cow never speaks
> A virgin is ever voiceless.

The two Amritas are the most celebrated Indian female artists of the twentieth century. While Sher-Gil dominates the visual scene, Pritam, with her volumes of poetry, short stories and novels, dominates the literary world. Both are highly successful in exposing the covert manipulation and exploitation of women in overtly festive scenes.

Sher-Gil's 'Woman on the Charpoi' (1940) is even more complicated than 'The Bride'. In a letter to Khandalavala, she excitedly describes the colors of her painting but nothing more.[60] It is as though Sher-Gil saw the world only in colors. In the painting, a young woman reclines on a 'yellowish off-white charpai' with her left knee up, while an attendant with a fan sits beside her on the floor. In the far left corner is a pot of water. The heat of the atmosphere resonates with the erotic posture of the woman, again dressed in brilliant red. In fact, the 'incandescent red' in the parting of her hair – the cultural symbol of marriage – inflames the posts of the bed rising 'round her like tongues of flame'. The red is also repeated in the wooden handle of the fan, the glass by the pot of water and the henna on the woman's feet. And yet, in spite of the seething sensuality of the scene, there is sheer ennui and indolence. Something is badly out of joint. The dark-blue drapery, 'embroidered with little magenta and cream colored flowers' falling off the bed, indicates her deflowered state. An emotional impoverishment dominates the scene. The man has been there and gone. The fan held by the attendant shows no motion. The women do not look at each other. The dark attendant ('ruddy blackish brown tones in the flesh very attractive') recedes into the 'darkish transparent yellow' background. Her foot, stretched indolently from under the bed, sneaks up to join in with the listless hand of her mistress on the bed. The blank stares and defeated body positions suggest their inauthentic mode of existence. Everything is in stasis. The upper-class, newly married woman and her maid – both pawns of their androcentric society.

A different mood is evoked in two paintings in which we discern distinct Sikh subjects. Also from 1940, they are entitled 'The Musicians' and 'The Ancient Story Teller'.[61] In both compositions, there are dynamic movement, emotions and aural resonance. In the first we see and hear a trio of Sikh musicians in white turbans against a midnight blue background, seated closely together on a typical Punjabi hand-woven cotton rug (*durri*) with geometric designs. The musician closest to us, with a *tanpura* in his hands, is a large, well-built figure – very different from the silhouettes that Sher-Gil painted in Simla or after her travels to the South of India. He is also the darkest of the three figures – in fact, he is so dark that the *kara* on his right wrist is barely visible. His startling white shirt forms a spellbinding contrast to his dark skin. As though that were not enough, the lover of colors paints a garland of flaming orange marigolds around his neck. The white is repeated in the turban of the middle musician and shifts to that of the drummer, the youngest of the trio. He is also the fairest and, with his eyes closed, exudes a quiet spiritual joy. The young drummer's wide horizontal *dholak* forms a rhythmic perpendicular with the leader's vertical *tanpura.* There is a proximity, a fluidity in the figures and a tonal equilibrium among them. The glowing white effectively illuminates their professional and spiritual bond. Peace radiates from their faces, along with the joyous notes from their instruments. They have something greater to celebrate. This seems to be one of Sher-Gil's happy paintings.

Her attraction for the composition and lyricism of Pahari miniatures comes out in 'The Ancient Storyteller'. The painting is reminiscent of the Janamsakhi illustration of Guru Nanak, seated in Kuruksheta with the pot of meat being cooked behind him. Sadly, it happens to be one of Sher-Gil's last completed works. It is as if she had moved from her mother's Hungarian world to search for her identity in Paris, to a discovery of the Indian subcontinent on her return to India and was now beginning to enter her father's Sikh world. This open-air scene takes us into a spacious, symmetrically-structured courtyard. In the center are two figures: a male and a female, sitting back-to-back on the ground. As their backs curve sinuously and the gentle colors of their respective outfits extend horizontally, they create two separate semicircles.

The figure on the right is an elderly man with a white turban and flowing white beard. Three small children avidly listen to him as he tells his story. His eloquently raised hand is a metonymic marker for his interesting content and his vibrant style of communication. Behind him is his wife, with a red dupatta covering her head and flowing to the ground. She is darker than him and more enigmatic. Instead of the three children, three large containers form her semicircle: an earthenware pot to pound the grain; a yogurt container to churn butter; and a flatter bowl (to knead flour for chappatis?). In contrast to her husband's animated left hand, hers lies on the floor. The gender roles are blatantly clear: the husband nurtures the mind; the wife, with all her paraphernalia to grind and churn and knead, is in charge of the body. He is actively engaged; she is disengaged. In the background is a large, sprawling domed house – all in a dazzling white that adds quiet drama to the composition. (From photographs, it appears to be the artist's home in Saraya.) The mansion juxtaposes the courtyard scene, with the husband and wife openly undertaking their chores. The panoramic view offers a segment of the different lifestyles of the upper and the lower classes, of the different gender roles between the husband and the wife and even portrays the generational gap between the ancient storyteller and his very young listeners. It is difficult to say exactly what Sher-Gil intended in her work. Is it purely art for art's sake, or was she trying to convey a symbolic message? Perhaps by disclosing the way life *is* in its ordinary rhythms, Sher-Gil was inviting her audience to speculate on the way life ought to be.

Had she the opportunity to continue with her work we would have learnt much more about her aspirations and perhaps would even be gifted with more Sikh themes and subjects. Unfortunately, she died prematurely in December 1941 at the age of 28. She had married her Hungarian cousin, a medical doctor and the two of them had moved to Lahore to start life on their own. Lahore at this point had acquired the reputation of being the 'Paris of India', and Sher-Gil reveled in its progressive cosmopolitan atmosphere. She was preparing for an important solo exhibition when her life was cut short in mysterious circumstances – a 'botched abortion' is generally assumed. Her last painting, though incomplete, is a rural view from the window of her studio, which swoops down to the ground where we see four black buffaloes. Two of them are lying down lethargically, the third stands near a trough and the fourth, also standing, is resigned to having a big black crow sitting on its muzzle. From beak to tail, the crow covers almost the whole of the buffalo's face. From the back of a shed, steps (with no railing) lead up to a rooftop, where a woman is making dung patties. Like the two buffaloes, she too is crouched on the floor and, like the buffalo with the crow, is resigned to her fate. She appears as a silhouette: societal codes shroud her face and being. In the far distance, the red and yellow buildings of Lahore can be seen. In this incomplete panoramic view, Sher-Gil's observant eyes and boundless empathy convey the theme of female oppression with a bold new freedom of space and form. In her unique sensibility, Paris and Punjab come together to open up unexplored territories for generations of artists to come.

S. G. Thakur Singh

Born in the village of Verka, near Amritsar, Thakur Singh (1899–1976) began his career painting stage sets in Bombay alongside his Muslim mentor, Mohammed Alam. He then moved to Calcutta, where the Tagore brothers became his patrons. His fame spread and Maharajas from all over India commissioned his works. In oils, pastels and watercolors, Thakur Singh created a vast repertoire that included heroes such as Mahatma Gandhi and Sir Sunder Singh Majithia, monuments like the Taj Mahal and the Golden Temple, and the landscapes of Ladakh, Bombay and Udaipur. His seductive painting 'After the Bath' won a prize in 1924 at an exhibition of Commonwealth Art in Britain. It shows a woman seen from behind, gently putting up her hair with both hands – quite unaware of her sensuous body softly showing through her wet, white sari. Ten years later, his 'Ganesh Puja' was acclaimed at an exhibition of Modern Indian Art held in London. In Calcutta, he started the Punjab Fine

Arts Society and when he moved back to Amritsar in 1931, he established the Thakur Singh School of Art, which continues to serve as a vital center for Punjabi artists. Members from his school played an important role in the creation of the Central Sikh Museum at the Golden Temple. Thakur Singh's painting of the first Indian Governor General taking office is displayed at the Rashtrapati Bhawan in New Delhi; that of the Taj Mahal (Mumtaz Mahal's 'Her Last Desire') at the National Art Gallery in Moscow; and that of the Qutab Minar at the Scottish National Gallery.

Sobha Singh

Sobha Singh (1901–86) painted figures across religious traditions. Having witnessed human violence during his service in the British Army, he dedicated his life to displaying prototypes of peace and love on his canvases. After the partition of the Punjab, he left Lahore and built a cottage in Andretta in the Kangra Valley. Its serene atmosphere was very beneficial to his artistic temperament and Sobha Singh was able to create a huge collection of oil paintings. Though he focused primarily on the Sikh Gurus, he also portrayed Jesus Christ, Lord Krishna, Lord Rama, Hindu and Muslim saints such as Bhagat Ravidas and Baba Farid, and national heroes such as Shaheed Bhagat Singh, Kartar Singh Sarabha, Mahatma Gandhi and Lal Bahadur Shastri. His rich legacy includes images of immortal lovers from the Punjabi folk romances of Heer–Ranjha, Sassi–Punnu and Sohni–Mahival. In fact, his painting of Sohni and Mahival is a classic. Here the lovers, seen in a sideways pose, lyrically echo each other: with the wet folds of her clothes clinging to her desirable body, Sohni is sinuously enfolded by her lover; and as her left arm glides down, his right arm stretches up lithely – uniting the male and the female in a profound metaphysics. However, dark blue and black clouds gather threateningly in the background and the clay pot beside Sohni foreshadows its treacherous replacement, leading to her death. That societal codes obstruct true love flows out poignantly from his canvas. In another painting, we see the poet Omar Khayyam reclining against a tree, with a book on his lap and a glass of wine in his hand, listening to a lovely young woman playing the mandolin. In yet another exquisite scene in pastel blues, yellows and earth tones, the Mughal Queen Mumtaz Mahal is locked in the arms of her husband, Shah Jahan, who is seated on her bed; her end may be near, but the

Figure 20: Eternal lovers Sohni and Mahival

closeness of their bodies clinging together, their swirling clothing and the pervasive circular momentum, betray the power of love over death.

Sobha Singh's great masterpiece is a portrait of Guru Nanak – inspiring comfort and serenity in viewers. In this composition, which is now deeply imprinted in the Sikh imagination, the Guru's face with his white beard is inclined tenderly, his turban and robe are a soft yellow, his eyes brim with spirituality and his hand gestures a gift of blessings. Prints of this painting are extremely popular and, as witnessed in Gurinder Chadha's film *Bend It Like Beckham*, serve as a prime marker of a Sikh home.

Phulan Rani

Born in Amritsar in 1923, the eminent female artist Phulan Rani continues to create the human form with subtle lines and evocative colors. She has illustrated biographies of Guru Nanak, Guru Tegh Bahadur and Guru Gobind Singh. In 1970 she visited the United Kingdom, performing 'Indian Ragas through Music and Painting' in Manchester, Birmingham, Liverpool and Glasgow. Dedicated to the advancement of women, youth and global peace, Phulan Rani has been instrumental in publishing illustrated souvenirs for the International Women's Year (1975), for the International Year of Youth (1985) and for the International Year of Peace (1986). She has served as the member and president of the Modern Academy of Fine Arts and Crafts at Amritsar and won many awards for her beautiful works. For Guru Nanak's Fifth Birth Centennial in 1969, she wrote the life of the Guru and illustrated it in a series of 40 remarkable paintings, for which she has received many honors. Phulan Rani's feminine eye captures the presence of women in the First Guru's life. Not only does she show us the female relatives of the Guru, but also women from his village and town, women who saw Nanak at school and those who attended his various rites of passage. There is one that strikingly portrays Nanak and his sister Nanaki walking together among the serenity of nature.[62] The older sister has her arm lovingly around her little brother, who in turn is holding on to her left arm as it gently rests on his shoulder. Both are wearing loose and rather similar outfits. Both are in a contemplative mood; while he looks down at the ground, she gazes at the far horizon. Her chin bends over him almost as a protection for his head with its halo, and they form a beautiful whole. Nanaki and Nanak, sister and brother, female and male, are physically and psychologically integrated. In this picture of oneness and harmony, Nanaki gently leads her little brother forward into a new world. *Her* love, guidance and togetherness at the core of the Sikh tradition is gracefully captured by Phulan Rani.

Arpita Singh

Born in 1937, Arpita has been a prolific painter and winner of numerous awards. Her illustrations for the *Hymns of Guru Nanak* (translated by Khushwant Singh)[63] convey Guru Nanak's spiritual longing, expressed in a wide range of musical melodies. Here she sets Punjabi folk tradition in Persian miniature layouts, and as these appear in her modernist style reminiscent of the biblical illustrations of Marc Chagall, Arpita's works underscore the universality of art.

Instead of scenes from his biography, Arpita highlights Guru Nanak's esthetics. Through her vibrant colors and tender forms, she evokes the specific emotion (*raga*, which literally means color) distinguishing the respective compositions. Therefore, her paintings accompanying Guru Nanak's hymns from Sri Raga color the mind with a gentle mystery – characteristic of the evening melody, which is the first in the Guru Granth (*Sri* means supreme). Likewise, Arpita illustrates the cooling impact of Guru Nanak's composition *Barah Mah* (Twelve Months), set to the melody called Tukhari, from the Sanskrit *tushar* (meaning winter frost), to be sung in the morning. Arpita articulates the psyche of Guru Nanak's protagonist as she goes through the different seasons of the year. In the spring she sits lonely on her terrace, her loneliness augmented by the bounty of nature around her. Shades of green and pink and her own bright yellow scarf and magenta shirt, manifest her angst. During the monsoon (following the scorching summer), when everybody buzzes with joy, the lonely woman is frightened by the thunder and lightning and so, with her large, anxious eyes, we see her holding on to a pillar. Dark purples, blues and greens, with a patch of dazzling white, dominate the landscape. Finally, at the end of the lunar year, the month of Phalgun (February/March), the woman discovers her Lover. During the tender coolness of the season, duality, and its ensuing anguish, dissolve. She is soothed. The smile on her face and the flowers in her hand perfectly render Guru Nanak's message: '*ghar var paia nari* – the woman found her Beloved in her own self' (GG: 1109).[64]

Arpita's visual translations appropriately depict the female figure at the center of Guru Nanak's imagination, which is often neglected or even altered into male syntax by translators and exegetes (see Chapter VI). In the *Barah Mah* hymn, it is the woman who pulls the Timeless Beloved into her personal and historical world. Likewise, an illustration for *Sri Raga* shows two women, dressed in striking green, gold, red and white outfits, embracing each other.[65] The joy of Guru Nanak's hymn, '*avahu bhaine gal milau ank saheleria* – Come O' sister let us embrace each other; we are intimate friends', radiates from their faces as they hold each other affectionately in their arms and gaze into each other's eyes. They validate female bonds and human relationships that are vital to the Guru's world view. In her illustration for *Rag Vadhans*, Arpita depicts a woman in a pink scarf sitting on the ground in her courtyard, braiding her hair in front of a mirror.[66] A pillow and neat bedspread, a basket of pink flowers, and a tray with two cups, signify the presence of her absent Lover. She must dress herself in ways that will bring union with the Beloved. Arpita's scenario replays Guru Nanak's affirmation of the feminine as a category of being with essential values and strengths; she is the one with a quest for her divine Lover and her adornment serves as a vital metaphor for spiritual refinement. If we look into *her* mirror, we too can see who we are and what we might hope to become.

Arpana Caur

Daughter of the renowned author Ajit Caur, Arpana was born in Delhi in 1954. Drawing on the Punjab hills for figuration, color and line, she explores the subjugation of Indian women, political violence and environmental issues. These social tragedies are woven into philosophical themes of time, life and death. By superimposing her modern sensibility on traditional folk drawings, Arpana creates powerful psychological and visual tensions. Her works appear surrealist, almost Dada-like. They provoke serious reflection and critical thought.

In 'Between Dualities', a green and a blue woman come together synchronically in a vortex to render the creative and destructive force of the universe: while the green one above sews a cloud, the lower cuts it away with her scissors. In 'Green Circle', a young female child is painting a circle around herself against the backdrop of urban traffic. While reminiscent of the circle drawn for the ancient Queen Sita in the *Ramayana*,[67] it forcefully brings to mind little girls who are being forced to go begging in bumper-to-bumper traffic in metropolises such as Delhi and Bombay. Arpana's contemporary protagonist desires a small space free from the pollution of three-wheelers, and free from human exploitation.

Sikh history is recorded by the artist in deep colors and innovative forms. Entitled '1947', Arpana's painting of her grandfather carrying the Guru Granth, wrapped in green material, on his head and a bundle of white cloud-like memories on his hunched back, registers the displacement and carnage during the Partition of the Punjab. Likewise, Arpana's '1984' is a traumatic reminder of the historic massacre at the Golden Temple by the Indian government and the killing of innocent Sikhs that followed the assassination of Prime Minister Indira Gandhi by her Sikh bodyguards. For Sikh spectators, the severed head in the painting entitled '1984' is also a reminder of the Ninth Guru's sacrifice for the freedom of religion in 1675 and of the Five Beloved Sikhs who were ready to offer their head to the Tenth Guru during his creation of the Khalsa in 1699.

Many of Arpana's works focus on the biography of Guru Nanak and render a postmodern perspective to the Janamsakhi narratives. In 'Sacred Thread', we see Guru Nanak with scissors in his hand, cutting the traditional ritual thread worn by upper-caste men in his society. In 'Endless Journeys', Guru Nanak is set within a large footprint, symbolic of his attempt to spread his message of love and peace 'wherever his feet would take him'. In a joint collaboration with another Sikh woman, Mala Dayal, Arpana has illustrated *Nanak: The Guru*, a book for children.[68] Her intriguing arrangement of colors reveals his spiritual radiance. Indeed, on Arpana's canvas, a white-bearded Nanak, dressed in solid black, with an orange mala, glows brilliantly.[69]

In 1995, Arpana was commissioned by the Hiroshima Museum of Modern Art to commemorate the 50th anniversary of the dropping of the A-bomb. In the last panel of her triptych, 'Where Have all the Flowers Gone?', Arpana paints a dark female figure crouched under a black cloud. Against a bright yellow backdrop, the contrasting darkness spells out her emotional and physical charring from the atomic bombing. The receding yellow intimates the first panel of the triptych, with its flowers emerging from a river. In a horrifying way, a stem extends into the next panel and becomes the strap of a gun of one of the many soldiers framed in the middle panel.

The recipient of numerous awards, Arpana's works are displayed in museums in Delhi, Mumbai, Chandigarh, Singapore, Hiroshima, Düsseldorf, Stockholm, Bradford, London, Boston and San Francisco. Religious pluralism is an important theme for this internationally renowned artist. For the 50th anniversary of India's independence, she created 'Where Many Streams Meet'. Figures from Sikhism, Jainism, Buddhism, Hinduism and Islam converge on Arpana's canvas to evoke India's rich legacy. Music from the harmoniums and *tanpura* fills the air. A royal blue river flows through the brown soil. Arpana's surreal depiction lingers in the imagination. How do we make sense of these figures and colors, and their juxtapositions? Do we celebrate our diversity? Or do we lament our religious divisions? As it opens up to new horizons, Sikh art confronts us with our essential humanity.

Chapter IX
Sikhs in the Diaspora

A dynamic movement to and from the Punjab is manifest in the life of the founder Guru, in Sikh Scripture canonized by Guru Arjan, and in the Khalsa institution created by the Tenth Guru. The Janamsakhis recount Guru Nanak embarking on odysseys to the east, south, north and west from his home in the Punjab; he is said to have visited Hardwar, Varanasi, Bodh Gaya, Bidar, Sri Lanka, Kashmir, Mecca, Medina and Baghdad. Sikh Scripture contains the sublime voices of saints from different regions, including Bhagat Kabir from Varanasi and Namdev from Sitara (in Maharashtra). The Five Beloved, who were ready to offer their lives to Guru Gobind Singh during the historic Baisakhi of 1699 at Anandpur, are believed to have come from diverse cultural centers in India – Lahore, Dwarka, Bidar, Hastinapur and Jagannath. The encounter with other faiths and ethnicities is fundamental to the shaping of the Sikh community. The interplay between the centrifugal force from the Punjab and the centripetal force to its homeland intrinsic to the Sikh psyche, is also characteristic of the Sikh diaspora. In an estimate made in 2005, there were about 15 million Sikhs living in the Punjab, 5 million in the rest of India, one-third of a million in Asia, half a million in Europe and over half a million in North America.[1] Wherever they may live, the soil of the Punjab sustains the Sikh spirit and is in turn fertilized by it.

Sikh communities developed in the places that the Sikh Gurus visited. There are tiny populations, such as those of the Nanakpanthis, found 15 miles north-west of Pilibhit in Uttar Pradesh, where Guru Nanak is remembered as having discourse with the Nath Yogis.[2] At the other end of the spectrum, there is a very large Sikh population living in Varanasi. The Gurubagh Gurdwara, located two miles from the city center, commemorates the visit of Guru Nanak. Its wall inscription records that he visited Varanasi in 1506 and a small garden in the courtyard blooms as a memento of the spot where he sat.[3] Similarly, Nichibagh Gurdwara, another important shrine in Varanasi, commemorates the visit of Guru Tegh Bahadur in 1666. The Guru's long shirt in Dhaka muslin, his sandals and 14 historical letters addressed by him to the local congregation, are displayed at this shrine. A special room marks the spot where he is believed to have meditated, and a lamp is constantly lit in front of its doorway. Over the years, such historic spots have attracted Sikh settlements in the north, south, east and west of India.

In the early part of the twentieth century, Sikh farmers bought land in Rajasthan, Uttar Pradesh and Haryana (of modern times), and settled beyond the Punjab. The partition of India in 1947, however, had a dramatic effect on the migration of Sikhs. Millions of Sikh refugees from Pakistan found new homes and professions in urban areas across India. Transportation, business, industry and administrative jobs took the enterprising Sikhs to distant parts of the country. Sikh traders have traveled to Afghanistan, Persia and Sri Lanka for centuries, and thus small Sikh communities began to flourish beyond India. Bhatra Sikhs, the earliest followers of Guru Nanak, are known to have traveled with him to Sri Lanka.

In general, the phenomenon of Sikh migration is traced to the British annexation of the Punjab in 1849. The transportation web of railways and ships for colonial enterprises intensified and accelerated Sikh mobility. The British extended the irrigation canals too, and the newly irrigated areas of West Punjab attracted Sikh farmers. New varieties of crops were introduced. New Orleans cotton, wheat, sugar cane, flax and tobacco were cultivated, making the Punjab one of the most agriculturally productive regions in the colonial world. The region had mulberry trees, and with the import of silkworms, its sericulture progressed even more. Tea was planted on the slopes of the Murree Hills and in the Kangra Valley. Italian merino rams were crossed with local breeds, which boosted the yield of both meat and wool.[4] By the 1920s, the Punjab produced one-third of British India's total cotton crop, and a tenth of its wheat. Using the railway network, Punjabi farmers were able to export their goods. The exports brought cash and credit, inspiring young Sikh men to venture out much farther afield – to the *tapu* (island) of 'Telia' (Australia) and 'Merika' (America), as the Punjabis commonly called them. Adventurous Sikhs were financially prepared to pay their fares to the Far East and further afield.

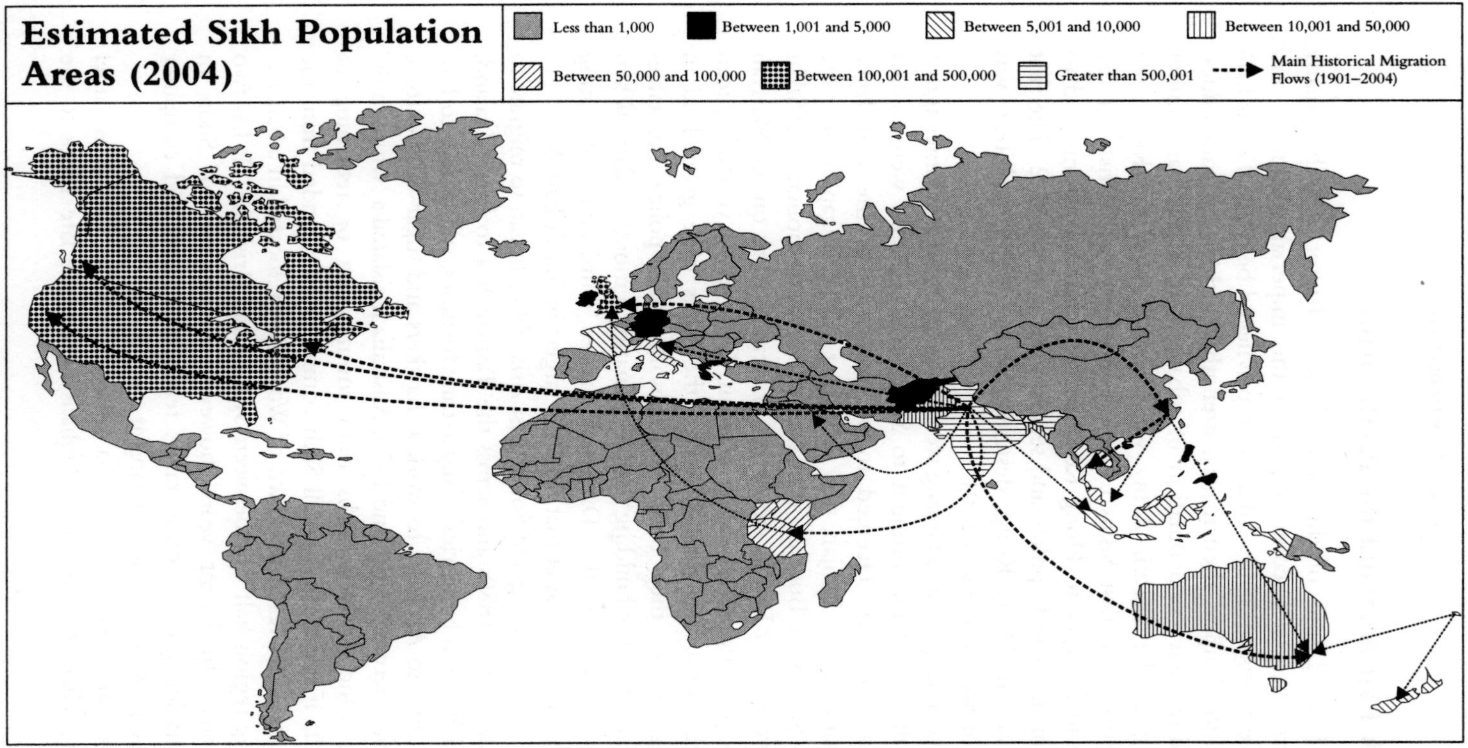

Map 2: World Sikh population map

South East Asia and the Pacific Rim

The 'favored sons of the Empire' (see Chapter VII) had many opportunities to become a part of the imperial workforce and migrate to distant lands. Sikhs were privileged because of their loyalty to the Empire, their martial strength and their religious values, including their condemnation of tobacco.[5] A substantial number serving in the British Army were posted to Hong Kong and Singapore. The first Sikhs to be recruited by the British for the police force went to Hong Kong in 1867 and they continued to serve in the island's police and security forces until 1952. The first Gurdwara in Hong Kong, designed by an English architect, was built for Sikh soldiers in 1901.

Since Singapore and Penang were designated penal colonies at that time, the first Sikhs brought to Singapore, in 1850, were in fact political prisoners. Deemed to be dangerous to the East India Company rule in Punjab, they were sent out to Singapore after the Anglo-Sikh wars. But they were soon followed by thousands of Sikhs who were either British employees or went to work on the Malayan rubber plantations and in dairy farms. During the year of Queen Victoria's Diamond Jubilee (1897), the Sikhs were given land in Penang, where they built a Gurdwara. Sikh police constables contributed to the building fund by donating a month's salary. When it was completed, the Diamond Jubilee Gurdwara, celebrating Queen Victoria, was at that time the largest in South East Asia.

From Hong Kong and South East Asia, Sikhs began to migrate to Australia in the 1880s and across the Tasman Sea to New Zealand. And then, lured by stories of sugar-cane fortunes, still farther to Fiji. They came to Australia to work as hawkers and sugar-cane cutters. However, between 1901 and 1973, Australia legislated a 'whites only' policy, which barred Sikhs from immigrating or returning to Australia if they left. A small Sikh community descended from the early migrants lives in the town of Woolgoolga, located in a banana-growing region half way between Sydney and Brisbane.[6] It has two Gurdwaras. In recent years, however, the number of Sikhs in Australia has grown considerably: teachers, doctors and computer software professionals are arriving at a rapid rate.

Some Sikhs went to Australia directly from the Punjab as camel drivers (called 'Ghans', from Afghans). From the late 1860s to the early 1920s, camel trains carried supplies to settlements in the isolated arid interior of central Australia. Though the Ghans were mainly Muslims from Afghanistan, a sizable minority were Sikhs from the Punjab.

The Sikhs who migrated to China, the Dutch East Indies and the Philippines left few traces, but significant groups remain in Singapore, Malaysia and Thailand.

East Africa

Following a similar pattern of army recruitment as that to Hong Kong and Singapore, Sikhs migrated to various colonies and protectorates of East Africa. Many were hired in 1895, when the British established the East African Rifles, a military base force with its headquarters in Mombasa. Two years later, more Sikhs were brought over by the Empire to put down the mutiny by Sudanese troops. Sikh men constituted a large proportion of the labor, imported from the Punjab for the construction of the Uganda Railways project during the late nineteenth century. Most of them were artisans. They built their first Gurdwara in East Africa in Kilindini in 1892. Once Kenya gained its independence in 1960, many Sikhs – even second- and third-generation – were forced to leave as a result of 'Africanization' policies. There was a major Sikh exodus from Uganda after Idi Amin gave orders for an immediate expulsion of 80,000 Asians in August 1972.

The United Kingdom and Ireland

Ironically, Sikhs migrated to other parts of the Empire before turning to Britain. The exiled Maharaja Dalip Singh (1838–93) is said to be the first Sikh settler in Britain. Since Britain had a special place in the colony's imagination, other Sikh Maharajas, travelers, writers, students, soldiers and even some workers came to the British Isles, the majority of them as visitors. London was the shopping and tourist jaunt for Sikh princes, who came with their entourages. The stories of Maharaja Bhupinder Singh of Patiala circulate widely: he would book an entire floor of the Savoy Hotel and drive around London in a huge motorcade of Rolls-Royces. As a representative of the Olympic team, Bhupinder Singh visited London frequently. He became the patron of the first Gurdwara in Britain, which was founded in Shepherd's Bush in 1911. The Maharaja was present at its opening ceremonies.

Sikh regiments came frequently to parade during gala State occasions. They came for Queen Victoria's Golden Jubilee, for her Diamond Jubilee and for the Coronations of Edward VII (1902), George V (1911) and George VI (1937). A contingent of wounded Sikh soldiers was brought to London during the First World War. Dalip Singh's daughter, Sophia, visited the wounded at convalescent camps and in their letters to their families back home the soldiers shared their delight at seeing the granddaughter of Maharaja Ranjit. The Royal Pavilion at Brighton, the seaside retreat of George IV in the nineteenth century, was used as a hospital for Indian soldiers fighting for the Empire. Patients were treated by orderlies from their own caste or faith, and they also had opportunities to attend their respective religious services.[7] In 1921, a monument (in the shape of *chattri*, or umbrella) was built on the spot where Hindu and Sikh soldiers were cremated. It is dedicated 'To the memory of all Indian soldiers who gave their lives for their King-Emperor in the Great War … in grateful admiration and brotherly affection.' Many Sikh soldiers discharged after the War chose to stay in Britain. Recent services at the Chattri Memorial show Sikhs offering wreaths and reciting the Ardas with their fellow British countrymen and women.[8]

Affluent Sikh families saw the cultural value of a British education and began to send their children (mainly their sons) to school in Britain. A relationship with England was seen as a way of signifying high-class status back home.[9] The opening of the Civil Service to Indians in the early twentieth century inspired youngsters to study at Oxford and Cambridge. The first turbaned Sikh to enroll at Cambridge was Teja Singh. He was in the early batch of Sikh students to arrive in London in 1907.[10] Teja Singh became the president of the London Gurdwara and gave regular lectures on Sikhism. The eminent Sikh historian, Khushwant Singh, was also educated in England.

As well as the transient group of princes, soldiers and students, the Bhatras were the earliest Sikh presence in the British Isles, and the first to settle permanently. They came from the Sialkot and Gurdaspur regions of the Punjab. Most of them lived in small groups, situated in ports and industrial towns. Expert in their traditional occupation as hawkers, they spread to northern England and Scotland, going from door to door, selling clothing in remote areas. They filled the need created by the migration of Jewish peddlers from Europe to the USA. With their commercial success, Bhatras today are prominent owners of market stalls, shops, supermarkets and wholesale warehouses. The community is credited with the building of many Gurdwaras.

Wartime labor shortages in Britain opened up doors previously closed to people of color, and Sikh pioneers immediately took advantage of this. The harrowing Partition of their homeland in 1947, when countless Sikhs lost their lives, homes, jobs and land, pushed them to search for employment elsewhere. The British Nationality Act of 1948, passed in response to India's independence, gave the citizens of the Commonwealth the right to settle and work in Britain. Sikh men flocked to work in foundries and textile mills, providing cheap labor in a depressed post-war economy. They did not mind the rigorous and monotonous work. Most new arrivals settled in London, Birmingham and West Yorkshire, with Southall in west London becoming the hub for the diasporic community. They frequently assisted their kinsmen and fellow villagers from back home to make their way to Britain and find jobs in factories and mines. Thus they set up an ever-expanding process of chain migration, of relative following relative. A dozen to two dozen men would live together in a house, working shifts and eating in a communal kitchen. A report on British race relations noted: 'Some of the beds were used during the day by the night shift workers and at night by the day workers.'[11] They lived to work so they could send their savings back home. With the post-war boom and the liberalization of immigration policies, Britain became the host for the largest Sikh diasporic community. Its rapid growth fueled xenophobic attitudes. Economic and social fears for the loss of jobs and the 'British way of life' led to aggression against those who displayed Sikh symbols. Immigration controls were reintroduced in 1962. The right to wear a turban in the workplace was denied, and young men became victims of virulent racism.

But the resilient Sikhs withstood the harsh challenges and soon proved themselves to be a worthy and prosperous community in Britain. They succeeded in overturning the ban on wearing turbans at work on buses and trains, and even in the police force. They brought their wives and children to Britain, and began to participate in local and national politics. Another wave of second- and third-generation Sikhs migrated from Tanzania, Uganda and Kenya in the 1970s. The East African Sikhs were highly skilled and employable, and having been a conspicuous minority for decades, they were used to keeping their Sikh symbols. They were an inspiration to those who had to shed the turban in order to work in British factories and mines. There are 336,179 Sikhs in Britain and they are influential in all spheres of British life.[12] Many have firmly established their roots, and 56.1 per cent of Sikhs are British born. Hard working and resourceful, they are making important contributions to business, industry, art, culture, the media and the law.

There are interesting chapters in the Sikhs' reception by the host country too. For example, in a futuristic novel entitled *The Devil's Children* (mentioned in my Introduction), Peter Dickinson presents a deep friendship full of love and trust between an English girl and some Sikh migrant children. During a mad anti-technology wave in Britain, 12-year-old Nicky is separated from her parents and eventually joins a group of Sikhs, who have made their way to Shepherd's Bush (historically significant, as that is where the first Gurdwara was established). They settle at a deserted farm, but nearby villagers view them as 'the Devil's Children'. Showing how easily racial stereotypes are constructed, Dickinson discloses the values of the migrant Sikh community: strong family bonds, loyalty, warrior legacy, sacrifice and resourcefulness in using skills brought from the Punjab, and those learnt as low-skilled workers in Britain. As a part of the Changes Trilogy, it was adapted as a BBC TV series in 1975 and may have changed people's attitudes toward their relationships with Sikhs.

At the community level, Sikhs have created an important place for themselves. There are about 200 Gurdwaras serving *langar* meals and providing services to the elderly and the needy. There are numerous cultural centers, and political and literary associations, in Britain, and many have global links. Gurdwara Singh Sabha, completed in 2003, is the largest in the UK. It was built in Southall to accommodate the burgeoning Sikh population. The building also serves as a community center, with facilities including a library, seminar room, a multi-use space and a dining hall that can serve 20,000 meals over a weekend during special celebrations.

With the passage of time, the diasporic experience has become even more psychologically complex. Instead of having a subordinate immigrant relationship, Sikhs desire equal partnership with their once 'host' country and colonial power. Memories are important for personal and communal identity, and Sikhs in Britain want access to their Anglo-Sikh past to enable them to build an authentic future for themselves. The Sikh sovereign, Dalip Singh, serves as an important symbol of the Anglo-Sikh relationship. He is remembered not solely as a Sikh, but also as a responsible Briton who contributed generously to local charities and institutions. His death centennial in 1993 was celebrated extensively all over Britain. It included worship and charity events in Gurdwaras, and outdoor festivals with performers, musicians and poets. Buses full of Sikh children from urban centers toured Dalip Singh's grave in the remote estate in Elveden, now owned by the Guinness family. The locals did not want Sikhs – the 'nightmarish intruders' with turbans – disturbing their peace and quiet, but for the Sikhs it was far more than just a simple visit. It was a claim and validation of their own past in a quintessential English space. The *Guardian* reported: 'The wrought iron gates, the empty mansion and the romantic sweep of parklands exert a snobbish fascination. All this once belonged to their co-religionist.'[13] But again, it was much more than a demonstration that Dalip Singh and the modern visitors were British, as the *Guardian* saw; for the second-, third- or fourth-generation Sikhs, this was their own history planted in British soil. Many other English sites where the Sikh icon lived or visited, and even where his mother, Queen Jindan, lived, are a part of Sikh geography, and even though they may be 7,000 miles away from the homeland, they promote a sense of selfhood. The borders of the Punjab are expanded by the Sikh diasporic experience.

During Dalip Singh's centennial, his portraits were widely marketed by the efforts of Nanaksar Thath Isher Darbar, an international organization based near Birmingham. A reproduction of the Winterhalter portrait was issued by the National Portrait Gallery. (The original was painted soon after Dalip Singh's arrival in England in 1854; for details, see Chapter VII.) The Dalip Singh Centenary Trust commissioned another reproduction, with some worthwhile changes. Here, the basic pose and the magnificent outfit and jewels are rather similar, but the vacuous Winterhalter stage is abundantly filled. Behind Dalip Singh is a throne with the Khalsa symbol, and a lion-skin carpet lies beneath his feet. Images of his father, Maharaja Ranjit Singh, and his mother, Queen Jindan, are on either side of Dalip Singh. Gone is the portrait of Queen Victoria from his pearl necklace, to be replaced by his father, the first Sikh Maharaja. And directly above Dalip Singh's royal plume is Guru Nanak's configuration *Ikk Oan Kar*, flashing within a golden light. The metaphysical Oneness dominates the opulent scene. By endowing the grandee of the English countryside with concrete markers of his personal history, politics and religion, the diasporic community was articulating its own Anglo-Sikh identity. Similarly, in 1999, during the 800th anniversary of Thetford's first mayor, a large bronze equestrian statue of Dalip Singh was unveiled by Prince Charles. The statue, erected close to the center of the English town, anchors the memories of the 150 years of Sikh presence in England; its unveiling by Prince Charles signifies the closeness between the English and Sikh royal families. Such occasions affirm the distinct heritage of the Sikhs and their British citizenship.

With the Celtic Tiger boom after the Republic of Ireland joined the European Community, Sikhs started entering the country to work in information technology, business, medicine, and the hotel and catering industry, as well as to attend technical colleges. They are now enlisting in the Garda Síochána as well. At this point there are almost 1,000 Sikhs energetically putting down their roots in Ireland. The Gurdwara in Dublin (once an old movie theater) is their religious and cultural center. In 2004, they formed the Irish Sikh Council to voice their concerns and needs. After the 7/7 attacks in Britain, a Sikh student in Athlone was stabbed and verbally abused. To raise awareness, Sikhs participate in interfaith programs and multicultural fairs. Colorful new mosaics of Celtic and Sikh festivities are being created: in 2007, for the first time, the St Patrick's Day parade included 90 Sikhs performing dances. Their bright saffron and blue colors combine well with the Irish green. In 2010, the Chester Beatty Library launched an exhibition called *A Sikh Face in Ireland*, an important step towards transcultural understanding. It includes Inderjit Kaur, who could not speak English when she arrived in Ireland, and now her children do not speak any Punjabi.

In post-colonial Britain, the interaction of diasporic Sikhs with other diasporas is an important process. On arrival in urban centers, Sikhs not only meet the host country, but other Punjabis as well – Hindu and Muslim, other South Asians and people from other commonwealth countries. They work in places with South Asians, Caribbeans, Africans and Irish; their children grow up in multiethnic and multifaith neighborhoods. Tension and conflicts are inevitable, but there has been meaningful exchange and creativity. Modern Bhangra is an exciting consequence of the social contacts and cultural crossovers between Punjabi youth and their Afro-Caribbean peers, who happened to live closely in places like Southall and Birmingham.[14] Traditionally performed in the Punjab during harvest festivals and weddings, Bhangra dance music is being fused with Western pop, hip-hop, house, rap and reggae; its distinctive drumbeat is being synthesized with drum machines, live percussion and other modern instrumentation; and its Punjabi language is being mixed with English. The content of the lyrics too has changed. Characteristic of the original Bhangra, they celebrate the beauty and joy of the Punjab, but in addition, the lyrics express nostalgia for the homeland left far behind, and, furthermore, voice the immigrant's anger and frustration against a hostile Britain. The innovative sounds and rhythms, the use of English, and the pan-communal anti-racist politics of Bhangra, are empowering for the young and help them to reach a wide audience. With their creative energy, young Sikhs are combining their inheritance – 'their parents' drumbeat' – with the cultures around them, and generating an exhilarating music and dance form, which is becoming the latest rage in all parts of the world. Indeed, the diasporic landscape is a rich resource for innovative ventures. We shall explore the contributions of a few Sikh women artists at the end of this chapter.

Continental Europe

In the rest of Europe there are around 100,000 Sikhs; Germany has the largest community, with 25,000, followed by Belgium and Italy with around 20,000 each. Ukraine, Greece, France, Spain, Denmark, Sweden, Switzerland, the Netherlands and Norway each have a few thousand.[15] Sikhs come to Europe primarily to work and earn money, and each time they visit their families and friends in India, their suitcases are bursting with expensive gifts. Even people who are employed in menial jobs will get dressed lavishly for their visit back home. Their success stories encourage others to make their way to the West. There are problems too. In France, a law adopted in 2004 bans the wearing of conspicuous religious symbols in state schools, which includes the wearing of turbans. Several Sikh boys have been expelled from schools in France for defying the ban. However, in most French schools, Sikhs have reached a compromise that allows them to wear the *keski*, a smaller version of the turban. In the migrant and minority communities, religion plays a crucial function. Sikhism becomes the primary channel for the transmission of language, culture and heritage. As such, it is vital to the construction of personal identity and serves as the crucial agent for shaping Sikh identity across multiple generations. It provides the infrastructure for organizing the community from within and at the same time serves as the primary identity marker for the general public.

North America

The first Sikhs to visit the New World were Sikh Lancers and Infantry in the Hong Kong Regiment, who went to Vancouver, British Columbia, after celebrating Queen Victoria's Diamond Jubilee in London in 1897. They were lured by the farming opportunities of the New World and dreamed about settling here. The four Sikhs mentioned in the news item were the first trickle of migrants who landed in San Francisco on 5 April 1899 in search of economic opportunities. When a severe famine in the Punjab drove them out, advertisements by steamship companies and recruitment to work on the Canadian Pacific Railroad attracted the first 'passenger' Sikh migrants to the North American continent. They usually came by boat through Hong Kong and disembarked either in Vancouver or at Angel Island (the West Coast equivalent of Ellis Island in New York). Since India and Canada were at that time both British dominions, a visa was not required for travel to Canada, so Vancouver was the preferred destination. On the way, they would stop in Hong Kong, receiving support from the local Gurdwara. On arrival in North America, the migrants rapidly moved to Southern California to work on farms throughout the Sacramento, San Joaquin and Imperial valleys, or settled in Washington, Oregon and British

Sikhs Allowed to Land.

The four Sikhs who arrived on the Nippon Maru the other day were permitted yesterday to land by the immigration officials. The quartet formed the most picturesque group that has been seen on the Pacific Mail dock for many a day. One of them, Bakkshlied Singh, speaks English with fluency, the others just a little. They are all fine-looking men, Bakkshlied Singh in particular being a marvel of physical beauty. He stands 6 feet 2 inches and is built in proportion. His companions—Bood Singh, Varlam Singh and Subava Singh—are not quite so big. All of them have been soldiers and policemen in China. They were in the Royal Artillery, and the tall one with the unpronounceable name was a police sergeant in Hongkong prior to coming to this country. They hope to make their fortunes here and return to their homes in the Lahore district, which they left some twenty years ago.

Figure 21: San Francisco Chronicle, 6 April 1899

Columbia to work in the lumber industries and on the Pacific railway. The new immigrants were hard-working and accepted lower wages than the local people. There was an influx of Sikh migrants between 1905 and 1908. They were able to build their first Gurdwara in North America in 1909 in Vancouver, followed by another in Victoria.

The local population was threatened by labor competition from the robust, low-paid newcomers. In 1908, Canada passed the Continuous Voyage Act, barring people who were not able to travel on a continuous voyage from their native land to Canada. This law put an end to migrations from the Punjab. Nevertheless, a group of determined Sikhs tried to fulfill the legal obligations and chartered a Japanese ship, *Komagata Maru*. Collecting 376 passengers from Hong Kong and Shanghai, they arrived at Victoria harbor but, with the exception of just a handful of passengers, the Canadian immigration officials would not allow them entry. After a protracted legal battle, the *Komagata Maru* was forced to return home, only to be met by a hostile police force on landing in Calcutta. This incident of the *Komagata Maru* damaged the psyche of these proud British subjects.[16]

American papers also began to report on the 'Hindu invasion'. Unfamiliar with the distinctive faith of the Sikhs, they gave them the generic 'Hindu' designation. Those who wore the turbans, the marker of their religious identity, were called 'Rag Heads'. In 1907 there were racist riots – 'anti-Hindoo' violence – in Washington, California and Alaska. Sikhs were included on the list of enemies of California's Asiatic Exclusion League, formed in 1907. The United States' laws were repressive and discriminatory. In May 1913, the California Alien Land Act restricted the right to register land only to American citizens, and in 1917, Sikhs were barred from entering the country. In 1923, they lost the right to become naturalized. In the oft-quoted *Bhagat Singh Thind Case*, the US Supreme Court ruled that Asian Indians were not 'free white persons', and therefore could not become American citizens. It even took away the citizenship from Sikhs who had already been naturalized. Asian immigrants could not vote, they could not own land, they could not become US citizens, and they could not sponsor their family members to follow them.

The land of their dreams had turned into a nightmare. Disgruntled about discrimination and exclusion from basic individual liberties, many began to leave the New World. The Sikh population dwindled. Sikhs who had refused to join the Sepoy Mutiny of 1857 against the British and had become the most fervent loyalists, lost their allegiance to their 'white masters'. Indians on the West Coast started campaigning for India's independence. In 1913, the revolutionary Ghadar Party was formed and many Sikhs joined it. The first issue of the *Ghadr* paper was published from the University of California in Berkeley, declaring its manifesto for a free and independent India with equal rights for all its citizens. The party published several magazines and pamphlets, and organized demonstrations against the British Raj and lectures to raise public awareness. Sikhs on the East Coast lobbied the White House to put pressure on Britain to give freedom to India. While many were actively engaged in such activities, a number of Sikhs returned home to join the Freedom Movement. The famous Ghadarite Kartar Singh Sarabha inspired a generation of nationalist revolutionaries, including Bhagat Singh, who died as a martyr for India's independence.

Those who stayed in the USA were severely isolated from their families. They lived like bachelors, even though some had been married back in India. Their expected temporary absence from the Punjab often became a lifetime spent abroad. There were barely any Sikh women in this early group of immigrants, and the Sikh men often married Spanish-speaking women on the western rim. Since couples applying to the county clerk for marriage licenses had to look alike to be considered as being of the same race, it was Hispanic women who met this requirement. Thus they created a bi-ethnic community erroneously termed 'Mexican-Hindus' (also 'Mexidus'). Some of their descendants today are among the most successful farmers, owning huge orchards of walnuts, peaches, plums and other fruit.[17]

A few Sikh immigrants returned home later in life. They had lost fluency in their mother tongue, Punjabi, but had not gained fluency in English. In the 1960s, there were cases like the one in the city of Patiala, where there was a gala 'remarriage' between a grandmother and a grandfather who had not seen each other for over half a century. The groom had left his newlywed wife with his extended family to work in America, and though he regularly sent back money, he barely knew his wife, and never had a chance to meet his son or his grandchildren.[18] As noted earlier, women were rare partners in the first wave of Sikh migrations and the pervasive anti-Asian feelings, allied to the series of exclusionary acts and immigration restrictions, made their entry almost impossible.

Since the relaxation of immigration laws after the Second World War, and in particular after the elimination of national quotas in 1965, there has been a dramatic surge in the Sikh population, both male and female, all over North America. The New Family Reunification policy opened doors to a second wave of Asian immigration through which Sikh men and women from all strata of society arrived in increasing numbers. Political crises in India have also impelled the increase in migration in recent decades. In the 1980s, the quest for an independent Khalistan led to a tragic political situation, driving many young Sikhs to North America, and their families have now found a home there. Another set is the case of the 'twice migrants' who were initially settled in Uganda, Kenya and Iran, but because of political turmoil in their adopted countries, families were forced to migrate a second time, and many settled in the USA and Canada.

There are more than 250,000 Sikhs in the United States and the numbers are even higher for Canada. In Vancouver they constitute 2.3 per cent of the population. The Punjab-like terrain of California still attracts the Sikhs (Yuba and Sutter counties form the largest and most prosperous Sikh farming communities outside India), recent Sikh migrants are strongly urban-based. History was made when the first Asian American won a seat in the United States Congress in 1956. A Sikh, Dalip Singh Saund, went to do graduate work in mathematics at the University of California at Berkeley and eventually became a successful farmer in the Imperial Valley. However, he fought numerous discriminatory laws against his people. In 1949, Indians finally earned the right to become US citizens and Saund was elected to Congress. In 2004, Ruby Dhalla made history as the first Sikh woman to be elected to a national parliament in the Western world. She is a Liberal Member of Parliament for Brampton-Springdale (Ontario, Canada). There are several other North American Sikhs now in the forefront of Canadian and American politics. Sikh women arrive in the New World not only on visas for wives, mothers, daughters and sisters, but also independently, to pursue education or enter a variety of careers. Like their male counterparts, they are energetic and enterprising, and highly successful in their professions.

The Middle East

The discovery of vast oil reserves, and the sudden wealth it brought to the Middle East in the early and mid-1970s, opened up another front for migrants. The new infrastructures and construction projects attracted thousands of Sikhs. From laborers to highly-skilled engineers, off they went to work in Dubai, Oman, Saudi Arabia, Bahrain and Iraq. Though exact figures for Sikh migration are unavailable, it is estimated that at the time of writing there are 60,000 to 175,000 Sikhs in the Gulf States, and the numbers may even have been higher in earlier times. The Middle East has frequently served as a stepping-stone for migration to the West or the Far East.

Clearly, Sikh migrations have followed unique patterns in different parts of the world, and have differed greatly depending on the historical moment. The different 'pull' factors from the host country, and the different 'push' factors from home, have been contingent on shifts in world economy and politics. The personality and talent of each individual migrant contributes greatly to the Sikh community's diasporic experience. Indeed, Sikhs have made their homes in extremely different cultural and religious landscapes. The recent revolution in communications – travel, electronic mail, telephones and skype – has eased the homesickness factor. With satellite television from India, they can enjoy their own films and shows. Star and Alpha Punjabi TV channels are available in several countries. In metropolitan centers, community members host radio and TV programs. With their boundless energy, hard work, entrepreneurship and cheerful attitude, Sikh men and women have been highly successful. Consciously or unconsciously, they live out their ethical maxim: '*kirat karni, nam japna, te vand chhakna* – work honestly, remember the Divine and share the goods'. Wherever they go, they adapt their distinct Sikh norms and values to new challenges.

Family

As noted earlier, the first immigrants were males who were either bachelors, or had left their wives and families in India when seeking their fortunes abroad. When the immigration rules relaxed and they had the opportunity to sponsor families, the demographics increased significantly. Since the typical Sikh family is not nuclear, the extended family would arrive, which would then begin another chain of migrations. A male could sponsor his wife and children, parents and unmarried siblings, who then in turn sponsored their spouses, and their spouses would subsequently sponsor their siblings and parents and so on. Such extended networks contributed to the concentration of Sikhs in areas such as Southall in England, Yuba City in America and Vancouver in Canada. A lonely visitor to a street like Girard in Toronto becomes envious of the chain of relatives running stores selling clothing, jewelry and groceries.

On the other hand, the success and affluence among diasporic communities is creating its own set of problems. The clash of traditional values and modern lifestyles is beginning to play out in individual homes. As people move on to live out their suburban dreams, the loneliness and depression of the transplanted elders is taking its toll. A recent *New York Times* lead story highlighted the aging parents of naturalized American citizens, who speak little or no English, do not drive and are culturally 'light years' away from the Punjab.[19] Its front page had a photograph of a group of white-bearded men with turbans sitting in a park in Fremont, California.

They made a sad group. Immigration to the West breaks down the joint family system to which they are accustomed. With their sons and daughters settled abroad, the aged parents are forced to follow them. Sometimes they come to take care of their grandchildren, for even those who are the most modern and well-established believe that their children should be taken care of by family members. The passing down of language and culture is important for diasporic Sikhs, and grandparents are called upon to play that crucial role. While the couples are busy with their professional life, parents and grandparents from the Punjab are confined to the home. Lonely and isolated, they find the West a golden cage and miss the rhythms of Punjabi life with the washerwoman, newspaper man, vegetable seller, and friends and relatives dropping by during the course of the day.

Gurdwara

The Gurdwara has always been the most important Sikh institution. In fact, the demography and prosperity of Sikh communities is reflected in the 'quantity' and 'quality' of its Gurdwara(s). The grandest Gurdwara outside India is the Sri Guru Singh Sabha Gurdwara in Southall. Soon after its opening in 2003, Prince Charles visited this prime symbol of Sikh presence in Britain. All across the globe, Gurdwaras serve as a central point for the local Sikh community: they are a source of information, assistance, food, shelter and fellowship. For the newly arrived Sikhs, locating the Gurdwara is an important initial step. The Sikh community creates and maintains its social, cultural, intellectual and political links through the Gurdwara. The first Gurdwara in the United States, built in Stockton, California in 1912 – was not only a religious hub, but also a storm center for political activities of the Ghadar Party. For decades, Stockton was the only Sikh center, but today there are more than 150 Gurdwaras in the USA.

Many started out on a rotational basis in homes, or in the basement of a church, or in a community hall. Stained glass windows with Gospel narratives can still be seen in some Gurdwaras. Where there are large Sikh populations, new buildings are being designed to accommodate the huge gatherings. Spacious Gurdwaras, such as the Ontario Khalsa Darbar, with 38 acres and over 35,000 square feet of buildings (located close to the airport in Toronto), or the Singh Sabha in Southall, help Sikhs to celebrate their special festivals in their thousands. Simultaneously, they enable people living in the neighborhood to pay daily homage before going to work – just as many Sikhs do back in India. Even for an occasional visitor, the Gurdwara offers a wonderful opportunity to pay homage, listen to *kirtan*, enjoy the delicious *langar*, visit the library and meet fellow Sikhs. With exactly the same sights, sounds, accents, smell and spirit as those in the Punjab, the Gurdwaras abroad transport immigrants back home in their imaginations, back into the recesses of their deepest self.

However, there is also a growing trend toward devotional services in smaller, more intimate groups. The dramatic increase in the Sikh population has led to some tension within the community. When the numbers were few, young or old, pioneer or newcomer, clean-shaven or Amrit-initiated, communist or Akali in their ideology, the migrants attended the same Gurdwara. Today, however, even minor differences within the burgeoning Sikh community tend to produce major factional conflicts. Consequently, even those who once were patrons of Gurdwaras now try to steer away from 'Gurdwara politics'. Instead, they organize smaller get-togethers for scriptural readings and devotional music. In lieu of fancy birthday parties and wedding anniversary celebrations, many Sikhs opt for worship and *kirtan* recitals in their homes.

Similarly, the younger generation of Sikhs is being attracted to the small, laity-led congregations. There was a recent report in *The New York Times* about a 'youth gurdwara' that a professional Sikh found on Facebook, posted by the Manhattan Sikh Association. Its information

> led him, on a Thursday night in late 2007, to the rented multipurpose room of a luxury condominium building in Battery Park City. There, in a setting usually deployed for residents' meetings and children's birthday parties, white cloths covered the carpet and white sheeting obscured the mirrors. At the far end of the room sat the hooded wooden platform, or palki, that held the Sikh holy book, the Adi Granth.
>
> What most caught Mr Singh's eye, though, were the other members of the congregation, or sangat. They were, like him, young professionals, the BlackBerry crowd, and as the worship service, or

> diwan, proceeded over the next several hours, these amateur clerics took turns leading the chanting of sacred poetry and the singing of devotional hymns.
>
> *The New York Times*, 22 August 2009

Whereas back in India, young Sikhs take their religion for granted, those abroad are keen to discover their heritage. Like this BlackBerry crowd, young diasporic Sikhs across the globe are organizing study groups and Cyber Gurdwaras so that they can understand the fundamental principles of their faith. Rather than Sikhism simply being handed down to them, they want discussion and debate, and seek an active role in their tradition.

The Gurdwaras too are making attempts to accommodate them. They are using plasma screens, with simultaneous English translation of the Scripture, so that the younger generation can follow the liturgy. Scholars from India and abroad are invited to lecture and explain philosophical and ethical concepts to the congregation. Many Gurdwaras organize youth camps, which provide religious knowledge, social bonding and athletic training. These camps are remarkably transnational, for they bring together children from North America, Europe and India. The *langar* meal in Gurdwaras typically consists of lentils, vegetables and wheat flatbread, but French fries and other local treats for children with Western palates are being added to the menu.

The Gurdwaras also reach out to people of other faiths. For Thanksgiving in the USA, Sikh congregations prepare meals in Gurdwaras and serve them to the needy and the homeless in their local communities. The Guru Nanak Nishkam Sewa Jatha in Birmingham has been involved with the Parliament of the World's Religions, the United Nations and NGO programs. It has organized interfaith forums at universities and Gurdwaras. At the Parliament of the World's Religions in Barcelona in 2004, the Jatha served *langar* meals to the thousands of men and women participants of the Interfaith Parliament. It also organized Kirtan recitations in the evening. As the verses of the Sikh Gurus merged with the lapping waves of the Mediterranean Sea, they set new currents in motion. The diasporic reality has expanded the meaning and experience of the Guru's verse: '*taha baikunthu jah kirtanu tera*: that place is paradise where we recite your praise' (GG: 749).

Gurpurabs

Wherever Sikhs migrate, they celebrate Gurpurabs (literally the day of the Guru). These include birth anniversaries of their Gurus, important historical events and the martyrdom of their heroes. During Gurpurabs, uninterrupted readings of the Scripture take place, intellectual symposiums are held and musical performances organized. Because of the large population of Sikhs in and around urban areas, a recent phenomenon has been to pool the resources of the various communities for the celebration of major events. For example, during the 300th anniversary of the Khalsa in 1999, Sikhs from the Washington DC area collectively held religious, cultural and intellectual activities at the National Convention Centre in the US capital.

While maintaining the foundations of their own faith and culture, Sikhs participate wholeheartedly in the customs and traditions prevalent in their adopted countries. In the West, they participate in traditions such as Easter, Thanksgiving and Christmas. Hanukkah candles and Christmas trees are making their entry into Sikh homes. Sikhs interact meaningfully with their neighbors and friends, exchanging gifts, sharing sweets. They also want to share their culture, so women and men relay *kirtan* and Sikh discourse on local television stations. Eager to reap the benefits of mutual friendship, Sikhs reach out to people of other faiths in their neighborhoods and communities.

Sikh Dharma of the Western Hemisphere

A Sikh immigrant, Harbhajan Singh Puri (1929–2004), had been teaching Kundalini yoga in Los Angeles when he founded the Sikh Healthy, Happy, Holy Organization (3HO) in 1969. The Organization soon developed into a formal religion, with ashrams across the USA and abroad. Under the guidance of Yogiji Maharaj, the 3HO adapted the philosophical and spiritual tenets of the Sikh religion to the needs of the counterculture and new age sensibilities, and reproduced a unique American Sikh community. Vietnam-era mistrust toward social and political institutions was rechanneled toward trust in the inner self and in the leader of the 3HO. The movement was a dramatic synthesis of Tantric Yoga, Sikhism, New Age spirituality and counterculture thought. The usually 'White'

(*Gora*) members adopt Sikh names, wear the five Sikh symbols and recite Sikh hymns. But they go beyond Sikhism by giving up meat and caffeine, wearing white outfits (though they are also beginning to wear light colors now), adopting yogic practices as an essential part of their spirituality, and being devoted to the leader – even entering into marriages arranged by him. The women members also wear the turban. In many parts of the Western hemisphere, the Khalsa Singhs (as they are commonly called) were the first to establish Gurdwaras. They continue to perform *kirtan*, prepare *langar* and make important contributions to Sikh scholarship. Through his collaboration with Punjabi Sikhs, Sardar Dr Sant Singh Khalsa made a valuable translation of Sikh scripture (see the website srigranth.org). Since the death of Yogiji Maharaj, his son-in-law, Bhai Sahib Satpal Singh Khalsa, serves as the ambassador of the Sikh Dharma of the Western hemisphere. Through his dedication, leadership, lectures and writings, Bhai Sahib Satpal Singh Khalsa is furthering the mission of Yogiji.

Kirtan

Sat Kartar Khalsa, also from the 3HO, has opened Sikh verse to a wide Western audience. She has recorded the Scripture by synthesizing Eastern and Western melodies. With her study and practice of Sikh Kirtan and yogic forms such as Kundalini and Naad (the yoga to access the inner Sound), she has added a new dimension to Sikh liturgical music.

An innovative figure in the Sikh diaspora is the twice migrant Dya Singh, who was born in Malaya and now lives in Australia. He and his music group present the traditional message of the Sikh Gurus through a new form of world music that fuses Eastern and Western melodies. In 2000, Dya Singh received the Male Artist of the Year World Music Award in Sydney. His group includes instrumentalists and musicians from various religious backgrounds, but all of them are in tune with the basic precepts of Sikhism. He has described his group's music as 'bringing Sikh music to the world and World music to the Sikhs'. Though some Sikhs object to his innovative style, his own mission is to take the universal message of the Sikh Gurus to diverse audiences.

Sikh Rites of Passage

Sikh rites basically remain the same as in India, except at death, when the body is taken to the mortuary and cremated according to the norms of the funeral home. The family members later take the ashes back to India and place them in the River Sutlej. In the interim, the ashes are left in the local Gurdwara. Death in the family is marked by the initiation of a reading of the Guru Granth. The *bhog* ceremony takes place on the tenth day, with final prayers being recited for peace to the deceased. In order to fit schedules, *bhog*, which can be at home or at the Gurdwara, is arranged over weekends. Family members try to keep the memory of their loved ones alive by making gifts to the needy, to schools, libraries, hospitals and to their Gurdwaras. At the death anniversary, the family will supply *langar* to the community. Sikh families may even send money to Gurdwaras back in the Punjab to have a continuous reading of the Guru Granth (*akhand path*) at shrines such as the Golden Temple. Incidentally, the Chair for the study of Sikhism at the University of California at Santa Barbara was endowed by Dr Kapany in memory of his mother, and the Chair for Sikhism at the University of California at Riverside by the Saini family in memory of Dr Jasbir Singh Saini.

Sikh weddings are extravagant affairs, and as the families become more affluent, so does their demonstration of conspicuous consumption. Since weddings are much more than a union between couples, they involve relatives across the Sikh diaspora and the exchange of expensive gifts. The ceremony of the Anand Karaj ('rite of bliss') is usually held in the local Gurdwara and follows the same pattern as those in the Punjab. But the pre-wedding and post-wedding rituals include Western customs: the exchanging of rings, cutting the cake, the popping of champagne corks and loud bands and discotheques have become standard. So are pre-wedding shopping sprees to the Punjab, and post-wedding honeymoons to exotic tropical islands. Contemporary Sikh weddings seem to be headed in opposite directions: they include Western-styled receptions and commodities as part of the daughter's dowry, but on the other hand, they are reviving traditions from the past. The standard *salwar-kameez* outfit has been replaced with elaborate *lahinga* skirts, and discarded customs such as putting on *mahindi*/henna are gaining importance. As always, the bride's family has to bear the burden of costs.

The rise in female education and female employment, the higher standard of living, and the stresses and challenges of modern life, have increased the break-up of marriages. Divorce, which was anathema in Sikh society, is becoming more accepted, and so is remarriage for women. (It used to be quite common for Sikh men to remarry, but remarriage for a woman, or even a widow, was dishonorable both for her and her family.)

Gender and Sexuality

Sikhs are transnational and remain closely tied to their families and communities in India. How to preserve Sikh identity in the modern West is a vital concern for diasporic Sikhs. To begin with, Sikh society has never quite freed itself from ancient Indian patriarchal structures. Threatened by the modern West, these patriarchal formulations are carried over the oceans and upheld with even greater urgency by the immigrants. Since women are literally the reproducers of the community, the preservation of 'Sikhness' in the New World falls primarily on them. As a result, they are subjected to strict controls. Control over their reproductive rights leads to the reproduction of the family's identity and that of the Sikh community at large. Alarmed by the permissive lifestyle of the West, some parents try to give their daughters a more traditional upbringing. A few send daughters back to the Punjab for education, and many have grandparents come here instead. Whereas sons are allowed western freedom, daughters have to uphold traditional values.

The honor (*izzat*) of the family depends on the mothers and daughters, so it is the Sikh mother who is held responsible for the upkeep of *kesha* among her sons and daughters. Living in the West, where boys have short hair, there is a real psychological struggle between her pride in preserving the Sikh format and the taunts aimed at her son by his peers, who have only seen girls with long hair and braids.

Most Sikh marriages are arranged. Parents and families of beautiful, talented young women respond to flashy advertisements for immigrant bachelors visiting home. Attracted by the wealth and lifestyle offered by alliances abroad, Sikh women from the Punjab immigrate as dependents. Many are married off to men settled in distant lands as a means of sponsoring their entire families.

Sociologists have interpreted this process as the 'sacrifice of the daughter for the sake of the son'.[20] A popular English-language newspaper in the Punjab captured this modern tragedy: 'Young, bright, promising girls are literally bartered away by their parents looking for an opportunity to send other members of the family to the land of lucre.'[21] Upon their arrival, some even discover that the 'successful doctor' is in fact a part-time pharmacologist; or a 'wealthy businessman' actually works at some 7-Eleven store belonging to a relative.

Cases of forced marriages, honor killings and female feticides are reported in diasporic communities.[22] Diasporic Sikhs are using different approaches to combat sexism and empower both women and men. There are scholars who return to the Guru Granth, urging their community to recognize the revolutionary spirit of their Gurus hidden by centuries of patriarchal accretions. They highlight gender disparity and challenge partriarchal assumptions. Artists, novelists and filmmakers are providing creative lenses for Sikhs to recognize the rampant sexism harming their society. Activists are leading campaigns to contest established structures of power. Members of the Sikh Coalition in America educate women about their basic rights. Members of the Sikh Nari Manch in the UK empower women to seek equality in public worship. The Southall Black Sisters Organization for Asians and African-Caribbeans courageously fights racism, domestic violence, arranged marriages, the dowry system and sexual abuse in the family, and provides support services to enable women and their children to escape violent relationships.

Sikhs are bringing their religion into contemporary debates on sexualities of difference. Jasbir Singh, a diasporic Sikh from London, affirms homosexuality and bisexuality on the basis of his Sikh faith. A law student, Singh is the founder of the Darshan group for lesbian, gay, bisexual and transgendered Sikhs, and the founder of the Masala group for gay and bisexual South Asian men. Situated in the modern West, he draws on the ideals of tolerance and equality expressed by Guru Gobind Singh. He cites historical examples in which the Sikh community stood up for the rights of others. A website for Lesbian, Gay, Bisexual and Transgendered Sikhs (sarbat.net) is based on the inclusive Sikh concept '*sarbat da bhala*' (welfare of each and all).

Academics

The establishment of institutions like the Punjabi University (in Patiala) and Guru Nanak Dev University (in Amritsar) in post-colonial Punjab has promoted academic interest in Sikhism all over the world. This interest is generating endowed Sikh Chairs across North America, including at the University of British Columbia, the University of California at Santa Barbara, Hofstra University on Long Island, the University of California at Riverside and the University of Michigan at Ann Arbor. A Chair in Musicology is also planned at Hofstra. As well as endowed Chairs, there is a growing number of professors in the USA, Canada, the UK and Europe whose teaching and research incorporate Sikhism, which should strengthen transnational connections and open the study of Sikhism to a larger audience. Both Sikhs and non-Sikhs are doing innovative research in a variety of areas: literature, history, philosophy, gender studies, post-colonial theory, performance theory, popular culture, art and architecture. As a result of the concerted efforts of Michael Hawley, a Canadian scholar, Sikh studies has recently established a distinct space at the American Academy of Religion. This critical forum fosters exchange among established scholars, graduate students and those new to Sikh studies on a range of critical issues. At the same time, it brings Sikhism to the attention of the Academy at large.

The community has played a very important role in promoting the academic study of Sikhism in the USA and is also engaged very actively in educating the general public. Under the visionary leadership of Dr Narinder Singh Kapany, the Sikh Foundation was established in 1967 to advance the heritage and future of the faith in the West. Kapany's unparalleled contributions have crystallized Sikh and Punjabi studies programs and permanent Chairs in several prestigious American universities, as well as the first Sikh permanent art gallery at the San Francisco Asian Art Museum. In more recent times, the Sikh Council on Religion and Education and the Kaur Foundation have started to organize educational activities to increase awareness and understanding of the Sikh religion, and its values, within local communities and political groups. They arrange workshops and conferences, and produce books and visual materials. Mirin Kaur, President of the Kaur Foundation, has collaborated with the United States Library of Congress to bring scholars, and host conferences in its auditoriums, and add 80 Sikh volumes to its collection. The Spinning Wheel Festival sponsors films by Sikhs or about Sikhs across the diaspora to provide education about their religion, history, culture and traditions. Valerie Kaur's *Divided We Fall*, the first feature documentary chronicling hate violence in the aftermath of 9/11, has traveled to many classrooms and lecture halls, sparking dialog and discussion. The goal of these enterprising individuals and organizations is to see Sikhism become a part of the mainstream American curriculum. They are steadily succeeding. On 21 May 2010, the Texas State Board of Education unanimously passed an amendment to its curriculum, to include information about Sikh culture and religion in social studies and history syllabuses.

Sense of Responsibility

The second generation of Sikhs takes great pride in its American constitution, and to ensure the civic rights of diasporic Sikhs in the land of liberty and equal opportunity, they are building community-based organizations. In 1996, a group of graduate students created the Sikh Mediawatch and Resource Task Force (SMART), a volunteer cyberspace organization with a focus on media analysis and the communication of accurate information about the Sikh faith. With the growing needs and challenges, it expanded to become the Sikh American Legal Defense and Education Fund (SALDEF), a national civil rights and educational organization based in Washington, DC. Immediately after 9/11, the Sikh Coalition came into existence in New York. Following the discrimination faced by many Sikhs after 9/11 and 7/7, they are taking seriously the responsibility of educating the general public. Mainstream media projections instilled such fear and hate for anybody with turban and beard that more than 200 Sikhs have been victims of hate crimes in the USA since 9/11. A Sikh gas station owner in Arizona, Sadar Amarjit Singh Sodhi, was murdered in an act of blind rage. In another act of violence, a young teenager had his turban torn off and his hair sheared by a fellow schoolmate in Queens, New York (*The New York Times*, 26 May 2007). Backed by an extensive network of volunteers, SALDEF and the Sikh Coalition have initiated numerous projects in the areas of advocacy, education and media relations. They take up the issue of wearing turbans in the workplace, carrying *kirpan* (the Sikh symbol of the sword) in public schools, and the religious rights of Sikhs during travel at airports. Young Sikh men and women are enthusiastically providing legal assistance, educational outreach at Federal and State levels, and legislative advocacy to protect the civil rights of Sikh Americans. They are quick and forceful in their response too. Within hours of South Carolina State Senator Jake Knotts' racist remark ('We've already got a raghead in the White House, we don't need another raghead in the governor's mansion') against South Carolina State Representative and Gubernatorial candidate Nikki Haley, daughter of Sikh migrants, SALDEF demanded an official apology.[23] When the Sikhs were called 'ragheads' a century ago there was hardly any reaction; but today politically conscious Sikhs demand the same respect that white Anglo-Saxon Americans are given. Numerous organizations and websites are working diligently to rectify past errors and deletions in the area of Sikhism, and to promote new channels of inter-religious understanding.

Diasporic Narratives

As already noted, Sikh women were few and far between in the first waves of migration, but today they are a vital presence and they are making phenomenal contributions in both local and international spheres. This concluding section focuses on the works of just a few women artists: Gurinder Chadha, Shauna Singh Baldwin, Inni Kaur, Jessi Kaur, and Amrit and Rabindra Kaur. From their unique diasporic locus, these women explore the intricate threads that make up the durable fabric of the Sikh diaspora. Their films, literary narratives and paintings offer a meaningful insight into the colorful past connecting Sikhs, from Singapore to Montreal. Most subtly, they introduce the complex strands of nostalgia, adaptation, prejudice, stereotype, hybridization and multiculturalism woven into the present reality of the diasporic experience. And their introspective artistic designs provoke reflections on the future of Sikhism in a rapidly shifting world.

Gurinder Chadha

Born in Kenya and brought up in the UK, Gurinder Chadha is the first British South Asian woman to direct feature films. From a family of 'twice migrants', her father worked for Barclays Bank in Kenya, but his Sikh turban and beard were deemed unsuitable for British customers. Subsequently, he set up a family business in Southall, where the family lived, and so Chadha grew up in the midst of a large group of working-class South Asians. She started her career as a news reporter for the BBC and directed several award-winning documentaries. As she recounts in an interview, her film *I'm British, But* was premiered with much jubilation in the Southall community center, and, ironically, the money she earned from her first commercial film, *Bhaji on the Beach* (1993), was deposited in Barclay's Bank![24]

With no formal training in filmmaking, Chadha's career has been a remarkable success, with films such as *What's Cooking?* (2000), *Bend It like Beckham* (2002), *Bride and Prejudice* (2004), *Angus, Thongs and Perfect Snogging* (2008) and *It's a Wonderful Afterlife* (2010) under her belt. So far, *Bend It Like Beckham* is her greatest box office hit. Made on a tiny budget and with no established stars, it has grossed over 77 million dollars worldwide, and quickly promoted its cast to premier league status and hefty incomes. As in many of her other films, Chadha's camera sensitively explores ethnic, racial, religious and gendered identities. So this classic coming-of-age comedy with its feel-good quality is acutely sharp. 'Bending the ball' is actually bending one's conventional roles so that dreams can come true. The images of Guru Nanak and David Beckham are frequently flashed on Chadha's screen, juxtaposing the protagonist's Sikh heritage with her Western dream. The Bamras want their daughter Jaswinder (Jess for short) to be educated, get married and take care of domestic matters, but Jess wants to play soccer. Her father's experience of racism and exclusion, when he wanted to join the cricket team on arriving in Britain, is replayed when Jess is called a 'Paki' during a match. The airplane flying above their home is a trope for their relocation. Chadha's powerful narrative and brilliant direction disclose the complexities of migration and cultural integration – not just for Sikhs, but for diasporas across the board. The film has an international appeal. It raises fundamental issues: generational conflicts, cultural tensions, and the clash between tradition and modernity.

Her resonating theme is that humans have the capacity to bond despite racial, religious, ethnic and cultural differences. Chadha's camera shows how people brought up in the same home can be far apart, while those who come from entirely different backgrounds can be very close. Indeed, the Bamra sisters, who grew up near Heathrow in a traditional Sikh home, are a total antithesis: while Pinky reproduces the stereotypical gender roles with a love for fashionable clothes, marriage and children, Jess – with her sole dream to play soccer – rejects these conventions entirely. On the other hand, Jess is able to relate closely with the tall, blonde Jules who comes from a white, middle-class 'modern' British family. Even Jules' 'white' mother and Jess' 'Sikh' mother who look, speak and act entirely differently from each other, are amazingly similar in the ideals they cherish for their daughters. Neither wants her daughter to play soccer! Victims of patriarchy, both want a sexy body for their daughters. Likewise, the 'white' coach and the 'brown' Jess are extremely similar – Indian or Irish, both have been victims of colonialism, both are disgruntled with their parents, both love soccer and both have had accidents that left scars on their legs. The budding love between them, and her friendship with Jules, reveals the human connections that transcend differences of birth or origin. The film projects global identities as culturally plural rather than fixed around some national or racial entity. The Punjabi lyrics of the film, combined with Western rhythms, celebrate the Britishness of diasporic Sikhs. The film points toward a new collective ethnic identity.

The possibility of seeing people like ourselves in mainstream cinema is a self-affirming phenomenon. To come across a Sikh family sharing their own problems, wearing their costume, speaking their language, cooking their food and celebrating their customs and symbols, brings a feeling of great pride and self-worth to the Sikhs. Socially located within the wider family and community, Chadha's protagonists provide meaningful associations. Overall, the Sikh experience has been marginal in both Indian and Western films. The spate of Bollywood films rarely has authentic Sikh protagonists. Hollywood's trivialization of Kirpal Singh in *The English Patient* is yet another example of the paradigm of neglect to which Sikhs have been subjected. Even Ondaatje's lengthy and beautiful description of the Golden Temple was completely deleted from Anthony Minghella's screen. Chadha's vibrant visual spectacle fills an important gap. Artist Sobha Singh's painting of Guru Nanak above the mantlepiece dominates the Bamra home, and a replica of the Golden Temple is also proudly displayed in their living room. Pinky's wedding takes place in Shepherd's Bush Gurdwara, the first Gurdwara in Britain. This is also the religious site where the director Chadha herself got married. The audience can thus participate in their ever-accumulating history.

Shauna Singh Baldwin

Continuing in this genre of the 'Empire writing back', Shauna Singh Baldwin focuses on the 'forgotten' religion of the Sikhs, and makes an important contribution by introducing this north Indian religion to the reading public. She is the acclaimed author of *English Lessons and Other Stories*. Her first novel, *What the Body Remembers*, received the 2000 Commonwealth Writer's Prize for Best Book in the Canada-Caribbean region. Her second novel, *The Tiger Claw*, was a finalist for the 2004 Giller Prize. The author was born into a Sikh family in Montreal, but grew up in India when her parents moved back, and subsequently went to the USA. Her work therefore spans many crossings. Her short story, *Montreal 1962*, for example, captures the predicament of a new migrant couple. The husband is told that he can have a job only if he takes off his turban and becomes clean-shaven. But his wife will not allow it. She takes an oath: 'I will not let you cut your strong rope of hair and go without a turban into this land of strangers.'[25] Many diasporic Sikhs in the New World, including the author's parents, have found themselves in such a situation.

Her novel, *What the Body Remembers*, gives a political-historical background to the Partition of the Punjab in 1947. Literary works on this traumatic period of Indian history are few and far between. Baldwin's rich novel joins Khushwant Singh's *Train to Pakistan*, Salman Rushdie's *Midnight's Children* and Bapsi Sidhwa's *Cracking India*. However, *What the Body Remembers* stands out because it leads us into the historical reality from the perspective of a Sikh woman. Roop, the young and fertile second wife of a wealthy Sikh Sardar, boldly crosses over the boundary mapped by the British as they give up their sovereignty over the Indian subcontinent. Furthermore, Baldwin's text reviews the political negotiations of that time from a Sikh point of view, and movingly articulates Sikh aspirations and despair. The novel is quite explicit in criticizing Indian politicians, whose strategic plans and maneuvers hurt the Sikh community. The great Mahatma Gandhi is sketched in a negative light: a 'shilly-shallying politician' – 'a man who says he is for all religions, Hindu, Sikh, Muslim, Christian, is a man of no conviction'.[26] The author hauntingly expresses the betrayal felt by her fellow Sikhs: 'The

Mahatma raised the national flag of a free India and it did not have a strip of deep Sikh blue as he promised'.[27]

Baldwin's fictional discourse offers an interesting window into the daily life of the Sikhs. Roop's grandmother personally contextualizes the centrality of the Guru Granth as she goes into the small prayer room with the holy book, and puts 'the Guru to bed for the night'.[28] Through the novel, readers meet Sikhs who proudly wear their five symbols – *kesha* (long hair), *kangha* (comb), *kara* (bracelet), *kirpan* (sword) and *kacha* (drawers); encounter Sikh Gurus and their families; visit Sikh shrines in both Pakistan and India; frequently hear the Sikh greeting *Sat Sri Akal*; and learn about many other Sikh customs and ceremonies, and even how these differ from those of their Hindu and Muslim counterparts. Sikh ideals, values and identity are woven into the texture of Baldwin's narrative. Her vivid descriptions take readers beyond stereotypical images and bring them face to face with authentic Sikh men and women. Having been raised on stories of Cinderella and Snow White in a postcolonial Punjab, even Sikhs are pleasantly surprised to discover affinities with characters penned in English. Such works of fiction published in the West empower Sikhs with a renewed sense of their own heritage.

Inni Kaur and Jessi Kaur

Inni Kaur (from the East Coast of the USA) and Jessi Kaur (from the West Coast) utilize the medium of stories and illustrations to introduce Sikhism to children in the diaspora. How to pass on traditions to the next generation is a major concern for the Sikh community. These innovative thinkers are relaying their Sikh legacy in modern idiom. Inni captures the founder Guru before he set out on his spiritual mission, narrating and illustrating events from his childhood and adolescence.[29] Her literary and visual focus is not on the Guru's miracles, but on his inner tensions and angst. Her young grade-school audience can thus access the Guru in personal ways. Rather than being a distant figure, Guru Nanak emerges in Inni's text as a three-dimensional person with whom young readers can share their anxieties, and with him they can think through ways to solve them too.

Jessi Kaur's fictional protagonists are young diasporic Sikh boys, growing up on the West Coast. They maintain long hair as a symbol of their faith in a culture where they are barely known and terribly misunderstood. The nine-year-old Simran's struggle for acceptance by his peers is effectively communicated in his letters to a pen pal in Japan – *Dear Takuya...Letters of a Sikh Boy*.[30] His schoolmates tease him about his turban and taunt him that he is a girl. During the summer, Simran attends a Sikh cultural camp, where he meets other children like himself and learns to appreciate his culture in the contemporary West. While affirming himself, the little boy informs outsiders about his Sikh faith and identity.

Jessi's protagonist Arjan, in *The Royal Falcon*, goes on a magical flight from his room in America with a falcon name Khushi under beautiful skies, over soccer matches, in unkempt apartments, and into the past to the royal court of Guru Gobind Singh in Anandpur.[31] A cultural symbol of sovereignty, the fearless falcon actually represents the essential human values of compassion, generosity and love, so prized by the Sikh Gurus. The little story takes readers into that vast interior world where they begin to understand one another beyond superficial differences. In a highly nuanced manner, the author links the sentiments of the Sikh Guru's falcon with those of the Western literary icon the Velveteen Rabbit – 'Love makes everyone real' – thus opening new emotional and cognitive channels for her society.

Amrit and Rabindra Kaur Singh

The Sikh diasporic experience acquires an exciting new multicultural perspective in the paintings of Amrit and Rabindra Kaur Singh. They are twin sisters who collaborate and have created a genre they call 'Past Modern'. It is a brilliant reworking of the traditional Indian miniature style and techniques developed in the Mughal Imperial Court – combined with their own post-colonial diasporic experience. They were born in a Sikh home in London in 1966 and attended a Catholic school. Close family and community ties were crucial to their development as artists. During postgraduate work on 'Religion and the Arts', the twins were struck by the lack of non-Western esthetic models in their curriculum. Because of their multiple identities – British, Asian, Sikh and women – their sensibilities are exceptionally refined. Using the universal medium of colors and lines, the twins offer a perceptive portrayal of displacement and hybridization, to which immigrants across cultures and ethnicities can easily relate. They have already become highly successful, exhibiting their work in several solo and group shows in the UK and abroad.

Just as the life of the Mughal Emperors was minutely recorded in the traditional miniatures, the Sikh Twins narrate their multilayered autobiography. In amazing detail they paint people, objects and scenes that have relevance for them. Consequently, episodes from their personal life as British Asian Sikh women living in a predominantly Western culture, offer valuable societal and political critiques. Each of their works is full of exquisite details and symbolism, and therefore elicits a close reading.

Having grown up in the Thatcher era, they are able to offer a biting critique of her policies. Their *Reagan and Thatcher* (1987) mimics the Mughal painting of the Indian Emperor Jahangir embracing Shah Abbas of Persia.[32] The embrace of the Muslim leaders is changed into a handshake between the American President and the British Prime Minister, symbolizing their close alignment as champions of Christianity, capitalism and the destruction of the Soviet Union. The Indo-Persian locus on Abul Hassan's map is shifted to the mid-Atlantic, and the halo behind Jahangir is metamorphosed into a red cloud to indicate Reagan and Thatcher's threatening nuclear ambitions. In this political satire, the lamb and the lion of the original painting are replaced by the mule and the vixen – upon which stand the modern leaders with big, sly smiles.

A more serious political critique emerges in *Nineteen Eighty-Four* (1998).[33] Here the Sikh Twins depict the tragic storming of the Golden Temple by Indian troops under the orders of Prime Minister Indira Gandhi. Armored tanks entered the most sacred precincts of the Sikhs. Though the diasporic community was geographically far from the tragic occurrence in Amritsar, the suffering and injustice were intimately felt by Sikhs in every corner of the world. In the twins' painting, the Golden Temple is framed in an angular perspective, and its pool of nectar is full of blood. Innocent men, women and children who had come to pay homage are panic stricken. Because of their biased reporting, the media is rendered blindfolded. A multiheaded Indira Gandhi stands in an armored tank, holding a bag of coins in her left hand. With her right, she rejects the martyred heads of the Ninth Sikh Guru Tegh Bahadur and the freedom fighter Bhagat Singh. The heads of Thatcher, Churchill and Bill Clinton constitute Indira Gandhi's identity. Like the Western politicians, she is shown to be obsessed with money and power. Every tiny part of Amrit and Rabindra's paintings has a nuanced significance.

In *All That I Am*, they vividly reproduce the immigrant story of their father.[34] A smiling Sikh man, with a yellow turban and a stethoscope around his neck, is in the center, with his memories and dreams interlacing his mental cartography. On the left is his carefree childhood of flying kites left far behind in the Punjab; on the right is his struggling start as a peddler in the industrial district of Manchester's Ancoats. Above him are three distinct sites: the Golden Temple that was his religious centre; Mahatma Gandhi walking on a bleeding area that evokes the traumatic 1947 Division; and the Bombay–Tilbury steamer that carried him to Britain. At the bottom right, books and diplomas begin to appear, signifying his successful career as a doctor. An English suburban house on his left is balanced by a globe centered on India on his right, so no matter how settled he may be in his new world, there is always nostalgia for 'Mother India'. In fact, the LP record of the popular 1957 Bollywood film, *Mother India* (directed by Mehboob Khan), is in his left hand. We also see his volume of Sikh verses and the *sitar* brought from India. The striking intersection between the framed photographs of his parents and that of his family held in his right hand, highlights his role in passing the culture and religion of his ancestors in the Punjab to the next generation in the UK. Any immigrant from any part of the globe can tap into the Singh Twins' intricate and ornate designs and draw sustenance from their poignant narrative. Their paintings repeatedly celebrate their multicultural reality.

Les Girls brings together Asian and Western cultures in the bedroom of the artists, where Punjabi handmade *juttis* lie next to high-heeled modern shoes.[35] In this interior space, the sisters are relaxing together with their friends and cousins. Brown and white friends sit together on the twin beds in a variety of Punjabi outfits and blue jeans. The Edenic imagery of the outside contextualizes their innocent and blissful chatting, eating samosas, drinking Coca-Cola, listening to music, dancing, sharing stories and photos, doing make up. Intriguingly, in this harmonious picture, distinct 'Indian' and 'Western' postures can be discerned: while one of the twins sits with her legs folded in, her Western friend seated beside her on the bed has her legs stretched out. Overall, the beaming yellow and gold colors bestow an extraordinary quality to ordinary moments experienced by the girls. Female icons dominate the landscape: a black and white photograph of the secular icon Marilyn Monroe is as much a presence as the ornate Madonna and Child. Brimming with joy and togetherness, this bedroom scene becomes a metonymic marker for the artists' multicultural existence.

Similarly, *The Last Supper* depicts their Sikh family having a Christmas feast and the entire scene overflows with icons, food, clothes and items belonging to the West, the East and the Middle East.[36] As the father sitting near the decorated Christmas tree carves a huge turkey, a cousin wearing a tee shirt with an Egyptian pharaoh print tries to catch a spilling bottle of Coke. A plurality of images from different religions – Guru Gobind Singh, Lord Buddha, Lord Ganesha, the Virgin Mary, the Taj Mahal – fill the space around the sumptuous table spread with English and Indian delicacies. The backdrop is Michelangelo's *The Last Supper*, evoking the significance of Christmas that is often lost in its commercial hype. And the typical plump snowman outside the window happens to be a sleek Sikh with a saffron turban and black beard! Facing the Christmas party, he seems to raise issues of hybridization, globalization and postmodernity. Clearly, multiple currents are at work: Sikhs in the diaspora ardently maintain their culture, adopt the customs of their new neighbors and dynamically forge new ways of being in the world.

Along with an urgent sense of responsibility, there is a new confidence among diasporic Sikhs that empowers them with an identity that is equally American, British or Canadian as it is Sikh. Musicians, novelists, short-story writers, fashion designers and film makers are exploring their Sikh heritage, as well as creating new arabesques with *other* cultures they encounter in their lives. Sikhs are proud citizens who celebrate their traditions with great jubilation at numerous cultural and academic venues. And they are making new ones. The air is especially abuzz with excitement around Baisakhi, the Sikh New Year (in the spring), and for Guru Nanak's birthday (in the autumn). Huge Sikh processions, with colorful floats carrying the Guru Granth and depicting different aspects of Sikh life, are becoming a familiar sight in metropolises all over the world. On 16 November 2009, Guru Nanak's birthday was celebrated in the White House for the first time. Sikh sacred music was performed by *ragis*, who were brought in from the Golden Temple in Amritsar, and hymns were sung by two American Sikhs from the 3HO. For the Sikh community it was a powerful affirmation of their own identity and of their presence in the USA. In their religious processions, Sikhs confidently carry both the Nishan Sahib and the Stars and Stripes flags – symbolic of their simultaneous allegiance to their faith and their new country.

Whether in the Punjab or abroad, Sikhs are not homogenous by any means. Differences in education, age, profession, gender, beliefs, practices (some keep their external symbols, some do not), and political and social interests, contribute to their manifold diversity. The social environment of their host country has its own impact, but there is a fundamental Sikh spirit that is shared by all. The transnational ties and social networks keep that spirit alive and link their practices. Entering a Gurdwara in Southall (UK) is the same as entering the one in Bobigny (France). With the same hymns, language, *langar*, Sikhs connect spatially with their communities everywhere, and even temporally with past and future generations. And the hospitality is uniform. Years later, the words of welcome continue to echo in my mind. A Bobigny group of *amritdhari* Sikhs came to deliver some *kirtan* music tapes while I was staying at a chateau with fellow American academics, and asked: 'Why don't you stay in our own Gurdwara, sister?' A clean-shaven Sikh taxi driver drove me from a hotel in Victoria (British Columbia) and said: 'Sister, why don't you stay with my family?' Their words belong to the Sikh tradition of hospitality and nurture migratory populations across the continents.

The first Sikhs who arrived in the USA were just a 'picturesque quartet', as the *San Francisco Chronicle* observed in 1899, but now the Sikh men and women are significant players on the global field. Their home is now in their new countries; they no longer have the myth of returning to the Punjab. Securely settled in different regions of the globe, they are funding educational, medical and business infrastructures for their fellow Sikhs in India. Sikhs abroad have also reached out to other Indian communities. Recently, a British Sikh funded the rebuilding of a mosque in his village near Ludhiana, which had been demolished during the Partition riots of 1947. Their regional religion from the Punjab has indeed become a world religion. It is an exciting time for the Sikhs.

[illegible] of their [illegible] as the USA. [illegible] their [illegible] pride these [illegible] confidently [illegible] the Punjabi [illegible] and the Sikhs [illegible] [illegible] [illegible] in their simultaneous allegiance to their [illegible] and their new country.

[illegible] the Punjab or abroad, Sikhs [illegible] [illegible] [illegible] [illegible]. Differences in education, [illegible], [illegible] [illegible] practice (some keep their external symbols, some do not), and political and social interests contribute to their [illegible] [illegible]. The social environment of their host country has [illegible] [illegible], but there is a fundamental Sikh spirit [illegible] [illegible] by [illegible] [illegible] traditional and [illegible] [illegible] to keep that spirit alive and [illegible] their [illegible] the Sikh tradition of [illegible] and [illegible] to [illegible] [illegible] [illegible] [illegible].

[illegible] funded the rebuilding of a mosque in the village that [illegible] [illegible] had been demolished [illegible] [illegible] [illegible]. Their [illegible] [illegible] [illegible] the Punjab [illegible] [illegible] [illegible] [illegible] [illegible] [illegible] [illegible] [illegible] [illegible].

Glossary of Names and Terms

3HO — Healthy Happy Holy Organization – the name of the Sikh Dharma of the Western hemisphere. It was founded by Yogi Harbhajan Singh, and after his death in 2004, Bhai Sahib Satpal Singh Khalsa serves as its ambassador.

Akali — 'A follower of the Timeless One'. Also the name of a Sikh political party.

Akal Takht — Building facing the Harimandar, the Sikhs' seat of religious authority.

Akhandpath — Uninterrupted reading of the entire Sikh Scripture by a sequence of readers. The reading is completed in 48 hours.

Amritdhari — Sikhs who have been initiated by the *amrit* (nectar) ceremony.

Amrit sanskar — Rite of Khalsa initiation.

Amrit vela — The period of early dawn conducive for spiritual contemplation.

Anandkaraj — 'Rite of bliss'; Sikh wedding.

Ardas — Liturgical prayer recited in solo by a representative of the congregation. It is recited at the conclusion of ceremonies with everybody standing up.

Baisakhi — New Year's Day, the first day of the month of Baisakh.

Bani — The divine word.

Bhai — Term for brother, often used to address male community members.

Bhangra — Punjabi folk dance.

Bhog — Ceremonial conclusion of a complete reading of the Guru Granth.

Chauri — Fan made from yak hair, waved over the Guru Granth; symbol of respect.

Darbar Sahib	Harmandar or Golden Temple, the revered 'Royal Court'.
Darshan	'To see'; being in the presence of the Guru Granth.
Dasam Granth	The book of the Tenth Guru created in his Court.
Deg tegh fateh	'Cauldron, sword, victory', the slogan of the Khalsa.
Gidda	Punjabi folk dance and music performed by women.
Granthi	'Reader of the Granth', custodian of a Gurdwara, and leads worship.
Gurdwara	Sikh place of worship (*dwara*/door to the Guru).
Gurmukh	Moral person (faces the Guru; not self-centered).
Gurmukhi	The script of the Sikhs.
Gurpurabs	Special days of the Sikh calendar (birth and death anniversaries of the Gurus).
Guru	Teacher, enlightener.
Guru Granth	Sacred scripture of the Sikhs; center of Sikh rites and ceremonies. Also called the Adi Granth, the First Book, to distinguish it from the Dasam Granth. In daily parlance this 1,430-page volume is addressed as Guru Granth Sahib; the suffix *sahib* or *sahibji* denotes respect.
Gutka	Small collections of hymns.
Hukam	'Command, or order' – the rite of reverently opening the Guru Granth at random, and the passage on the top left is read as the Guru's direct response.
Haumai	The narrow, self-centered 'I' or 'me'.
Ikk Oan Kar	'One Being Is', the Sikh precept of the singular Divine.
Janamsakhis	Narratives about the birth and life of the first Sikh Guru.
Jap	Composed by Guru Nanak, this is the first hymn in the Guru Granth. It is recited by devout Sikhs every morning. The suffix *'ji'* (*Japji*) is added for respect.
Jhatka	Animal killed in one stroke, approved for consumption.
Kacha	Underwear, a symbol of the Khalsa.

Kangha	Comb, tucked into the hair as a symbol of the Khalsa.
Kara	Bracelet, worn as a symbol of the Khalsa.
Karahprashad	Sacrament distributed at the end of Sikh worship. It is warm and delicious, consisting of equal portions of butter, flour, sugar and water.
Karam	Action as well as the fruit of action.
Kar Seva	Voluntary service, denotes the cleaning of the pool surrounding the Harmandar.
Kaur	'Princess' – surname for Sikh women.
Kesh	Unshorn hair, a symbol of the Khalsa.
Keshdhari	Those who do not cut their hair as a symbol of the Khalsa.
Keski	A smaller version of the Sikh turban.
Khalsa	'Pure'; often used as a synonym for Sikhs; the distinct Sikh identity, which Sikhs firmly believe was created by their Tenth Guru in 1699 at Anandpur.
Khanda	Double-edged sword; also a symbol of the Khalsa, comprising a vertical double-edged sword (like the axis mundi) set within a circle – with two crossed swords below it.
Khande di pahul	Initiation with the double-edged sword, the Sikh initiation rite.
Kirpan	Sword, one of the five symbols of the Khalsa.
Kirtan	Singing of sacred verses accompanied by harmonium and *tabla* drums.
Kuka	Belonging to the Namdhari sect of Sikhs.
Langar	Community meal; everybody sits on the floor and eats together.
Lavan	(Four) circumambulations of the Guru Granth for the marriage ceremony.
Manmukh	Facing the self – a selfish person.
Matha tekana	To bow down before the Guru Granth with forehead touching the ground.
Mubarak	'Congratulations'.
Mul Mantar	The prelude to Guru Nanak's Jap. Set at the beginning of the Guru Granth, it forms the quintessence of Sikh thought.

Nishan Sahib	Sikh flag. Serves as a marker for gurdwaras. It is saffron in color, triangular in shape, and imprinted with the design of the *khanda*.
Nitnem	Daily prayers.
Panj pyare	The five beloved: Daya Singh, Dharam Singh, Himmat Singh, Sahib Singh and Muhakam Singh. They were the first five volunteers at the inauguration of the Khalsa.
Panth	Sikh community.
Path	Reading of scripture.
Prakash karna	'Bring to light'; the morning ritual of opening the Guru Granth.
Purdah	Practice that confines women to their private world by having their faces veiled, and keeping them behind the walls of the home.
Rag	Musical mode.
Ragi	Musicians who perform kirtan.
Rahit Maryada	Ethical code.
Rumala	Covering for the sacred text.
Sahajdhari	'Slow adopter'; Sikhs who do not keep long hair.
Salwar-kameez	The general loose pants and shirts worn by Sikh women.
Sangat	Sikh congregation.
Sant-sipahi	Saint-soldier; the ideal Sikh who is both pious and brave.
Sardar, Sardarni	Titles for Sikh men and women (equivalent of Mr and Mrs).
Sat	Truth.
Sati	The custom of self-immolation of women on the funeral pyre of their husband.
Sat Sri Akal	Sikh greeting: 'Truth is the Timeless One'.
Seva	Selfless action, a means to build moral character.
Shahid	Martyr.
Shromani Gurdwara Prabhandak Committee	SGPC for short. The elected committee that governs Sikh shrines.
Sikh	Disciple or student from Sanskrit *shishya*, Pali *sekha*.

Singh	'Lion-hearted'; surname for Sikh men.
Singh Sabha	Sikh renaissance movement begun in 1873.
Sukhasan	'Resting posture'; evening ceremony of closing the Guru Granth.
Udasi	An ascetic order of Sikhs founded by Guru Nanak's son, Siri Chand.
Waheguru	'Wonderful Guru'; common Sikh exclamation (before meals or even after a sneeze).

Illustration, Map and Picture Credits

Notes

Introduction

1 Mark Juergensmeyer, 'The Forgotten Tradition: Sikhism in the Study of World Religions', in M. Juergensmeyer and N. G. Barrier (eds), *Sikh Studies* (Berkeley, CA: University of California Press, 1979), 13–23.

2 W. C. Smith, 'Comparative Religion: Whither – and Why?', in Mircea Eliade and Joseph Kitagawa (eds), *The History of Religion* (Chicago, IL: University of Chicago Press, 1959), 34.

3 Peter Dickinson, *The Devil's Children* (*The Changes*: Book 1) (New York: Dell, 1970), 89.

4 In 'What Is Feminist Theory?', C. Pateman and E. Gross (eds), *Feminist Challenges: Social and Political Theory* (Boston, MA: Northeastern University Press, 1986), 199.

Chapter I

1 For the population statistics, I have relied on Gurharpal Singh and Darshan Singh Tatla, *Sikhs in Britain: The Making of a Community* (London/New York: Zed Books, 2006), 32. The authors provide the global Sikh population in 2005. The numbers would have increased by now. More data will be available in the soon to come 2011 census.

2 Harbans Singh, *Guru Nanak and Origins of the Sikh Faith* (Bombay: Asia Publishing House, 1969), 20–1.

3 Otto Rank, *The Myth of the Birth of the Hero* (New York: Vintage, 1959).

4 Most likely, Guru Nanak was named after his older sister 'Nanaki'. Since she was born at her maternal grandparents' home, called *nanake* in Punjabi, she got the name 'Nanaki'.

5 A few centuries later, the Sufi poet Bulleh Shah asks: 'Why must I turn towards the Ka'ba, when my lover lives in the village of Takht Hazara?'

6 Recorded in the Guru Granth, Rag Asa, 471.

7 Victor Turner, *The Forest of Symbols: Aspects of Ndembu Ritual* (Ithaca, NY: Cornell University Press, 1967), 96.

8 *Puratan Janamsakhi Guru Nanak Devji*. Published in Amritsar by Khalsa Samachar, 1946; 'Bein Parvesh', 16–19.

9 Hans-Georg Gadamer, *Truth and Method* (New York: Crossroad, 1989), 575.

10 For a fuller typological analysis, see my book, *The Birth of the Khalsa: A Feminist Re-Memory of Sikh Identity* (Albany, NY: SUNY Press, 2005).

11 Darshan Singh, *Bhai Gurdas: Sikhi de Pahile Viakhiakar* (Patiala, India: Punjabi University, 1986), 6.

12 For Bhai Gurdas' ballads, I have used the volume edited by Bhai Vir Singh, *Varan Bhai Gurdas* (Amritsar, India: Khalsa Samachar, 1977).

13 Earlier in his text, Bhai Gurdas mentions that Guru Nanak on his travels carried a manuscript tucked under his arm (Var I: 32), so it is likely that the jasmine flower he brings out from under his arm symbolizes his poetic utterances.

14 The composition he recited during his revelatory account from the Janamsakhi and mentioned by Bhai Gurdas.

15 S. H. Nasr, *Knowledge and the Sacred* (NY: Crossroad, 1981), 12.

Chapter II

1 For studies on the development of the Guru Granth, see Pashaura Singh, *The Guru Granth: Canon, Meaning and Authority* (New Delhi: Oxford University Press, 2000); Gurinder Singh Mann, *The Making of Sikh Scripture* (Oxford University Press, 2001), and S. S. Kohli, *A Critical Study of the Adi Granth* (Delhi: Punjabi Writers Coop, 1961).

2 Rudolph Otto, *Idea of the Holy* (New York: Galaxy, 1958).

3 For a study of the Harmandar, see Madanjit Kaur, *The Golden Temple: Past and Present* (Amritsar: Guru Nanak Dev University Press, 1983); and Patwant Singh, *The Golden Temple* (New Delhi: Time Books International, 1988).

4 Stella Kramrisch, *The Hindu Temple*, Vol. 1 (Delhi: Motilal Banarsidass, 1976), 6.

5 Michael Ondaatje, *The English Patient* (New York: Vintage International, 1992), 271.

6 Ahmad Shah Sirhindi died in 1624 at Sirhind, near Patiala. A mystic and theologian, he is responsible for the revival of Sunnite Islam in India. Annemarie Schimmel mentions that in '1598 Akbar visited the prolific Guru Ajran'. See her book, *The Empire of the Great Mughals: History, Art and Culture* (London: Reaktion Books, 2004), 118. In this work Schimmel writes, 'Akbar's tolerance and his syncretism were completely at odds with Ahmad's narrow conception of true Islam' (p. 132).

7 *Tuzuk-i-Jahangiri or Memoirs of Jahangir*, translated by Alexander Rogers and edited by Henry Beveridge (London: Royal Asiatic Society, 1909), 72.

According to Pashaura Singh, under the Yasa Mongolian law, the blood of princes and honored persons could not be spilled, so without shedding his blood, extreme torture was inflicted on the Guru. See Pashaura Singh, *Life and Work of Guru Arjan: History, Memory, and Biography in the Sikh Tradition* (New Delhi: Oxford University Press, 2006), 207.

8 *Tuzuk-i-Jahangiri*, 72–3.

9 Father Jerome Xavier's letter is included by Ganda Singh (ed.), *Early European Accounts of the Sikhs* (reprinted as *Indian Studies: Past and Present*) (Calcutta: A. Guha, 1962), 48–9.

Chapter III

1 Jizya was also a means of replenishing the treasury, which had been drained by the Emperor's southern campaigns.

2 An excellent resource is Robin Rinehart, *Debating the Dasam Granth* (forthcoming 2011, Oxford University Press).

3 According to Dr S. Radhakrishnan, Mahatma Gandhi got the idea for his popular public prayer ('*ishvara allah tere nama mandira masjida tere dhama sabko sanmati de bhagavana* – Ishvara and Allah are your names; temples and mosques are your homes; may the Divine give wisdom to all') from Guru Gobind Singh. See S. Radhakrishnan, *The Principal Upanishads* (London: George Allen & Unwin, 1953), 139.

4 For a fuller analysis, see Gurharbhagat Singh, *Transcultural Poetics: Comparative Studies of Ezra Pound's Cantos and Guru Gobind Singh's Bachittra Natak* (Delhi: Ajanta Publications, 1988); and Nikky-Guninder Kaur Singh, *The Birth of the Khalsa: A Feminist Re-Memory of Sikh Identity* (Albany, NY: SUNY, 2005), Ch. 1.

5 Derived from Arabic, *khalsa* means pure.

6 W. H. McLeod, *Who Is a Sikh: The Problem of Sikh Identity* (Oxford: Clarendon Press, 1989), 29.

7 David Shulman, *The Hungry God: Hindu Tales of Filicide and Devotion* (Chicago, IL: University of Chicago Press, 1993), 136.

8 Quoted in Kapur Singh, *The Baisakhi of Guru Gobind Singh* (Jalandhar, Punjab, India: Hind Publishers, 1959), 4–5.

9 Doris Jakobsh has made a valuable entry in this area. See her book, *Relocating Gender in Sikh History* (New Delhi: Oxford University Press, 2003).

10 See Nikky-Guninder Kaur Singh, *The Birth of the Khalsa*, Ch. 4.

11 According to Giani Garja Singh, the author of this entry is Narbud Singh Bhatt, who was with Guru Gobind Singh at Nander at that time. For a detailed account, see Harbans Singh, *Sri Guru Granth Sahib: The Guru Eternal for the Sikhs* (Patiala, Punjab, India: Academy of Sikh Religion and Culture, 1988).

12 Quoted in the original in Harbans Singh, *The Heritage of the Sikhs* (New Delhi: Manohar Publications, 1983), 108–9. See also, Jeevan

Deol, 'The Eighteenth Century Khalsa Identity: Discourse, Praxis and Narrative', in Christopher Shackle, Gurharpal Singh and Arvind-Pal Mandair (eds), *Sikh Religion, Culture and Ethnicity* (Richmond, UK: Curzon Press, 2001), 28.

13 Harbans Singh, *The Heritage of the Sikhs* (New Delhi: Manohar, 1985), 110.

14 Harbans Singh, *Sri Guru Granth Sahib: Guru Eternal for the Sikhs*, 19.

15 George Lakoff and Mark Johnson, *Metaphors We Live By* (Chicago and London: University of Chicago Press, 1980). For 'ontological metaphors', see 25–32; for 'orientational metaphors', see 14–21; and for 'structural metaphors', see 61–8.

16 W. H. McLeod, *Historical Dictionary of Sikhism* (Lanham, MD: The Scarecrow Press, 2005), 2.

Chapter IV

1 S. Radhakrishnan, *The Principal Upanishads* (London: George Allen & Unwin, 1953), 695–705.

2 In the Preface to Carol P. Christ, *Diving Deep and Surfacing: Women Writers on Spiritual Quest* (Boston, MA: Beacon Press, 1980), xxvii.

3 *ma* + *i* = Laxmi and Sarasvati. G. S. Talib acknowledges the three goddesses, Parvati, Laxmi and Sarasvati in his translation, *Japji: The Immortal Prayer-Chant* (New Delhi: Munshiram Manoharlal, 1976), 42.

4 I have discussed these five stages in depth in my chapter on 'The Spiritual Experience in Sikhism', in K. R. Sundararajan and Bithika Mukerji (eds), *Hindu Spirituality: Postclassical and Modern World Spirituality* (New York: Crossroad Publications, 1997), 530–61.

5 The influential religious philosopher Søren Kierkegaard distinguished three realms – esthetics, ethics and religions – with esthetics at the lowest level.

6 Wassily Kandinsky, *Concerning the Spiritual in Art* (New York: Dover, 1977), 54.

Chapter V

1 For a detailed analysis of *akhandpath*, see Kristina Myrvold's excellent work: *Inside the Guru's Gate: Ritual Uses of Texts Among the Sikhs in Varanasi* (Lund, Sweden: Lund University Press, 2007), 269.

2 Barbara Meyeroff, in Victor Turner, *Celebration: Studies in Festivity and Ritual* (Washington, DC: Smithsonian Institute Press, 1982), 109–35.

3 For more details on Guru Ram Das's hymn 'Lavan', see Chapter II.

4 Owen Cole, *The Sikhs: Their Religious Beliefs and Practices* (Eastbourne, UK: Sussex Academy Press, 1995), 124.

5 Harvey Cox, *Feast of Fools: A Theological Essay on Festivity and Fantasy* (Cambridge, MA: Harvard University Press), 7.

6 Satwant Kaur Rait, *Sikh Women in England: Their Religious and Cultural Beliefs and Social Practices* (Stoke-on-Trent, UK: Trentham Books, 2005), 55–94.

Chapter VI

1 Elisabeth Bumiller, *May You Be the Mother of a Hundred Sons* (New York: Random House, 1990).
2 The Laws of Manu are generally dated to between 200 BCE and 200 CE.
3 Dated between 1740 and 1765, 'no existing rahit-nama carries us nearer to the time of Guru Gobind Singh than this work…': W. H. McLeod, in his Introduction to his translation and edition of the text, *The Chaupa Singh Rahit-Nama* (Dunedin, New Zealand: University of Otago Press, 1987), 10.
4 McLeod, *The Chaupa Singh Rahit-Nama*, 111–13.
5 A painting from the Victoria and Albert Museum in London depicts the tragic scene. For details, see Chapter VIII, on Sikh art.
6 C. C. Fair, 'Female Foeticide among Vancouver Sikhs: Recontexualizing Sex Selection in the North American Diaspora', *International Journal of Punjab Studies* (Sage) 3/1 (1996), 1–44. See also Anshu Malhotra, 'Shameful Continuities: The Practice of Female Infanticide in Colonial Punjab', in Doris Jakobsh, *Sikhism and Women* (Delhi: Oxford), 83–114.
7 Mary Daly, *Gyn-Ecology: The Metaethics of Radical Feminism* (Boston, MA: Beacon Press, 1978), 1–42.
8 Ibn al'Arabi, *The Bezels of Wisdom* (trans. R. W. J. Austin, *The Classics of Western Spirituality*) (Mahwah, NJ: Paulist Press, 1980), 29.
9 Phyllis Trible, *God and the Rhetoric of Sexuality* (Philadelphia, PA: Fortress Press, 1978), 31–59.
10 H. Cixous and C. Clement, *The Newly Born Woman* (trans. B. Wing) (Minneapolis, MN: University of Minnesota Press, 1986), 93.
11 S. McFague, *Models of God: Theology for an Ecological, Nuclear Age* (Philadelphia, PA: Fortress Press, 1987).
12 See Rosemary Ruether, *Sexism and God-Talk: Toward a Feminist Theology* (Boston, MA: Beacon Press, 1983).
13 Naomi Goldenberg, 'The Return of the Goddess: Psychoanalytic Reflections on the Shift from Theology to Thealogy', in Ursula King, *Religion and Gender* (Oxford UK/Cambridge MA: Basil Blackwell, 1995), 155.
14 Rudolph Otto, *The Idea of the Holy* (New York: Galaxy, 1958), 29.
15 Tillich, Paul, *Systematic Theology*, Vol. 1 (Chicago, IL: University of Chicago Press, 1951), 241.

16 Carol Christ, 'Symbols of Goddess and God in Feminist Theology', in *Book of the Goddess*, ed. Carol Olsen (New York: Crossroad Press, 1985), 250.
17 For a graphic account of the condition of Indian widows, see Deepa Mehta's film *Water* (2005). See also Nikky-Guninder Kaur Singh, 'The Kanjak Ritual in the Land of Disappearing Kanjaks', in *South Asian Review* (University of Pittsburgh) 29/2 (2008), 109–32.
18 Nikky-Guninder Kaur Singh, 'Translating Sikh Scripture into English', *Sikh Formations* (Routledge, UK) 3/1 (June 2007), 1–17.
19 Grace Jantzen, *Becoming Divine: Towards a Feminist Philosophy of Religion* (Bloomington, IN: Indiana University Press, 1999).
20 Both Preneet Kaur and Harsimrat Kaur are daughters-in-law of powerful Sikh families. They belong to the Patiala royal family and the ruling Badal family, respectively.

Chapter VII

1 All the citations from Charles Wilkins in this section are from *Early European Accounts of the Sikhs*, ed. Ganda Singh (Calcutta: A. Guha, 1962), 71–5.
2 As Note 1, 74–5.
3 Colonel Antoine Louis Henri Polier, 'The Siques', in Singh (ed.), *Early European Accounts of the Sikhs*, 63.
4 Fauja Singh (ed.), *Historians and Historiography of the Sikhs* (New Delhi: Oriental Publishers, 1978), 2.
5 James Browne, 'History of the Origin and Progress of the Sikhs', in Singh (ed.), *Early European Accounts of the Sikhs*, 13–43. My citations from Browne in this section are from his Introduction, 13–19.
6 Identified by F. S. Aijazuddin, *Sikh Portraits by European Artists* (London/New York: Sotheby's Parke-Bernet, 1979), illustrations XI–XVII. The painting used to be in Elveden Hall, Dalip Singh's English home. It is now displayed in Lahore as part of the collection of his daughter, Princess Bamba.
7 Alex Burnes, *Travels into Bokhara: Being the Account of Journey from India to Cabool, Tartary and Persia* (Philadelphia, PA: Carey and Hart, 1835), 107.
8 Burnes, *Travels into Bokhara*, 106.
9 Burnes, *Travels into Bokhara*, 117–18.
10 Burnes, *Travels into Bokhara*, 116.
11 Burnes, *Travels into Bokhara*, 114.
12 Burnes, *Travels into Bokhara*, 117.
13 Burnes, *Travels into Bokhara*, 116.
14 Burnes, *Travels into Bokhara*, 122.
15 K. S. Duggal, *Maharaja Ranjit Singh: The Last to Lay Arms* (New Delhi: Abhinav Publications, 2001), 102.

16 Sir William Wilson Hunter (ed.), *Lord William Bentinck* (Oxford: Clarendon Press, 1897), 169.

17 Emily Eden, *Up the Country: Letters Written to her Sister from the Upper Provinces of India* (London: Richard Bentley, 1867), 236.

18 Eden, *Up the Country*, 227.

19 Eden, *Up the Country*, 228.

20 Eden, *Up the Country*, 230.

21 Eden, *Up the Country*, 200.

22 Eden, *Up the Country*, 201.

23 Eden, *Up the Country*, 209.

24 Eden, *Up the Country*, 216.

25 Arthur Benson and Viscount Esher, *The Letters of Queen Victoria, Vol. 2: 1844–1853* (London: John Murray, 1908), 217.

26 Cited by Brian Axel, *The Nation's Tortured Body: Violence, Representation, and the Formation of a Sikh 'Diaspora'* (Durham, NC: Duke University Press, 2001), 55. In "Maharaja's Glorious Body" (chapter 1 of the book) Axel splendidly describes the many happenings during the week Winterhalter painted the young Dalip. For Winterhalter's painting, see p. 138 of this book.

27 *Hindustan Times*, 28 March 2006.

28 Khushwant Singh, *History of the Sikhs*, Vol. 2 (Princeton, NJ: Princeton University Press, 1966), 101–2.

29 Arthur Moffat, quoted by Tony Ballantyne, *Between Colonialism and Diaspora: Sikh Cultural Formations in an Imperial World* (Durham, NC: Duke University Press, 2006), 63.

30 *Lahore Chronicle*, 17 November 1858; quoted by Ballantyne, *Between Colonialism and Diaspora*, 64.

31 Veena Talwar Oldenburg, *Dowry Murder: The Imperial Origins of a Cultural Crime* (Oxford, UK: Oxford University Press, 2002), 154.

32 DeWitt C. Ellinwood, 'An Historical Study of the Punjabi Soldier in World War I,' in Harbans Singh (ed.), *Punjab Past and Present: Essays in Honor of Ganda Singh* (Patiala: Punjabi University, 1976), 344.

33 For many of the historical details, I have relied on Khushwant Singh's *History of the Sikhs*; see esp. 160.

34 In *Historical Sketches of the Indian Missions* (Allahabad, 1886), 27.

35 Khushwant Singh, *History of the Sikhs*, 142–3.

36 Bhai Vir Singh, *Sundari* (New Delhi: Bhai Vir Singh Sahitya Sadan, 1985), 127–8.

37 Khushwant Singh, in his Foreword to K. C. Gulati, *The Akalis Past and Present* (New Delhi: Ashajanak Publications, 1974), 7.

38 See entry *"Morcha Chabian"* in Harbans Singh, *Encyclopaedia of Sikhism*, Vol. 3 (Patiala: Punjabi University, 1992), 124–5.

39 For official and unofficial numbers please see Kavita Daiya, *Violent Belongings: Partition, Gender, and National Culture in Postcolonial India* (Philadelphia: Temple University, 2008), 6.

Chapter VIII

1 Susan Stronge (ed.), *The Arts of the Sikh Kingdoms* (London: V&A Publishing, 1999).

2 B. N. Goswamy, *Piety and Splendour: Sikh Heritage in Art* (New Delhi: National Museum, 2000). I feel deeply indebted to Professor Goswamy for his inspiring scholarship on Sikh art.

3 Kerry Brown (ed.), *Sikh Art and Literature* (London/New York: Routledge, 1999); Stronge, *The Arts of the Sikh Kingdoms*; Goswamy, *Piety and Splendour*, and B. N. Goswamy and Caron Smith, *I See No Stranger: Early Sikh Art and Devotion* (New York: Rubin Museum of Art, 2006).

4 The B-40 Janamsakhi surfaced in Lahore in the nineteenth century and was acquired by the India Office Library in 1907. It has been edited by Professor Surjit Hans: *B-40 Janamsakhi: Guru Baba Nanak Paintings* (Amritsar: Guru Nanak Dev University, 1987). The image of Guru Nanak on p. 3 in this book is from the B-40 Janamsakhi. For information cited here, see Hew McLeod, *Popular Sikh Art* (Delhi: Oxford University Press, 1991), 5–6.

5 Goswamy and Smith, *I See No Stranger*, 36–7.

6 From the Kapany collection, in Brown, *Sikh Art and Literature*, Fig. 36.

7 Opaque watercolor at the Government Museum and Art Gallery in Chandigarh. See Goswamy and Smith, *I See No Stranger*, 69.

8 Goswamy and Smith, *I See No Stranger*, 93. It is now in the Asian Art Museum in San Francisco.

9 Also in the Asian Art Museum in San Francisco. In Goswamy and Smith, *I See No Stranger*, 89.

10 Guru Nanak converses with two Muslim holy men from the Pahari workshop of Nainsukh of Guler. In Goswamy and Smith, *I See No Stranger*, 61.

11 Goswamy and Smith, *I See No Stranger*, 94.

12 Goswamy and Smith, *I See No Stranger*, 30.

13 M. S. Randhawa, 'Paintings of the Sikh Gurus in the collection of Mahant of Gurdwara Ram Rai, Dehradun', *Roopa-Lekha* XXXIX/1, 13–20.

14 McLeod, *Popular Sikh Art*, 7–8.

15 According to B. P. Kamboj, these murals on the walls of Bhai Bahlo Darwaza 'are probably the oldest wall paintings of the Sikh Gurus

available in India so far'. See B. P. Kamboj, *Early Wall Painting of Garhwal* (New Delhi: Indus Publishing Company, 2003), 35.

16 It is at the Government Museum and Art Gallery, Chandigarh. Stronge, *The Arts of the Sikh Kingdoms*, illustration 30.

17 At the Himachal Pradesh State Museum in Simla. Goswamy, *Piety and Splendour*, 48.

18 Goswamy, *Piety and Splendour*, 38–9. Goswamy provides details of script and verses on Guru Nanak's robe. For the image, see p. 15 of this book.

19 Goswamy, *Piety and Splendour*, 38.

20 Translation of the Islamic invocation: 'In the name of God, Most Gracious, Most Merciful.' The translation of the Sikh verse: 'Truth it always was, is and will be evermore.'

21 Jeevan Deol, 'Illustration and Illumination in Sikh Scriptural Manuscripts', in Kavita Singh (ed.), *New Insights into Sikh Art* (Mumbai: Marg Publications, 2003), 50–67.

22 The Mul Mantar follows Guru Nanak's configuration of *Ikk Oan Kar.* It is set at the very beginning of the Sikh Scripture and at the start of different sections.

23 Goswamy and Smith, *I See No Stranger*, 38.

24 But we do not know its present whereabouts. See Deol, 'Illustration and Illumination in Sikh Scriptural Manuscripts', 55.

25 For translation and discussion, see A. S. Melikian-Chirvani, 'Ranjit Singh and the Image of the Past', in Stronge, *The Arts of the Sikh Kingdoms*, 63.

26 Goswamy, *Piety and Splendour*, 184.

27 At the National Museum in New Delhi.

28 Gold token, Goswamy, *Piety and Splendour*, 186.

29 Goswamy, *Piety and Splendour*, 188.

30 Goswamy, *Piety and Splendour*, 71.

31 Goswamy, *Piety and Splendour*, 70–1.

32 Goswamy, *Piety and Splendour*, 73.

33 Goswamy, *Piety and Splendour*, 78–9.

34 Goswamy, *Piety and Splendour*, 77.

35 Rosemary Crill, 'Textiles in the Punjab', in Stronge, *The Arts of the Sikh Kingdoms*, 119.

36 As noted by Rosemary Crill: 'early nineteenth century paintings by Ingres and David are valued by historians for dating Kashmiri shawls, which were extremely popular in France at that time'. See her chapter, 'Textiles in the Punjab', in Stronge, *The Arts of the Sikh Kingdoms*, 119.

37 Stronge, *Arts of the Sikh Kingdoms*, plates 143, 144. See also Goswamy, *Piety and Splendour*, 191.

38 F. S. Aijazuddin, *Sikh Portraits by European Artists* (London/New York: Sotheby's Parke-Bernet, 1979), 30.

39 Kanwarjit Kang, 'Art and Architecture of the Golden Temple', in *Marg*, XXX/3, June 1977, 24.

40 B. N. Goswamy, 'A Matter of Taste: Some Notes on the Context of Painting in Sikh Punjab', *Marg*, Special Issue: *Appreciation of Creative Arts under Maharaja Ranjit Singh* (Bombay: 1982), 55.

41 Aijazuddin, *Sikh Portraits by European Artists*, 30.

42 Aijazuddin, *Sikh Portraits by European Artists*, illustration II. (Reproduced by Amrit and Rabindra, *Twin Perspectives* (London: Twin Studios), plate 40.)

43 Aijazuddin, *Sikh Portraits by European Artists*, illustration III.

44 Aijazuddin, *Sikh Portraits by European Artists*, illustration V. For painting of Maharani Jindan by George Richmond, see p. 176 of this book.

45 Born Bannou Pan Del, Mrs Allard was the daughter of an Indian noble. Stronge, *Arts of the Sikh Kingdoms*, illustration 118. For painting of the Allard family, see p. 130 of this book.

46 Stronge, *Arts of the Sikh Kingdoms*, illustration 105 (Rietberg Museum, Zurich).

47 Goswamy, *Piety and Splendour*, illustration 129. For image, see p. 116 of this book.

48 Goswamy, 'A Matter of Taste', *Marg*, Special Issue: *Appreciation of Creative Arts under Maharaja Ranjit Singh* (Bombay: 1982), 49.

49 Illustration 63 in *Marg*, XXX/3, June 1977.

50 W. G. Archer, *The Paintings of the Sikhs* (London: HMSO, 1966), 30.

51 Wendy Moonan, 'An Heirloom Is Resurrected at Cartier', *The New York Times*, 29 November 2002.

52 Kavita Singh, 'Allegories of Good Kingship: Wall Paintings in the Qila Mubarak at Patiala', in *New Insights into Sikh Art* (Mumbai: Marg Publications, 2003), 68–85.

53 Goswamy, 'Continuing Traditions in the Later Sikh Kingdoms', in Stronge (ed.), *The Arts of the Sikh Kingdoms*, 175–7.

54 M. Milford-Lutzker, 'Five Artists from India', *Woman's Art Journal* 23/2 (Autumn 2002/Winter 2003), 21.

55 Deepak Ananth, *Amrita Sher-Gil: An Indian Art Family of the Twentieth Century* (Munich: Schirmer/Mosel, 2007), 14. Sher-Gil's paintings discussed in this chapter are reproduced in Ananth's volume.

56 Ananth, *Amrita Sher-Gil*, 22.

57 Ananth, *Amrita Sher-Gil*, 19–20.

58 Ananth, *Amrita Sher-Gil*, 20.

59 Yashodhara Dalmia, *Amrita Sher-Gil: A Life* (New Delhi: Viking/Penguin, 2006), 20

60 The citations in this paragraph come from Sher-Gil's letter to Karl Khandalvala, dated 1 July 1940, in Ananth, *Amrita Sher-Gil*, 98.

61 In Ananth, *Amrita Sher-Gil*, illustrations 82 and 84.
62 Painting by Phulan Rani, in *Life of Guru Nanak Through Pictures* (Amritsar: Modern Sahit Academy, 1969), 17.
63 Khuswant Singh and Arpita Kaur, *Hymns of Guru Nanak* (Hyderabad: Orient Longman, 1991).
64 Arpita's painting in *Hymns of Guru Nanak*, 109.
65 *Hymns of Guru Nanak*, 27.
66 *Hymns of Guru Nanak*, 81.
67 Line drawn for Sita's protection by her brother-in-law, Laxman.
68 By Arpana Caur and Mala Kaur Dayal (New Delhi: Rupa, 2005).
69 Displayed at the National Gallery of Modern Art in New Delhi.

Chapter IX

1 Gurharpal Singh and Darshan Singh Tatla, *Sikhs in Britain: The Making of a Community* (London/New York: Zed Books, 2006), 32. The authors provide global Sikh population data for 2005. The numbers would have increased by the time of writing.
2 Harbans Singh, *Guru Nanak and Origins of the Sikh Faith* (Patiala: Punjabi University, 1969), 116–17.
3 Details are from Kristina Myrvold, *Inside the Guru's Gate: Ritual Uses of Texts Among the Sikhs in Varanasi* (Lund, Sweden: Lund University, 2007), 34, 98–101.
4 Details are from Khushwant Singh, *History of the Sikhs*, Vol. 2 (Princeton, NJ: Princeton University Press, 1966), 91–2.
5 See Tony Ballantyne, *Between Colonialism and Diaspora: Sikh Cultural Formations in an Imperial World* (Durham, NC: Duke University Press, 2006), 72.
6 Hew McLeod, *Sikhism* (Harmondsworth: Penguin, 1997), 255.
7 Interesting photos are available on the BBC website: http://news.bbc.co.uk/2/hi/uk_news/8589634.stm; accessed 1 June 2010.
8 http://www.black-history.org.uk/chattri.asp.
9 Sandhya Shukla, *India Abroad: Diasporic Cultures of Postwar America and England* (Princeton, NJ: Princeton University Press, 2003), 38.
10 Singh and Tatla, *Sikhs in Britain*, 47.
11 Quoted by Singh and Tatla, *Sikhs in Britain*, 52.
12 Again, these figures are from Singh and Tatla, *Sikhs in Britain*.
13 The *Guardian*, cited in Ballantyne, *Between Colonialism and Diaspora*, 114.
14 For a fuller discussion, see Ballantyne, 'Displacement, Diaspora, and Difference in the Making of Bhangra', in *Between Colonialism and Diaspora*, 121–74.
15 Darshan Singh Tatla, 'Sikh Diaspora', in Melvin Ember, Carol Ember and Ian A. Skoggard (eds), *Encyclopedia of Diasporas: Immigrant and*

Refugee Cultures around the World, Vol. 1 (Springer Science+Business Media, 2005), 276. Also, Singh and Tatla, *Sikhs in Britain*, 32.

16 Acclaimed film director Deepa Mehta is making a film on the tragedy of the Komagata Maru.

17 Film: *Roots in the Sand*. Also, *New Puritans: Sikhs of Yuba City*.

18 The son of the returnee was married to the sister of the famous Sikh historian, Dr Ganda Singh. They were close family friends of the author.

19 *The New York Times* front page, 31 August 2009.

20 Gurpreet Bal, 'Migration of Sikh Women to Canada: A Social Construction of Gender', *Guru Nanak Journal of Sociology* (Amritsar, 1997).

21 *The Tribune*, 15 June 1996.

22 C. C. Fair, 'Female Foeticide Among Vancouver Sikhs: Recontexualizing Sex Selection in the North American Diaspora', *International Journal of Punjab Studies* (Sage Publications) 3/1 (1996), 1–44.

23 4 June 2010 http://www.saldef.org/pr/statement-on-sc-sen-jack-knotts-use-of-term-%E2%80%9Craghead%E2%80%9D/.

24 Susan Koshy and Gurinder Chadha, 'Turning Color: Conversation with Gurinder Chadha', in *Transition*, No. 72 (Indiana University, 1996), 148–61.

25 Shauna Singh Baldwin, *English Lessons and Other Stories* (Fredericton, NB, Canada: Goose Lane, 1996), 16.

26 Shauna Singh Baldwin, *What the Body Remembers* (New York: Doubleday, 1999), 335.

27 Baldwin, *What the Body Remembers*, 83.

28 Baldwin, *What the Body Remembers*, 34.

29 Inni Kaur, *Journey with the Gurus* (illustrated by Pardeep Singh) (Norwalk, CT: Sikh Education & Cultural Foundation, 2010).

30 Jessi Kaur, *Dear Takuya: Letters of a Sikh Boy* (illustrated by Brian Johnston) (Los Angeles: International Institute of Gurmat Studies, 2008).

31 Jessi Kaur, *The Royal Falcon* (illustrated by Pammy Kapoor) (Los Angeles: International Institute of Gurmat Studies, 2009).

32 *Twin Perspectives: Paintings by Amrit and Rabindra KD Kaur Singh*, with contributions by Julian Spalding, Raj Pal and Dr Deborah Swallow (London: Twin Studios, 1999), 29.

33 *Twin Perspectives: Paintings by Amrit and Rabindra KD Kaur Singh*, 67.

34 *Twin Perspectives: Paintings by Amrit and Rabindra KD Kaur Singh*, 81.

35 *Twin Perspectives: Paintings by Amrit and Rabindra KD Kaur Singh*, 53.

36 *Twin Perspectives: Paintings by Amrit and Rabindra KD Kaur Singh*, 49.

Select Bibliography

Reference Works

McLeod, W. H., *Historical Dictionary of Sikhism*, 2nd edn (Lanham, MD/Toronto/Oxford: The Scarecrow Press, 2005).

Nabha, Bhai Kahn Singh, *Gurushabad Ratanakar Mahan Kosh* (Patiala: Punjab Bhasha Vibhag, reprint 1930).

Singh, Harbans, *Encyclopedia of Sikhism*, 4 volumes (Patiala: Punjabi University, 1992–8).

Basic Works

Banga, Indu (ed.), *Five Punjabi Centuries: Politics, Economy, Society and Culture, c. 1500–1990. Essays for J. S. Grewal* (New Delhi: Manohar, 1997).

Cole, Owen and Sambhi, Piara Singh, *The Sikhs: Their Religious Beliefs and Practices* (London/Boston, MA: Routledge & Kegan Paul, 1978).

Duggal, K. S., *Maharaja Ranjit Singh: The Last to Lay Arms* (New Delhi: Abhinav Publications, 2001).

Dusenbery, Verne (ed.), *Sikhs at Large: Religion, Culture and Politics in Global Perspective* (New Delhi: Oxford University Press, 2008).

Fenech, Louis, *Martyrdom in the Sikh Tradition* (New Delhi: Oxford University Press, 2000).

——, *The Darbar of the Sikh Gurus: Court of God in the World of Men* (New Delhi/New York: Oxford University Press, 2008).

Grewal, J. S., *From Guru Nanak to Maharaja Ranjit Singh: Essays in Sikh History* (Amritsar: Guru Nanak Dev University, 1972).

——, *The Sikhs of the Punjab. New Cambridge History of India, Vol. II, 3* (Cambridge: Cambridge University Press, 1990).

Hans, Surjit, *A Reconstruction of Sikh History from Sikh Literature* (Jalandhar: ABS, 1988).

Juergensmeyer, Mark and Barrier, N. G., *Sikh Studies* (Berkeley, CA: University of California Press, 1979).

Macauliffe, Max Arthur, *The Sikh Religion: Its Gurus, Sacred Writings, and Authors* (Oxford: Oxford University Press, 1909).

Madra, Amandeep Singh and Singh, Parmjit, *Warrior Saints: Three Centuries of the Sikh Military Tradition* (London/New York: I.B.Tauris, 1999).

Mahmood, Cynthia, *Fighting for Faith and Nation: Dialogues with Sikh Militants* (Philadelphia, PA: University of Pennsylvania, 1997).

Mandair, Arvind-Pal S., *Religion and the Specter of the West: Sikhism, India, Postcoloniality, and the Politics of Translation* (New York: Columbia University Press, 2009).

Mann, Gurinder Singh, *Sikhism* (Upper Saddle River, NJ: Prentice Hall, 2004).

Mann, Jasbir Singh and Singh, Kharak, *Recent Researches in Sikhism* (Patiala: Punjabi University Publication Bureau, 1992).

McLeod, W. H., *Guru Nanak and the Sikh Religion* (Oxford: Clarendon Press, 1968).

——, *Who Is a Sikh: The Problem of Sikh Identity* (Oxford: Clarendon Press, 1989).

——, *Sikhism* (London: Penguin, 1997).

Myrvold, Kristina, *Inside the Guru's Gate: Ritual Uses of Texts Among the Sikhs in Varanasi* (Lund, Sweden: Lund University Press, 2007).

Nasr, S. H., *Knowledge and the Sacred* (NY: Crossroad, 1981).

Nesbitt, Eleanor, *Sikhism: A Very Short Introduction* (Oxford: Oxford University Press, 2005).

Nijhawan, Michael, *Dhadi Darbar: Religion, Violence, and the Performance of Sikh History* (New Delhi: Oxford University Press, 2006).

Oberoi, Harjot, *The Construction of Religious Boundaries: Culture, Identity, and Diversity in the Sikh Tradition* (Chicago, IL: University of Chicago Press, 1994).

O'Connell, J. T., *Sikh History and Religion in the Twentieth Century* (Toronto: University of Toronto, 1988).

Rinehart, Robin, *Debating the Dasam Granth* (New York, Oxford University Press, forthcoming).

Rogers, Alexander (trans. and ed. Henry Beveridge), *Tuzuk-i-Jahangiri, or Memoirs of Jahangir* (London: Royal Asiatic Society, 1909).

Schimmel, Annemarie, *The Empire of the Great Mughals: History, Art and Culture* (London: Reaktion Books, 2004).

Shackle, Christopher, Singh, Gurharpal and Mandair, Arvind-Pal, *Sikh Religion, Culture and Ethnicity* (London: Curzon, 2001).

Singh, Bhai Vir (ed.), *Varan Bhai Gurdas* (Amritsar: Khalsa Samachar, 1977),

Singh, Fauja (ed.), *Historians and Historiography of the Sikhs* (New Delhi: Oriental Publishers, 1978).

Singh, Gurdev, *Perspectives on the Sikh Tradition* (Chandigarh: Siddhartha, 1986).

Singh, Harbans, *Guru Nanak and Origins of the Sikh Faith* (Bombay: Asia Publishing House, 1969).

——, *The Heritage of the Sikhs* (New Delhi: Manohar, 1985).

Singh, I. J., *The World According to Sikhi* (Guelph, Canada: Centennial Foundation, 2008).

Singh, Kapur, *The Baisakhi of Guru Gobind Singh* (Jullundur: Hind Publishers, 1959).

Singh, Khushwant, *A History of the Sikhs* (Princeton, NJ: Princeton University Press, 1966).

Singh, Nikky-Guninder Kaur, *Sikhism* (New York: Facts on File, 1993).

Singh, Nripinder, *The Sikh Moral Tradition* (New Delhi: Manohar, 1990).

Singh, Pashaura, *Life and Work of Guru Arjan: History, Memory, and Biography in the Sikh Tradition* (New Delhi: Oxford University Press, 2006).

Singh, Pashaura and Barrier, N. G. (eds), *Sikhism in the Light of History* (New Delhi: Oxford University Press, 2004).

Talbot, Ian and Singh, Gurharpal, *The Partition of India* (NY: Cambridge University Press, 2009).

Sikh Scripture and Textual Studies

Chahil, Pritam Singh (trans.), *Sri Guru Granth Sahib*, 4 vols (New Delhi: Pritam Singh Chahil, 1992).

Kohli, S. S., *A Critical Study of the Adi Granth* (New Delhi: Punjabi Writers Coop, 1961).

Maken, G. S., *The Essence of Sri Guru Granth Sahib*, 5 vols (Chandigarh: Guru Tegh Bahadur Educational Centre, 2001).

Mandair, Arvind and Shackle, C. (eds and trans.), *Teachings of the Sikh Gurus: Selections from the Sikh Scriptures* (London/New York: Routledge, 2005).

Mann, Gurinder Singh, *The Making of Sikh Scripture* (New York: Oxford University Press, 2001).

McLeod, W. H., *Textual Sources for the Study of Sikhism* (Chicago, IL: University of Chicago Press, 1990).

Shackle, C., *An Introduction to the Sacred Language of the Sikhs* (London: SOAS, University of London, 1983).

Singh, Gopal, *Sri Guru Granth Sahib: English Version* (Chandigarh: The World Sikh University Press, 1978).

Singh, Harbans, *Sri Guru Granth Sahib: The Guru Eternal for the Sikhs* (Patiala: Academy of Sikh Religion and Culture, 1988).

Singh, Manmohan (trans.), *Sri Guru Granth Sahib*, 8 vols (Amritsar: SGPC, 1969).

Singh, Nikky-Guninder Kaur, *The Name of My Beloved: Verses of the Sikh Gurus* (New Delhi: Penguin, 2001).

Singh, Pashaura, *The Guru Granth: Canon, Meaning and Authority* (New Delhi: Oxford University Press, 2000).

Talib, G. S. (trans.), *Sri Guru Granth Sahib*, 4 vols (Patiala: Punjabi University, 1984).

Sikh Art

Aijazuddin, F. S., *Sikh Portraits by European Artists* (London/New York: Sotheby's Parke-Bernet, 1979).

Ananth, Deepak, *Amrita Sher-Gil: An Indian Art Family of the Twentieth Century* (Munich: Schirmer/Mosel, 2007).

Archer, W. G., *The Paintings of the Sikhs* (London: HMSO, 1966).

Bigelow, Anna, *Sharing the Sacred: Practicing Pluralism in Muslim India* (New York: Oxford University Press, 2010).

Brown, Kerry (ed.), *Sikh Art and Literature* (London/New York: Routledge, 1999).

Caur, Arpana and Dayal, Mala Kaur, *Nanak: the Guru* (New Delhi: Rupa, 2005).

Crill, Rosemary, 'Textiles in the Punjab', in Susan Stronge (ed.), *The Arts of the Sikh Kingdoms*.

Dalmia, Yashodhara, *Amrita Sher-Gil: A Life* (New Delhi: Viking/Penguin, 2006).

Deol, Jeevan, 'Illustration and Illumination in Sikh Scriptural Manuscripts', in Kavita Singh (ed.), *New Insights into Sikh Art* (Mumbai: Marg Publications, 2003).

Goswamy, B. N., 'A Matter of Taste: Some Notes on the Context of Painting in Sikh Punjab', in *Marg: Appreciation of Creative Arts under Maharaja Ranjit Singh* (Bombay: Marg Publications, 1982).

——, *Piety and Splendour: Sikh Heritage in Art* (New Delhi: National Museum, 2000).

Goswamy, B. N. and Smith, Caron, *I See No Stranger: Early Sikh Art and Devotion* (New York: Rubin Museum of Art, 2006).

Hans, Surjit (ed.), *B-40 Janamsakhi: Guru Baba Nanak Paintings* (Amritsar: Guru Nanak Dev University, 1987).

Kamboj, B. P., *Early Wall Painting of Garhwal* (New Delhi: Indus Publishing Company, 2003).

Kaur, Madanjit, *The Golden Temple: Past and Present* (Amritsar: Guru Nanak Dev University, 1983).

McLeod, W. H., *Popular Sikh Art* (New Delhi: Oxford University Press, 1991).

Melikian-Chirvani, A. S., 'Ranjit Singh and the Image of the Past', in Susan Stronge (ed.), *The Arts of the Sikh Kingdoms* (London: V&A Publishing, 1999).

Milford-Lutzker, M., 'Five Artists from India', *Woman's Art Journal* 23/2 (Autumn 2002–Winter 2003).
Mitter, Partha, *The Triumph of Modernism: India's artists and the avant-garde, 1922–1947* (London: Reaktion Books, 2007).
Moonan, Wendy, 'An Heirloom Is Resurrected at Cartier', *The New York Times*, 29 November 2002.
Murphy, Ann, 'The Guru's Weapons', *Journal of the American Academy of Religion*, June 2009.
Randhawa, M. S., 'Paintings of the Sikh Gurus in the collection of Mahant of Gurdwara Ram Rai, Dehradun', *Roopa-Lekha* XXXIX/1.
Rani, Phulan, *Life of Guru Nanak Through Pictures* (Amritsar: Modern Sahit Academy, 1969).
Singh, Kavita, 'Allegories of Good Kingship: Wall Paintings in the Qila Mubarak at Patiala', in Kavita Singh, *New Insights into Sikh Art* (Mumbai: Marg Publications, 2003).
Singh, Khuswant and Kaur, Arpita, *Hymns of Guru Nanak* (Hyderabad: Orient Longman, 1991).
Singh, Patwant, *The Golden Temple* (Hong Kong: ET Publishing, 1988).
Spalding, Julian, Pal, Raj and Swallow, Deborah, *Twin Perspectives: Paintings by Amrit and Rabindra KD Kaur Singh* (London: Twin Studios, 1999).
Stronge, Susan (ed.), *The Arts of the Sikh Kingdoms* (London: V&A Publishing, 1999).

Women and Gender

Bal, Gurpreet, 'Migration of Sikh Women to Canada: A Social Construction of Gender', *Guru Nanak Journal of Sociology*, Amritsar, 1997.
Baldwin, Shauna Singh, *English Lessons and Other Stories* (Canada, Fredericton, NB: Goose Lane, 1996).
——, *What the Body Remembers* (New York: Doubleday, 1999).
Bhachu, Parminder, *Dangerous Designs: Asian Women Fashion the Diaspora Economies* (London/New York: Routledge, 2004).
Daiya, Kavita, *Violent Belongings: Partition, Gender, and National Culture in Postcolonial India* (Philadelphia: Temple University, 2008).
Elsberg, Constance, *Graceful Women: Gender and Identity in an American Community* (Knoxville, TN: University of Tennessee Press, 2003).
Fair, C. C., 'Female Foeticide among Vancouver Sikhs: Recontexualizing Sex Selection in the North American Diaspora', *International Journal of Punjab Studies* 3/1 (Sage, 1996).
Jakobsh, Doris, *Relocating Gender in Sikh History: Transformation, Meaning and Identity* (New Delhi: Oxford University Press, 2003).

——, *Sikhism and Women: History, Texts, and Experience* (New Delhi: Oxford University Press, 2010).

Kaur, Kanwaljit, *Sikh Women: Fundamental Issues in Sikh Studies* (Chandigarh: Institute of Sikh Studies, 1992).

Kaur, Upinderjit, *Sikh Religion and Economic Development* (New Delhi: National Book Organization, 1990).

Mahmood, Cynthia and Brady, Stacy, *Guru's Gift: An Ethnography Exploring Gender Equality with North American Sikh Women* (Mountain View, CA: Mayfield Publishing Company, 2000).

Oldenburg, Veena Talwar, *Dowry Murder: The Imperial Origins of a Cultural Crime* (Oxford/New York: Oxford University Press, 2002).

Rait, Satwant Kaur, *Sikh Women in England: Their Religious and Cultural Beliefs and Social Practices* (Stoke-on-Trent UK/Sterling USA: Trentham Books, 2005).

Sasson, Vanessa, *Imagining the Fetus: The Unborn in Myth, Religion and Culture* (Oxford/New York: Oxford University Press, 2008).

Singh, Nikky-Guninder Kaur, *Feminine Principle in the Sikh Vision of the Transcendent* (Cambridge: Cambridge University Press, 1993).

——, 'The Kanjak Ritual in the Land of Disappearing Kanjaks', in *South Asian Review* (University of Pittsburgh) 29/2 (2008), 109–32.

——, 'Translating Sikh Scripture into English', in *Sikh Formations* (Routledge: United Kingdom) 3/1 (June 2007), 1–17.

Westwood, Sallie and Bhachu, Parminder (eds), *Enterprising Women: Ethnicity, Economy and Gender Relations* (London/New York: Routledge, 1988).

Colonialism and Diaspora

Ali, N., Lara, V. S. and Sayyid, S. (eds), *A Postcolonial People: South Asians in Britain* (New York: Columbia University Press, 2008).

Axel, Brian, *The Nation's Tortured Body: Violence, Representation, and the Formation of a Sikh Diaspora* (Durham, NC: Duke University Press, 2001).

Ballantyne, Tony, *Between Colonialism and Diaspora: Sikh Cultural Formations in an Imperial World* (Durham, NC: Duke University Press, 2006).

Barrier, N. Gerald and Dusenbery, Verne A. (eds), *The Sikh Diaspora* (Delhi: Chanakya, 1989).

Benson, Arthur and Esher, Viscount, *The Letters of Queen Victoria, Volume 2: 1844–1853* (London: John Murray, 1908).

Bhachu, Parminder, *Twice Migrants: East African Sikh Settlers in Britain* (London: Tavistock, 1985).

Burnes, Alex, *Travels into Bokhara: Being the Account of Journey from India to Cabool, Tartary and Persia* (Philadelphia, PA: Carey and Hart, 1835).

Coward, Harold (ed.), *The South Asian Religious Diaspora in Britain, Canada, and the United States* (New York: State University of New York Press, 2000).

Dusenbery, Verne and Tatla, Darshan S. (eds), *Sikh Diaspora: Philanthropy in Punjab* (New Delhi: Oxford University Press, 2009).

Eden, Emily, *Up the Country: Letters Written to Her Sister from the Upper Provinces of India* (London: Richard Bentley, 1867).

Ellinwood, DeWitt C., 'An Historical Study of the Punjabi Soldier in World War I', in Harbans Singh (ed.), *Punjab Past and Present: Essays in Honor of Ganda Singh* (Patiala: Punjabi University, 1976).

Grewal, Inderpal, *Transnational America; Feminisms, Diasporas, Neoliberalisms* (Durham, NC: Duke University Press, 2005).

Hunter, Sir William Wilson (ed.), *Lord William Bentinck* (Oxford: The Clarendon Press, 1897).

Kaur, Inni, *Journey with the Gurus* (illustrations Pardeep Singh) (Norwalk, CT: Sikh Education & Cultural Foundation, 2010).

Kaur, Jessi, *Dear Takuya: Letters of a Sikh Boy* (illustrations Brian Johnston) (Tustin, CA: International Institute of Gurmat Studies, 2008).

Kaur, Jessi, *The Royal Falcon* (illustrations Pammy Kapoor) (Tustin, CA: International Institute of Gurmat Studies, 2009).

La Brack, Bruce, *The Sikhs of Northern California 1904–1975* (New York: AMS, 1988).

Leonard, Karen, *Making Ethnic Choices: California's Punjabi Mexican Americans* (Philadelphia: Temple University, 1992).

Mukherjee, Bharati, *Jasmine* (New York: Grove Press, 1989).

Nayar, Kamala Elizabeth, *The Sikh Diaspora in Vancouver: Three Generations Amid Tradition, Modernity, and Multiculturalism* (Toronto: University of Toronto Press, 2004).

Ondaatje, Michael, *The English Patient* (New York: Vintage International, 1992).

Shukla, Sandhya, *India Abroad: Diasporic Cultures of Postwar America and England* (Princeton, NJ: Princeton University Press, 2003).

Sidhwa, Bapsi, *Cracking India* (Minneapolis, MN: Milkweed Editions, 1993).

Singh, Ganda (ed.), *Early European Accounts of the Sikhs* (reprint from *Indian Studies: Past and Present*) (Calcutta: A. Guha, 1962).

Singh, Gurharpal and Tatla, Darshan S., *Sikhs in Britain: The Making of a Community* (London/New York: Zed Books, 2006).

Singh, Pashaura and Barrier, Gerry (eds), *Sikh Identity: Continuity and Change* (New Delhi: Manohar, 1999).

Tatla, Darshan Singh, *Sikhs in North America: An Annotated Bibliography* (Westport, CT: Greenwood Press, 1991).

Tatla, Darshan Singh, 'Sikh Diaspora', in Melvin Ember, Carol Ember and Ian A. Skoggard (eds), *Encyclopedia of Diasporas: Immigrant and Refugee Cultures around the World*, Vol. 1 (Springer Science+Business Media Inc., 2005).

Tweed, Thomas A. and Prothero, Stephen, 'Things That Make You Ask Kion?', in *Asian Religions in America: A Documentary History* (New York: Oxford University Press, 1999), 312–14.

Index

I.B.TAURIS INTRODUCTIONS TO RELIGION

Daoism: An Introduction – Ronnie L Littlejohn
HB 9781845116385
PB 9781845116392

Jainism: An Introduction – Jeffery D Long
HB 9781845116255
PB 9781845116262

Judaism: An Introduction – Oliver Leaman
HB 9781848853942
PB 9781848853959

Zoroastrianism: An Introduction – Jenny Rose
HB 9781848850873
PB 9781848850880

Confucianism: An Introduction – Ronnie L Littlejohn
HB 9781848851733
PB 9781848851740

Sikhism: An Introduction – Nikky-Guninder Kaur Singh
HB 9781848853201
PB 9781848853218

Islam: An Introduction – Catharina Raudvere
HB 9781848850835
PB 9781848850842

Christianity: An Introduction – Philip Kennedy
HB 9781848853829
PB 9781848853836

Hinduism: An Introduction – Will Sweetman
HB 9781848853270
PB 9781848853287

Buddhism: An Introduction – Alexander Wynne
HB 9781848853966
PB 9781848853973